MW00337688

TENNIS GAME
THEORY

To David,
Thanks for the support.
Enjoy the read.
Best,
Jake

TENNIS GAME THEORY

THEORY

DIALING-IN YOUR A-GAME EVERYDAY

JAK BEARDSWORTH

Copyright © 2016 by Jak Beardsworth
All rights reserved, including the right of reproduction in whole or
in part in any form.

All previously published magazine articles reprinted by permission
of Harbor Style Magazine Inc., Punta Gorda, Florida.

Cover Art by Scott Spear

On court photos of author by Shaun Ondak

ISBN: 978-1-48356-574-3

Printed in the United States of America

DEDICATION

To all the players who do their best, always aspire higher, and love the game.

ACKNOWLEDGEMENTS

Many thanks to so many who have contributed to the production of this book.

Jimmy Dean, Harbor Style Magazine publisher, for granting permission to use my previous articles.

Candee Gulick, my long time webmaster, for organizing all of my tennis writing.

Scott Spear for his excellent cover design.

And especially to Terry Yonker, friend and dedicated student of the game, his associates Regie Belarmino and Elvis Oano, and the folks at Book Baby for their collective digital know how in bringing this work to fruition.

Finally, to all my many mentors and colleagues over the years who have supported me, especially those who have contributed their praise for this work.

Contents

THE ART OF DOUBLES

AUTHOR'S NOTE

Tennis Game Theory is the culmination of my tennis writing over the past few of years. Magazine articles – Harbor Style (Punta Gorda, FL), newspaper columns – Lake Placid News (NY), and essays dedicated to my website – www. JakBeardsworthTennis.com).

My love for the game, and commitment to it, began 57 years ago when a motley group of 12 year old boys sat on the New England stone wall that bordered my backyard, and watched the area's best players on the brand new, adjoining private court that was completely out of context in a middle class working neighborhood in coastal Massachusetts.

I was hooked.

Five years later I was invited, as a promising up and comer, to play in the prestigious Newport Grass Court Invitational (now the ATP Hall of Fame Championships), a lead-up to the then U.S. Nationals (precursor to the U.S. Open) later in the summer at Forest Hills. This was four years before tennis entered the "open era" of above the table prize money when the sport was still mired in the prevailing shamateurism of the day.

I had previously played doubles on a couple of occasions with Jimmy Van Alen, the originator of today's tie-breaker and now iconic founder of the International Tennis Hall of Fame at the historic Newport Casino. I, as was said back in the day, "played out of my mind" both times.

The rest is, as they say, history, with a successful college career – when college was the preferred vehicle to develop one's game - and now over 50 years logged-in playing, teaching, coaching, and being involved in the game at every level from the club trenches to rarified experiences at the top.

The three sections inside – consisting of original stand-alone pieces that have been adapted into a comprehensive work - share my career insights into ball striking, movement, match management, and inner toughness, the quartet of core fundamentals and skills necessary, above *and* below the neck, to be a successful player at any level.

Additionally, in the magazine section, you'll find a few human interest articles along with my take on some important state of the game issues.

You will also experience some repetitive themes throughout – subliminal conditioning if you will - much like your own pro having to periodically remind you, for example, to get your racket back, track the ball, energize your footwork, visualize, breathe, relax, etcetera.

Pro player positive examples, past and present, historical individuals with apropos messages, and noted contributors in other related genres are frequently referenced since tennis is most definitely a very repetitive, cumulative game that demands a positive redundancy if one is going to be able to reflexively perform their very best – dialing-in one's A-Game, win or lose, every time out.

Enjoy the read and the accompanying improvements to your game readily available in the pages within.

PART ONE : Magazine Articles

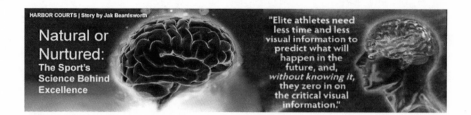

Natural or Nurtured:
The Sport's
Science Behind
Excellence

"Elite athletes need less time and less visual information to predict what will happen in the future, and, *without knowing it,* they zero in on the critical visual information."

What if you could flash forward to the 2016 Summer Olympics in Rio de Janeiro and actually walk in the opening ceremonies among some of the world's most elite athletes? What do you think would you see?

David Epstein, a mediocre athlete, one-time science graduate student and Sports Illustrated contributor, aptly describes the scene in his new book, *The Sports Gene: Inside the Science of Extraordinary Performance.* "The 4'9" gymnast beside the 310 pound shot putter who is looking up at the 6'10" basketball player whose arms are seven and a half feet from fingertip to fingertip. Or the 6'4" swimmer who strides into the stadium beside his countryman, the 5'9" miler, both men wearing the same length pants."

Very convincing evidence for, at the very least, how genetic gifts (varying body types) lend themselves to the potential for superior performance in particular sports.

But physique predisposition is not always so discernible. Take Epstein's high school track team teammate who, because of his "bulging paunch," was the brunt of his fellow runner's jokes. Yet, young Micheno, the son of Jamaican parents — the island nation known for its track stars — was the fastest sprinter on the team and led them to win state championships.

So, things are not always as they outwardly seem.

Long before Stein's very readable review of the science and genetics of sports, others believed that there had to be more than just physical gifts to explain how elite athletes, who could repeat extraordinary performances practically routinely, were just that, elite.

Case in point: Albert Pujols versus Jennie Finch. In the spring of 2004, Pujols was regarded as the best hitter in all of baseball. Jennie Finch was about to pitch the USA Olympic Softball team to the gold medal later that summer.

Pujols hit 95 mph fastballs for a living. Finch's pitches maxed out in the upper 60 mph range. But, when adjustments were calculated for the closer mound location in softball, her pitches took about the same time to reach home plate as a 95 mph baseball. Fair match-up. Right? And geez, c'mon, against a "girl" with a bigger ball.

Wrong. Very wrong. He couldn't even foul one off. Strike three. So much for the long standing theory that the gift of lightning quick reflexes, that long standing frame of reference, was *the* primary difference maker to be among the best in a sport. In fact, Pujols, when measured for simple reaction time among random college students at Washington University in St. Louis, rated no better than the 66th percentile!

So, it follows that there has to be more.

The first hint came in the early 1940s in a study conducted by a Dutch chess master and psychologist, Adriaan de Groot, who flashed still photographs of in-game chessboards to both grandmasters and lesser but still very good players. It turned out that the indisputable advantage of the masters was their superior ability to accurately reconstruct the staged game boards in only a matter of seconds of viewing it.

De Groot concluded, "It is evident that experience is the foundation of the superior achievements of the masters." The theory of "chunking" - unconsciously grouping information into smaller chunks triggered by patterns of play seen previously - had its beginnings.

Thirty years later, Dr. Janet Starkes, a former basketball point guard on the Canadian national team, invented the sports "occlusion" test based on her graduate school research in what became known as "perceptual cognitive skills."

Bruce Abernathy, an inquisitive cricket player at the University of Queensland in Australia, rode the occlusion wave further.

He showed a wide variety of batsmen film of cricket bowlers, cutting it off just prior to the throw and then asking where the ball was headed in the batsman's striking zone. The star players far surpassed the lesser players at predicting its resulting path.

Epstein, from his own research information, concluded that "elite athletes need less time and less visual information to predict what will happen in the future, and, *without knowing it*, they zero in on the critical visual information." So, the very best athletes in any sport "chunk" opponent's body information and positions, based on *their* database of experience, in the same way that the chess grandmasters could "see" the board so quickly.

Because Pujols had never seen Finch pitch before, with her completely different underhanded softball delivery compared to the overhand baseball pitch delivery, he was at an insurmountable disadvantage facing her for the first time.

Roger Federer, like Pujols, is among the very best at gleaning subtle information from opponent's physical cues, in his instance regarding their intended shot direction, from years of game experience. This references the conventional wisdom, coined by Florida State University psychologist K. Anders Ericsson, that it takes 10,000 hours of practice to acquire really extraordinary skills. Exactly why on court, Federer can read the monster groundies of today's players and effortlessly almost casually, chase them down and do something with them.

In terms of your own game, how can you take your own perceptual cognitive skills to another level, the one you realize every now and then, but cannot deliver on a relatively consistent basis?

First, you have to aspire to not having any holes in your game. Owning rock solid, shot making, *core fundamentals* is essential in enabling a just-do-it auto pilot game, one based upon whatever your innate and developed talent is. This

3

will facilitate a greater consistency and trust.

Making an investment, even a small one, in coaching can pay big dividends. All the new rackets and strings, the ones that always manage to offer the perfect blend of power and control, can only do so much.

It will also be essential to develop "triple vision" a phrase coined by Canadian pro Peter Burwash in the '80s, referring to a technique that fully utilizes your visual dexterity to "see" the game that's in front of you in the blink of an eye - like Fed - and not be undermined by a slow, distracting, overly conscious paint by the numbers approach, a sign of less experienced players.

Triple vision means never focusing primarily on the court or the opponent (some exceptions in doubles). Direct sighting is on the ball, and only the ball, incoming and outgoing. The opponent and the court are "seen" only through your periphery, which is where the "cues" mentioned earlier are ultimately unconsciously recognized through experience, exactly what Pujols found himself without against the unfamiliar Finch. The main focus remains on the flight of the ball, triggering auto responses, the quality of which will be dependent upon both your game nurturing - the time you've put in learning, practicing efficient mechanics - and your predisposed genetic gifts.

Federer once stated that he believed his greatest singular skill to be "seeing" his shot response faster than anyone else.

Start nurturing your inner Fed today!

The Tennis Mind-Set Universality

The beginning of a new year always symbolically represents an opportunity to set new goals in life, work, play and tennis!

One's tennis game, always a work in progress, can reap immediate rewards without even stepping on the court. Sure, you'd like to develop that one-handed backhand slice that skids suddenly into unsuspecting opponents. But focusing instead on becoming a better game manager of your existing skills has an even greater upside. Who better than Yogi Berra to explain the crucial role the mind plays in sport: "Baseball is 90 percent mental, and the other half is physical."

In More Than Just The Strokes, I convey that a common thread exists in all of sport — one that is simultaneously universal — particularly in tennis, with its mano a mano dynamic that has always made it both inviting and frustrating to its more than 60-milion worldwide participants.

This thread is thoroughly represented in mind-sets put forth by tennis greats past and present as well as some of the very best in other individual sports and disciplines, but also, far more intriguingly, by some of history's greatest thinkers. Whenever I come across one of their gems, not tennis specific but strikingly not out of context either, I always surmise that these individuals would have been, in spirit, accomplished tennis players even without skidding backhands.

We observe in collective awe the wizardry tennis' best are, and were, able to produce. Seeing it on the Tennis Channel is extraordinary enough. At a live venue, it's jaw dropping. How they are able to synergistically run, jump, twist and turn to connect perfectly with a fast moving small yellow sphere that's approaching with myriad spins and trajectories, and then redirect it back in-kind, is truly amazing. Not exactly "death-defying" as an earlier generation of circus performers were promoted, but defying for mere mortal clubbers nonetheless.

Yet, when these incredibly athletic and fit superstars are asked how they elevated their games to experience even greater successes than achieved earlier in their careers — none better represented than by Novak Djokovic's 2011 campaign — they consistently credit not better ball striking but mostly improved mental and emotional control as the difference maker in their play.

The ideal mind-set that facilitates this optimal state of body performance goes deep into the human psyche. When I experienced my 15 minutes of fame eons ago, sports psychologists didn't even exist. Now these mind coaches populate any and every sport you can think of.

Sports psychologists' training programs have capitalized on the sports metaphor that has successfully lent itself to now popular corporate training programs, especially those involving high stress occupations. One in particular, spawned by Dr. Jim Loehr — the father of mental toughness training, whom Arthur Ashe once referred to as "the most important person in tennis today" — is a by-product of Loehr's earlier work with tennis pros who, back then, were viewed as "head cases."

In tennis, their role is to simplify, clarify, and quiet the conscious mind to "settle to the task," as retired ESPN announcer Fred Stolle liked to say. His contemporary, the incomparable Rod Laver, still regarded by many as the best player of all-time, once quipped, "Tennis is a simple game. It's just not easy."

None other than Leonardo da Vinci would have been one of those in-spirit players referred to earlier. He proclaimed, "The greatest sophistication is found in simplicity." Clearly one of the world's greatest minds was on to something.

But our minds can play cruel tricks at the most inopportune times, and simple is not so simple. Frustrated with the dismal performance of an Olympic medal contender at the 2002 winter games, U.S. coach Marjan Cernigoj classically observed, "The fear of failure overcame the desire for success."

Likewise, the fire breathing Rafael Nadal admitted a few months ago, "I do not fear losing. I fear the fear of losing." Such is the delicate mental-emotional balance that one's performance in any endeavor is vulnerable to.

Jean Butler, the spectacular lead dancer in the original stage production of Riverdance, explained her performances this way, "On a good night nothing goes through my mind."

And the Swedish philosopher Kierkegaard would have had that Sampras ice water running through his veins had he been a player with this pearl, "Be with what is, so that what is to be, may become." Easier said than done."

Four centuries after Leonardo thought light years out of his box, Albert Einstein, who actually did play tennis, distilled problem solving into his Three Rules of Work: 1) Out of clutter, find simplicity; 2) From discord, find harmony; 3) In the middle of difficulty lies opportunity. Now there's a mind-set for aspiring players.

This clutter, discord and difficulty inhabit the minds of too many club tennis players like some incurable contagion. A rudderless stagnation occurs with predictable results: an exercise in frustration. Zen master Shunryu Suzuki's take on this paralysis evokes the simplicity theme once more, "In the beginner's mind there are many possibilities, but in the expert's mind there are few."

Before there was a Michael Phelps, Ian Thorpe was the world's dominant swimmer. In addressing the expectations of others regarding winning Olympic medals he said, "I don't swim for medals; I swim for performances. You have control over your performance. You don't have control over where you finish in a race. I think that's the right way, the best way to approach it." Success is empty if there's no possibility of failure, but the primary focus must remain on performing well, not the winning and losing.

Open water swimmer Lynne Cox openly acknowledged the tricky mind-body relationship manifested in her constant inner battles with fear and self-doubt, particularly in her Antarctic Ocean swim in life threatening 32 degree water. How you manage these normal human emotions is the key to unlocking your game.

Daniel Kahneman's experiences in the Israeli army's psychology corps included conducting tests designed to identify an individual's most innately predisposed to poise under fire. "We saw who seemed to be stubborn, submissive, arrogant, patient, hot-tempered, persistent or a quitter" he said, all strengths and liabilities applicable to the tennis quest. He believed the initial evaluations were a slam dunk. But individual results reported months later at officer training schools were often completely contradictory to the initial data. So yes, more positive, productive mental and emotional skills can indeed be developed.

"Taming the beast," my reference to eliminating the useless cacophony of noise in one's head that typically occurs when the task is seemingly moving too fast, involves never underestimating the importance of monitoring and orchestrating one's mind state. Creating the right climate by calmly thinking the right thoughts when it's time to think, and then pulling off the ultimate tennis mind trick of thinking no thoughts at all when it's time to physically execute what you've practiced —Just Do It — is indeed an acquired ability.

For starters, this takes a day in and day out commitment to conviction, courage and trust in what you know is already doable by playing within your existing game, nothing more. It's being with it, not against it. And it's making the time to practice regularly to maintain and sharpen your skills. It's not match play, match play and more match play, the self-defeating dead end street of far too many.

First You RELAX, Then You Do NOTHING

I wish that was an original line. It's not. A former frequent student, one Mickey Suarez, rattled that off to me in Spanish with a huge smile of satisfaction a number of years ago after a game epiphany session.

Mickey was a fit, physical player, a former eights collegiate rower, who loved to spar from the back of the court, an eager dirt baller. A bad shoulder had put his serving on the backburner. But he was a solid ball striker off both wings - a 4.0 with occasional 4.5 flash - sporting a two-handed backhand that he learned and honed at one of the many Spanish academies he had previously attended long before Rafael Nadal came to prominence.

He was also a self-destructor once he got deep into a back court rally, typically at the fifth or sixth ball. He could hold his own and create extended stalemate exchanges, but then he would blink first and go for too much without an inviting opportunity. Too close to the lines, or not enough safe margin over the net, or both. Suddenly, for no good reason, trying to force square pegs into round holes.

He would huff and puff and ultimately blow his own house down. I wouldn't give up trying to convince him that he was his own worst enemy, and that he should chill a bit, just go with the flow. That stalemating out of the gate was winning, not losing, as it is perceived by so many clubbers playing with their hair on fire, in singles or doubles. And that he should forget about trying to hit winners and glory shots, the source of almost all of his impatient, unforced errors.

He could dance, but he was unwilling to tango.

One day, after his usual stellar and nearly error free warm-up - when he was always okay with the back-and-forth cooperative rhythms of a proper warm-up - I suggested that during our rally points he should focus on still being aggressive but with very safe margins to the lines along with optimal margins above the net to keep his shots deep, or low to the net to place the ball at my feet when I came in. And to also stop pressing early on for something special, to make me play more balls to draw some errors, and to play within himself regarding average pace of shot and accompanying racket speed through the ball.

That's when Mickey exclaimed, "Primero se relaja, y despues hace nada," after finally committing to playing the points with the same willing-to-engage mind set he always warmed-up with. Fearlessly engaging me in racket-to-racket combat, he then played his A-game consistently throughout the session with unforced errors dramatically reduced.

He got it.

When you're all about performing well versus being outcome oriented - anxious about winning/losing - you'll begin to be with the game instead of being against it. Winning then becomes a by-product of your ability to execute your shots without the self-induced pressure from an overly judgmental self.

Playing at the very edge of your ball-striking skills, just because you made a couple of truly outstanding shots in the match's second game, is asking for a bad day at the office. Understand that your truly best stuff, your $100 shots if you will, are typically a spontaneously occurring perfect storm of high-level ball tracking, clear shot visualization, energized footwork and perfectly timed racket-on-ball contact with accompanying breathing. Buying into your own headline, and then attempting to replicate those personal best results on a consistent basis, is a recipe for handing the match over.

The classic example of "first you relax, then you do nothing" occurs all the time on returns of serves, the ones when you're anticipating that the serve is going to be in, but then realizing it just missed. At the last moment, already committed and in motion, you completely relax physically and emotionally, the point suddenly no longer at stake, and hit an effortless return with both big pace and spot-on placement.

Eureka.

Although the sport of boxing doesn't appeal to most - although Andy Murray is both a huge fan and student of it - the mano-a-mano similarity to tennis is undeniable. Bernard Hopkins, who until recently held two of the world light-heavyweight titles at age 49 in a young man's game far more punishing than tennis (Roger Federer has been declared by pundits "old" at 33), would have been an excellent tennis player.

In a recent in-depth magazine profile, Carl Rotella nailed the Hopkins essence this way: "Opponents don't worry about facing his speed or power anymore. They fear what's going on in his head."

Now in the latter part of his career, Hopkins never throws more punches than he needs to win and never goes for the knockout. Think constant placements versus winners, which decrease his chances of being hit - think reducing errors. He makes nuanced adjustments in spacing and timing - think changing pace and spin - that neutralizes an opponent's rhythm.

"Figuring out what the other guy wants to do and not letting him do it is a matter of policy for Hopkins," Rotella reports. Just like using the drop shot, or even a short chip, to bring in those maddening, incessant lobbers to take away, typically, their only strength.

A disciple of Sun Tzu's Art of War, he is also the "wise general" who wins by attacking an opponent's strategy versus a go-for-broke all-out slug fest. Or, in tennis, that could be succumbing to playing a slow motion lobbing contest.

Speaking of Federer, who has had a resurgence this year that has answered his critics following an injury-plagued 2013 campaign, Tennis Channel commentator Darin Cahill commented on his denial of Father Time: "In general, I think Roger has done a wonderful job of holding on to his youth. He's a young 33-year-old, and he still moves beautifully, but he doesn't move as well as he did 10 years ago".

Cahill also noted that with all of the Federer shot wizardry still intact, tactically he has reduced his myriad options in order to be more efficient and effective in his current older state.

Simplify.

When one of the all-time best now pays far more attention to playing more within himself, it's time to listen.

Back in club land, my regular lesson clients soon learn the correct response to my repeated query regarding exactly what was it that they did so well after a great point or practice exchange - "nothing special" Yet, doing nothing special is special in club tennis when you are not in possession of Federer's shot-making genius. It's important to know your limitations and that all club level matches are lost in on-paper even match-ups, such as 3.5s versus 3.5s. They are not won with consistently spectacular shot making. They are given away by far too many completely unforced, unnecessary errors.

The late Vic Braden, a Tennis Hall of Famer and respected coach with a comedic bent who gained notoriety during the 1970s tennis boom, would always say a couple of things for on-court success that caught on: "Keep hitting the same old boring shots over and over," and "Keep giving them another chance to screw-up."

Victory belongs to those who believe in that the longest.

How To Be
A Solid
Competitor

At the 2010 South African Open in Johannesburg this past February, surprising on-the-rise Frenchmen Stephan Robert reached the final before bowing out to Spain's highly ranked Feliciano Lopez. The announcing team, impressed with Robert's break-out performance, succinctly described his game this way: "No real weapons, but he competes so well." Yes, you can be successful at any level by being extremely difficult to beat by *always* competing well.

In an emotionally charged individual game like tennis, you must overcome your opponent(s), but yourself as well, which is often the most difficult task. Losing the inner mental-emotional match will always result in a sub-par performance, and typically a loss in a close but winnable contest.

When you're humming along, firing on all eight cylinders with your tail up, it's all good. Yet, when things go wrong, and they usually do at some point during a match, it often has little to do with your ball-striking skills. One of the very best competitors of all time, Rafael Nadal, lost all three of his matches at the 2009 Barclays ATP World Tour Finals without winning a single set. Afterwards, he summed up his poor play: "I was unable to stay calm in the important moments."

Some players - certainly not Nadal — in the face of adversity, put the flippers on and go in the tank. They fail to give 100 percent, not only physically, but mentally and emotionally as well. They've always got numerous post-match excuses aimed squarely at saving face and insulating themselves from assuming responsibility for their poor effort: "All they did was lob." "It was so windy I couldn't play my game." "I don't like playing at 8 a.m." "The court was slippery." "I had a bad partner."

Accept the conditions. Adapt.

Caving in to adverse circumstances is the worst possible scenario for any competitor. It's an embarrassment to yourself and disrespectful to both your opponent(s) and the game itself.

Anger management is another obstacle to overcome. It's well established that it's very difficult to transform negative emotions and outbursts into a positive result. Most know that, so why do we do it? More often than not, it's an appeal to one's partner, and opponent(s), and anyone who happens to be watching, that this is just not the real you and you're not happy about it. Not exactly a good fix.

Jimmy Connors, widely recognized as one of tennis' all-time bad boys, never directed any expressed anger inward. His venom was directed at the umpire, the linesmen or even a boisterous fan giving him a hard time. Despite his sometimes over the line behavior, Connors was always all about finding solutions regarding any match play difficulties. Tanking was never an option. Playing in the present, and always going forward, was.

Okay, good competitors never tank, and rarely ever allow anger to be directed inward, but they do choke. Yes, everybody chokes on occasion. No one is choke proof. Even the world's best, in any sport, experience choking. In tennis, I challenge you to watch any tight match on television and then tell me that player X did not choke one single time. No way! Just recall Andy Roddick's botched routine backhand volley that would have given him a most likely insurmountable two sets to none lead over Roger Federer in the 2009 Wimbledon final.

Since it's a given that even occasional tanking and the habitual expression of anger are not acceptable if you're going to play your best, how can you minimize choking in the big moments?

The intrusion of negative thoughts, conscious thoughts occurring in your analytical left brain, is anything but conducive to producing your best brand of play. When your judgmental self overcomes your just-do-it player self at the ball-striking moment of truth, you're pretty much toast and well on your way into a downward spiral. Whenever negativity, in the form of defeatist thought or naysayer self-talk, rears its ugly head, immediately say to yourself, "Stop it." Get rid of the whining and replace it with positive self-talk: "C'mon, you can do it!" Then embrace both in-point and out' of-point visualizations of successful shot "flight plans." These occur in the brain's more friendly right hemisphere, where your hard- earned shot-making skills are readily available. Simply put, thinking in pictures is a far more effective way to play versus reciting to yourself some ill-fated, by the numbers, how-to-play checklist right when you're striking the ball. Paralysis through analysis.

You have to love the report that Cornell University's men's basketball team, upon arriving early to the arena for their NCAA March Madness game against the favored Temple University, was not allowed to use basketballs for warm-ups until exactly :57 seconds prior to tip-off. So, being a motivated group with a good coach, they still started early and first performed all of their drills without basketballs! Visualization at its best. And, yes, they won the game.

The other technique that serves as an excellent choking counter measure is always breathing audibly through the moment of ball-on- string impact, and even a bit louder in the big or nervous moments. The sheer physicality of the act not only prevents the obvious — going into oxygen debt — but considerably reduces emotional stress by effectively negating conscious over-thinking.

Back in the day, I can remember playing a match at my very best from start to finish. Afterwards I heard the opposing player's coach, in a consoling effort, telling his player that I was "unconscious" and that I "played out of my mind" as was commonly said back then. Exactly, although that would have been my left-mind.

You can too. Start today!

Playing *Within* Yourself

The art of maximizing shot effectiveness while minimizing errors.

Playing within yourself. What exactly does that mean? Try this: not over hitting, not under hitting, but playing mostly in between.

Maximizing shot making effectiveness while simultaneously minimizing unforced errors is the end-all to performing at one's peak. Race car driver Danica Patrick's take on this balancing act — in a go-fast sport where possible loss of life and limb is a constant — strikes a relevant chord: "We're always right on the brink of crashing." Back on court, go for your shots, but know your limitations. Being outplayed and outgunned by a better player or team is one thing, but at the end of the day, a self-destructive pattern of unforced errors leaves a very bad taste.

A number of components contribute to tweaking the most out of your game, win or lose. Shot margins-to-the-lines and margins- to-the-net particularly represent the PWY core, whether you're on offense, defense, just playing "rally ball" neutral, red hot or stone cold.

The lines on the court merely inform you of what's in and what's out. A different set of boundaries, pictured in your mind's eye, should represent your realistic placement goals. "Play calling," or visualizing where the ball is intended to land should provide a bit of safety, be forgiving and, as a result, actually promote aggressiveness. It might be surprising to learn that Roger Federer's self-proclaimed greatest ability is just that: "...recognizing what's coming and then seeing my shot. I think I do that faster than anybody."

Committing to safe parameters — that's venturing no closer than 3-5 feet from the lines (still a very effective shot!) — will immediately reduce overzealous, needless, frustrating mistakes that can ruin your day. It will also foster a more relaxed brand of ball striking — playing freely — that eliminates the self-induced pressure to hit well-intentioned but unforgiving thread-the-needle bulls-eyes in the corner, for example. If your shot does get away from you despite good "quarterbacking," the built-in safety often results in a shot that may be dangerously close to going out, but that often wins the point. This is the unintended reward of PWY. Of course, always act like you meant it, but don't buy into it!

Understand that even a very average club player makes the majority of their mistakes either in the net, where there is zero chance for success, or long, with shots passing over the net at too great a height for the pace they were hit, causing them to sail beyond the baseline. Errors made to the left or the right of the sidelines are comparatively few and far between. Yet, when I ask aspiring players how much they intended to clear the net by, particularly after they've dumped one

13

into the net or hit the back windscreen, it's not at all unusual for them to pause and then glaze over without a definitive response. Being unaware of vertical intentions is a recipe for poor play.

Realize that since you can see through the net, the fact that it's a formidable barrier is easily forgotten. If it were a brick wall instead, there would be far fewer mistakes made in the net or beyond the baseline, and no one would have to be made aware of the necessity of visualizing a "flight plan." It would be that obvious. In fact, if you were to stand at the baseline and imagine that brick wall net, none of the court lines would be visible...unless you were John Isner. The net is not your friend, so turn it into a positive by making use of it as a "fly-over" reference point, or connecting dot A above the net to the dot B on the court.

Safe margins-to-the-net intentions come into play on every shot. Instantaneously determining your intended amount of clearance (like Federer does) is a blend of several components. Shot trajectory — varying rainbow topspin, floaty underspin and laser-like balls hit flat — along with shot speed and your court position all factor into zeroing in on the degree of clearance that fits each opportunity.

Playing to the score — by always knowing the score before the next point is played — also plays an important role in shot selection. With a 40-0 lead, for example, margins can be narrowed since you have "one to waste." Go big if you've got an inviting ball. Why not! Flatten your shot out with less net clearance, and go ahead and flirt with the lines. Some of the time you'll succeed and make a winner, or cause a forced error. When you make the error, no worries; you've still got two game points and, believe me, a message has been sent that you will jump on any meatballs served up.

Then there are the pivotal "swing points," where it's 15-30 and you need to level the score at 30-30 or fall precariously behind to 15-40. Here's where you pull back a bit and engage opponents with bigger margins all around, along with slightly less pace, looking to draw an unforced error by luring an opponent into playing outside of themselves. Commenting on playing Serena Williams at Wimbledon, Lindsey Davenport said: "Serena is the best at taking pace off her shots and concentrating instead on placement in key moments." Other score lines dictate their own strategies and tactics along, factoring in how well you're playing at the time. Adapt to the task at hand.

It's interesting to note that many are not cognizant that, with the obvious exception of the game winner, the very first point played in each game is the most important. That first point is instrumental in setting the tone for how the game will play out. Statistics reveal that those who win the first point, among players of similar ability, are far more likely to be successful, not to mention the impacting built-in psychological advantage. This is not the time to "waste one" as so many do by playing a loose, out-on-the-jazz first point that immediately puts them in a hole.

Be real. Make them play. Stick to it.

Putting a Face on Your Game

Nearly everyone is familiar with the term "body language" as it relates to everyday life. Many people, especially those who play sports, also recognize its significance as it relates to athletic performance. Many of these sporting individuals are, to varying degrees, in touch with their own body language, but are particularly aware of it in others. Typically, body language manifests itself in one of three categories: positive, negative and neutral.

Tennis players spend much of their match time playing in between points, and the more experienced and successful players are very aware of exhibiting positive body language during these non-playing moments, whether they're winning or losing.

Sure, players can become demonstrative in brief celebrations after winning a key or hard fought point — the fist pump, thigh slap and "c'mon" outbursts are common. But then it's right back to the same ritualistic, emotionally even-keeled routine leading up to the start of the next point. This type of positive behavior is paramount in maintaining one's optimal body chemistry in a mano-a-mano, finite sport like tennis.

But another manifestation — though rarely, if ever, mentioned by even the best television analysts — exists in facial expression, traditionally referred to as one's "game face." Rafael Nadal's snarl as he begins his service toss immediately comes to mind as does the classic Boris Becker penchant for extending his tongue out of the side of his mouth.

In our post-9/11 world, intelligence experts have developed a technique of studying facial expressions to identify potential terrorists. Vic Braden, a long-time tennis coach, author and psychologist, attended a seminar on facial analysis by leading computer science professor Dr. Gerard Medioni. Braden then applied what he learned to the study of facial expressions of tour players, particularly those of Roger Federer.

He discovered that Federer played with a straight-ahead visual focus along with a slightly upward-turned mouth against all opponents but one: Nadal. When facing his nemesis, and only his nemesis, he tended to look downward and wear a slight frown. So, yes, one's external facade — face and body — can absolutely be a window into one's mental and emotional state.

Taken further, the fleeting moment of ball on string contact is especially telling. Go ahead and observe the facial expressions, right at shot impact, of the

15

players on your own tour. You'll be amazed, and occasionally amused. Facial expressions can even vary from stroke to stroke depending on one's right at shot impact, of the players on your own tour. You'll be amazed, and occasionally amused. Facial expressions can even vary from stroke to stroke depending on one's expertise or lack thereof. They can also be heavily influenced depending upon the match moment at hand.

On the wrong side of what might be called "the game lace ledger" are three unfortunate, albeit common, responses during impact. First, there's the "deer in the headlights" expression, which suggests they player doesn't know what to do and indicates they're completely overcome by the task at hand. Then there's the "fraidy- cat" look: the tear of failure is clearly present and accounted for, psych 101 conflict avoidance at its best. Finally, the "clenched jaw breaker" is quite another story: standing fast, which is a step in the right direction, bur taking on the ball like an enemy in battle, totally over-amped with excessive muscle tension, eliminating any chance of playing consistently.

For the better side, there are two modes. The "gunfighter" look is steely eyed, exuding confidence, unafraid, clearly in charge of the proceedings in the present and going forward into the fray. The other desirable look that can pay dividends over the long haul is the classic "poker player" face: deadpan, slack jawed, emotionless, revealing nothing at all, yet totally comfortable and fully engaged. Tim Adams, in his book *On Being John McEnroe*, described the often over-the-top demeanor and psychodrama of McEnroe in his heyday.

"Others, like Borg and Sampras," he wrote, "managed to make their faces a mask that revealed little of what was going on inside — only to be criticized [mistakenly] as 'dull'..."

I'm looking forward to viewing a good image of Andy Roddick's facial expression right as he was blowing that easy backhand volley on set point versus Federer previously mentioned. Had he made it — no doubt keenly aware of what was at stake, the Wimbledon title — it would have given him a two-sets-to-none lead, one that even Federer, the eventual winner, would most likely not be able to overcome considering Roddick's stellar level of play.

At this juncture in my own tennis lite, although no longer competing, I still occasionally find myself in high-pressure situations where pride is definitely on the line. The odd Pro-Am or friendly exhibition are ripe with possibilities of a moment of uncertainty creeping in on my second serve, just when it counts the most — the club pro's least-hit shot and most embarrassing if butchered.

As a young, junior player coach, well before Braden's sophisticated research was published, I stumbled upon the benefit of trying to maintain the "right" facial expression at the split-second, shot- making moment by observing tour players. I learned then that the "right" look definitely equated to better results. Much like the technique of visualizing shot success on every ball — a skill valued in all sports — the "right" facial expression greatly enhance one's prospects of fending off negative mind sets and real or perceived vulnerability.

For me, the "gunfighter" look usually keeps me afloat during the bad patches, but otherwise it's the "poker player" persona that is instrumental in keeping me on an even keel, thus maximizing my game.

So, it's a pretty good idea to begin identifying your best peak performing persona — both below and above the neck — and then employing it point-in and point-out no matter the circumstance.

In the end, if all is going wrong, you're unable to dial it in and you're feeling conflicted and emotionally at odds with yourself, at least fake it. Chances are you'll be pleasantly surprised!

To Grunt  or Not To Grunt

When classically trained sopranos begin sending letters to newspaper sports editors regarding the high-pitched grunting, no, make that screaming, in women's tennis today, you know that trouble is just around the corner. And well it should, despite the slow moving, ultra-conservative, currently voluntarily toothless hierarchy of the Women's Tennis Association.

Marilyn Vondra, a self-described "big tennis fan," did just that at the conclusion of this year's Australian Open women's final, ironically played in the Rod Laver Arena, named after the legendary player who always displayed fierce competitiveness but never without the highest level of gentility Curious about the musical pitches of the two finalists, the reigning "queens-of- scream" Maria Sharapova and Victoria Azarenka, she went to her piano during their match, first voicing their "sounds" and then locating the exact match on the keyboard.

It turns out that they both are also sopranos, Azarenka emitting high G's with Sharapova blasting out high A-flats. Who knew? What interested Vondra even more was that their post-match voices were completely unaffected. She incredulously noted that she and her classical performing peers would be "hoarse for days."

With negative fan reaction growing and media coverage spiking, the two combatants remain completely indifferent and defiant. After dispatching another elite player — Agnie Radwanska — just prior to the finals, Sharapova, after learning her competitor complained openly that "It's pretty annoying, and it's just too loud," deadpanned, "Isn't she back in Poland already?"

Azarenka, for her part, whined that she's so tired of answering the same questions about her grunting, over and over. Poor child. Her equally out-of-touch coach, Sam Sumyk, smirked prior to the queen's final showdown, "It's going to be a very musical final." I'm betting that it's all heavy metal on his iPod.

Former world No. 1 Caroline Wozniacki is no shrinking violet on the subject. "I think there are some players who do it on purpose," she told reporters. "They don't do it in practice, and then they come into the match and they grunt" She also accused some of trying to gain an edge by drowning out the "sound" of their shot, a key auditory marker in judging an opponent's ball speed and spin.

"I've run into a lot of people who tell me if they're watching tennis on TV, they turn off the sound," noted revered announcer emeritus Bud Collins. "I'm sure players don't need to do it because you don't hear a peep from them when they're

18

practicing. It's gamesmanship." Yes, the same Bud Collins who, back in the day, referred to Jimmy Connors — the father of the modern grunt — as "sounding like a wounded seal."

Enter WTA CEO Stacey Allaster who stated that the "grunting issue" would be addressed last summer but did nothing. Her most recent comment, or justification, played the men's grunting card, "But our female DNA transmits it in a different way." Okay fair point. But does that condone breaking the sound barrier? Andrew Walker, a spokesman for the tour, emerged and ultimately did Allaster's bidding by indicating that "the landscape has changed, and we owe it to the fans to take a look at it." And he added, "It's a matter of degree: grunting is fine, but excessive grunting is not." Promising.

But out of that comes the WTA's most recent position that it wouldn't be fair to "alter the way they play." Instead they've decided that educating coaches, academies and young players is the best way to proceed while leaving the existing assault on the senses of both opposing players and fans alike as is. Where's my blue blazer?

A British tabloid once alleged that Monica Seles' — the first queen- of-scream — loudest grunts at Wimbledon back in the '90s reached 98.1 decibels, which reportedly is only a tick or two lower than a pneumatic drill. Yet, when she tried to smother her distinct two-syllable grunt in the '92 finals versus Steffi Graf, after Martina Navratolova got the Wimbledon brass all fired-up about it disturbing her play in the preceding semis, she got drilled in straight sets. Or was it the death threat that unhinged her? And this was a year before she was stabbed in the back, right on-court, in a Hamburg, Germany event by a deranged Graf supporter. The incident literally muted her and her career.

Mary Jo Fernandez, current U.S. Fed Cup coach and former top 10 player, is the first and only commentator, or player for that matter, who has mentioned the underlying emotional component involved in grunting. It has become increasingly apparent as volume levels vary from shot to shot. The bigger the moment, the more important the point, the more the "grunt-o-meter" needle gets buried. And, to Allaster's point, this is definitely not limited to the women. The impressive stable of Spanish men — the "moaners" — in particular have also embraced louder is better when their nerves are under assault, including Rafael Nadal.

Yet no one, and I mean no one, explains that loud grunting is really a guttural escalation of breathing, more specifically exhaling. Certainly not Ken Benson in his New York Times post-Australian Open article. But that omission was a major faux pas in that all professional players breathe through the racket-on-ball moment. But the court has to be heavily mic'd to hear a Roger Federer, or Graf back then, but trust me, they both are and were breathing out on every shot.

Another flaw in Benson's reporting was that "few coaches specifically teach their players to grunt..." Ground control to Benson! All good coaches teach their players, at any level, to breathe, otherwise they're doomed to becoming inefficient breath holders who tire prematurely both physically and mentally. An oxygen-starved brain undermines decision making and ball watching, not to mention the triggered, excessive accompanying muscle tension.

Appropriate breathing absolutely should be minimally audible to be effective, at least to the ball striking player, at every level. Not only to stave off oxygen depletion, but to reduce emotional stress and promote physical relaxation and its accompanying elevation in power. It's very much a multi-dimensional technique. As a welcome by-product, one's potentially over active, eager beaver, analytical left brain is dumbed-down into momentary optimal unconsciousness, which is precisely where that elusive "zone" of excellence that players and commentators talk about resides.

So what could be done at least at the tour level? Simple. Install an on-court decibel meter as first implied by that British tabloid in '92. Screaming and high-pitched shrieking serve no purpose and certainly has no place in the professional game, or at your neighborhood club and public parks. Radwanska had it right: "Pretty annoying."

If professional tennis can come up with an incredibly high-tech, multiple camera, computer-managed Hawkeye line calling system to virtually end the previously never-ending contentious disputes over line calls, then surely they can add simple decibel meters (set with reasonable noise thresholds) on the courts and include a no-nonsense point penalty system to penalize flagrant offenders. Start taking points away and the pro player adaptation will happen overnight.

It's long past the time the WTA, and all other tennis governing bodies, step up and put an end to behavior that's destructive to, and disrespects, the game.

ON
BEING A
COOL OPERATOR

Joey is not someone you cross paths with very often. Still relatively new to tennis, but not consumed by its allure despite his preternatural skill for that combative *mano-a-mano* dynamic of the game, he is undoubtedly off the everyday tennis player scale and operates at a level very few experience. He is emotionally gifted.

Tennis is indeed extremely emotional, which is the biggest difference maker among its four encompassing components, the other three being technical, physical and mental. Managing one's emotions in a productive manner is not always easy, just observe some of the world's best dealing negatively, and unsuccessfully, with their adverse circumstances.

Young Joey is an anomaly He is cool-wired. Without any previous exposure to sports psychology and with only periodic tennis coaching, he is, at 13, amazingly predisposed to be a cool, calm and completely collected operator no matter his still- developing playing skills.

When then-11-year-old Magnus Carlsen, the Norwegian chess prodigy, played the reigning world champion, Gary Kasparov, to a draw in a 2004 exhibition, it was interesting to observe the 41-year- old Kasparov exhibiting all sorts of emotional stress and duress while the youngster Carlsen deadpanned a walk in the park.

Albeit not destined to be a tennis world champion, Joey has the same attitude and mind-set. He just goes about playing the game on a completely even emotional keel. There's no anger over a missed shot. There's no mounting frustration if things are not going his way, as can commonly happen with still-developing youngsters. And, refreshingly, there's no overly demonstrative fist pumping at every possible opportunity or looking over at his supportive dad for confirmation, now a commonplace occurrence on tour with players constantly looking to their coaches and support team after every point.

Ideally, although there are variations on the theme, it's best when there's nothing, which is a very, very big something. And that's exactly the way Joey rolls.

I recall his dad, a run through a brick wall, make it happen over-achiever, enthusiastically urging Joey, with a hint of frustration, "C'mon, let's go," based upon his misperception of Joey's passive, seemingly cavalier, neutral on-court demeanor, which indicated, to him, a lack of fire and commitment. Not so.

Different circuits for sure, but still competitive to the Nth degree. It was hard wiring unlike his own.

In an elite junior development pilot program I once co-directed with Dr. Jim Loehr, the highly respected innovator in sports psychology's tactics and strategies for peak performance as we know them today, we would periodically videotape players in the facility's stadium court, a very big deal to the kids since most had previously been a ball kid for their heroes in tour events on the same court.

Unknown to them, we were only recording in between points while feigning shooting during points. Later, gathering in the academy playback room, we asked the mates of the two players involved to decide who won each point based upon their post-point body language, facial language, self-talk, if any, and behavior in general.

The kids were on to it quickly and were able to repeatedly and accurately determine the point winners and losers. Seamlessly they recognized how inept and ridiculous they appeared when carrying on negatively or when being way over the top celebrating as well. Then came the epiphany that habitual, histrionic engagement could not only fuel an opponent's fire and resolve but also undermine any necessary solution-oriented tweaking of their own game when needed.

Ivan Lendl, the world # 1 at that time and eventually coach of the hot-wired Andy Murray, provided them with a model of an above-it-all deportment. They had seen him dominate Jimmy Connors, the facility's touring pro, two years running in an ATP event finals. He was the new age, stone faced model, a polar opposite to Connors and especially John McEnroe, who preceded his ascent to the top of the game.

Then along came Pete Sampras who, strangely, was criticized because of his emotionless, laid back, quiet demeanor. Today, the Swiss neutral example of Roger Federer Is accepted and admired. After his win over Murray in this year's Wimbledon final, he confided, "I know we put on the poker face out there when we play, but we are trying hard. We do care so deeply about winning and losing"

There have been several career studies, way ahead of their time, of the sport warrior's ideal performance state, including Loehr who, in his 1980's *Mental Toughness Training for Sports: Achieving Athletic Excellence*, was the very first to mainstream the key mental and emotional markers. But Timothy Gallwey's *The Inner Game*, although far less clinical and somewhat mystical, was the forerunner in the performance psychology field back in 1974.

Others were impactful and remain so today, such as martial arts expert Bruce Lee, whose Eastern take is laid out in *Bruce Lee: Artist of Life*, and Dan Millman, who gave us *The Warrior Athlete: Body, Mind & Spirit, and Body Mind Mastery: Training for Sport and Life.*

Loehr's enduring in point mantra at the time was: "The ball, and only the ball." Losing the ball for even an instant, or worse, only seeing it in your periphery to begin with, equals playing somewhat blind. Tension and emotional stress is then suddenly triggered in the crucial ball-striking split second, a very bad timing. He also was the first to openly advocate breathing — exhaling through the racket-on-ball moment — as a very effective countermeasure to uptightness and was the first to preach pre-shot visualization as an emotionally calming tool as well.

Gallwey's originally coined, now fairly well known, "self-one and self-two" depictions teach that we need to be cognizant of which persona we're channeling under pressure: the accepting, unencumbered, this is my game, just do it, pure player self-one ideal, or the judgmental self-two that cannot, will not completely let go and trust the process.

For the peaceful warrior, Dan Millman explains, "Your fears are not walls, but hurdles. Courage is not the absence of fear, but the conquering of it." And also that, "Self-awareness leads to change; harsh self-criticism only holds the pattern in place."

Bruce Lee's personal letters are filled with enlightening passages: "Remember my friend that it is not what happens that counts; it is how you react to it." Another that's wonderfully relevant to doubles: "One who is possessed by worry not only lacks the poise to solve his own problems, but by his nervousness and irritability creates additional problems for those around him."

In the end, we consistently achieve the best outcome when we resolve to treat every point played the same, best exemplified by the storied Rudyard Kipling quote on a sign at the player s entrance to Wimbledon's fabled centre court: "If you can meet with triumph and disaster and treat those two imposters just the same."

Bobble Heads
A Guide to
Understanding
Ball Watching

Swivel Heads

It is well established that there is a big difference between "sight" and "vision," and that we, at best, utilize only about 30-40 percent of our visual potential. Factor in that athletes in ball sports, at all levels, are required to focus on small spheres moving very quickly through the air — far more demanding than simple static or "near point" acuity — and you've got a daunting task that is, ironically, often taken mostly for granted.

The great baseball hitter Manny Ramirez, when asked about his seemingly preternatural ability to successfully connect a round bat with a ground ball being thrown at him by trickster pitchers also armed with raw power, unassumingly quipped, "I see the ball, I hit the ball."

Compared to the ball-striking skills of a great tennis shot maker — think Roger Federer — club tennis players routinely sabotage themselves in the same stick-on-ball, moment-of-truth dynamic. They are inadvertent victims of bobble-heading (suddenly looking up) and swivel-heading (rapidly turning back). They have "seen" the ball, but they have failed to fully "track" it. Ball game over.

There's more. The eyes are absolutely affected by outside influences like stress and fatigue, both serious detriments in undermining one's performance. The stress of the ball-striking moment, particularly on the big points, as well as physical fatigue, can be overwhelming and result in an ineffective, "glazed-over" peripheral-only ball watching.

I ask players all the time, "Are you good enough to play tennis without watching the ball?" Naturally, they answer "no." I correct them by explaining, "Yes you can, that's what you're doing, and it won't be very good."

The eyes are, of course, required to work together, as a team if you will. This is referred to as "binocularity," the ability to quickly, and smoothly, blend stimuli — the ball — into a clear three-dimensional image. The most difficult task in tennis!

Leaders and innovators in the field of dynamic visual skills, Drs. Leon Revien and Donald Teig, have identified a number of key visual skills for ball sport athletes: accommodation - the adjustment of one's eyes to see objects at varying distances clearly; convergence - fixing both eyes on a specific point simultaneously; depth perception - judging the distance between objects at different points in space; peripheral vision - perceiving and recognizing objects to either side at the corners of the eyes outside the "normal" area of acuity; span and speed of recognition - recognizing, interpreting and reacting to what is seen; spatial awareness - maintaining good posture, balance and orientation while moving.

Sports vision trainers also address player's minds as well as their eyes. By eliminating distracting thought patterns, "visual concentration" is improved. And they strive to improve an athlete's ability to block out unimportant images known as "visual noise." You can't be looking primarily at the opponent, or court, and expect that your attention to the ball isn't going to suffer.

Back to Federer, at the height of his powers a few years ago, he indicated that he thought his greatest skill was his split second recognition of incoming shot speed, spin, trajectory and projected bounce point, and then "seeing" in his mind's eye, his response. The always modest Swiss superstar believed that he was able to achieve all of that faster than anybody in the game.

On the specific difference between sight and vision referred to earlier, well known optometrist Joseph Shapiro maintains "sight" as the perception of objects around us, but regards "vision" as involving our powers of interpretation. Because interpretation depends greatly on one's experience level, "vision" is learned.

The eyes are the body's prime mover and are the first sensory apparatus involved in any physical activity. The sooner the eyes can correctly inform the brain about the incoming ball's flight, the quicker one can correctly respond.

Bottom line: the more flying tennis balls you have seen and experienced in your tennis life, the more accurately the brain and the eyes, working very much in concert, can in large measure predict when and where it can be engaged, and, as a result, how it should be struck back.

Indeed, the role of visualization plays a large part in maximizing ball tracking. Those who hope for a good shot, or hope they don't miss, without visualizing their own shot response "flight plan" are guaranteed a sub-par performance. Stress, a by-product of not clearly visualizing your shots, will rear its ugly head and result in a disconnected peripheral sighting at best. Try catching a ball while staring at nothing in particular and thinking "don't drop it"

Beyond a better understanding of how the eyes and the ball-tracking process really work, and since you're probably not going to seek out a professional sports vision trainer, you can still markedly improve your visual acuity by, simply, keeping your head still while motoring around the court and especially at the shot- making moment.

Unfortunately, club players are often guilty of bobble-heading and swivel-heading while swinging the racket through the ball. The head moves, the body follows, the stroke is altered from its originally intended path, you lose the ball, and you've got a mishit or worse.

Making it a point to always keep the ball in front of you — right-off in the warm-up each and every day since good habits get grooved into our minds, too — will eliminate any last second swivel-heading. And monitoring not looking up at the court or the opponent, instead tracking the ball both "in" and "out" to the best of one's visual ability — watching it both ways — with a relatively still head (think Fed again) will end the auto rear window bobble head doll imitation. You will also experience a completely unexpected and startling perception that the ball is moving slower and that you have more time.

In a moment of zoned clarity, experienced as I warmed-up with a fellow pro at Stanford University just prior to presenting an on-court seminar to the USPTA Northern California pros a couple of years ago, I was able to simultaneously track the ball in-and-out to the nth degree, effectively visualize my shots with a high success rate, breathe and, out of curiosity, manage to peripherally locate a couple of dignitaries as they entered (the latter is not recommended!) Over a half-century of playing experience provides you with lots of practice and a pre-loaded hard drive of good habits.

In the final analysis, once the point is on-going there are only two primary tasks at hand: tracking the ball as described and visualizing your shots — a right brain activity that does not interfere with tracking — immediately upon recognizing the approaching ball. It's all you can manage. Sure, you're monitoring footwork and technique as well, but that's kinesthetically. You're not thinking about it, you're feeling it on a sensory level. You cannot think (interfering left brain activity) and hit at the same time!

Breathing
equals Better Game

A few years back, Joe Obidegwa, an outstanding pro from Naples, joined me at Gilchrist Park in Punta Gorda, Florida for a USTA-sponsored grass roots program for young juniors. He offered a unique perspective on the indispensable nature of breathing and how it significantly can improve one's game.

Immediately after we demonstrated some forehands and backhands, one of the youngsters in the group, itching to play and eyeing the demo rackets waiting by the fence, wanted to know why we "made a noise" when we were hitting the ball. Obidegwa spontaneously took charge and proceeded to explain why.

First, he asked the curious kid how long he could survive without food. With "a long time" quickly established, he then asked another kid how long she could survive without water. An "even longer time," she responded proudly, confident in her answer. Lastly, he asked the group how long they could go without breathing. After having one of them stand and hold his breath for as long as he could, quite a few simultaneously raised their hands and excitedly shouted out what amounted to, "Not very long!" Now, with their full attention, Obidegwa explained, "That's why we breathe out and make a little noise too when we hit the ball, so we can keep playing all day and never run out of air."

Virtually all club-level tennis players, both frequent and occasional participants, thoroughly enjoy, and always benefit from, watching the very best players on television and especially live at a tour venue. They instinctively assimilate what they've seen into their own games, which is readily noticed by their peers when they're back in action at their home club or park.

Yet, mostly, these same players are curiously reluctant, or self-conscious about, adopting what they've heard, that being the audible sound of players exhaling right as they're striking their shots. They unfortunately remain "breath holders" at the all-important racket-on-ball moment, a practice that sharply elevates muscle tension, undermines performance and, far more importantly, is detrimental tmo one's on-court health — including upper body injuries — and overall wellbeing.

There are a number of reasons why proper breathing is so beneficial — at any level of play — in the physically demanding game of tennis. The most obvious is to prevent the cumulative onset of oxygen debt, which invariably leads to unnecessarily elevated and potentially dangerous heart rates along with accelerated dehydration. If that's not enough, oxygen deprivation also results in difficulty concentrating on the ball and the poor decision making that accompanies it. I make it a point to remind players, those who are able to sustain long physical rallies from the baseline, "If you're going to play that well, you're going to have to start breathing!"

Breathing can also help you become more powerful in your shot making — widi less effort — and ennjoy greater stamina over the course of a match, particularly as it relates to your overall muscle tension. Think of your breathing regimen when you're in the gym weight training, or doing crunches and push-ups on your lanai. You inhale while doing the "negative" movement of the exercise and exhale during the "positive" movement. No personal trainer would ever allow you to hold your breath.

Something that's barely ever mentioned is the synergistic benefit of exhaling on impact. The very physicality of the act — you *do not have to be loud* for it to be effective — substantially diffuses any inadvertent, counter productive, over analytical, left-brain thinking that makes top-notch ball watching extremely difficult.

The strange case of Jay Lapidus always comes up when exploring this topic. As a former Princeton #1 and journeyman tour player, Lapidus, who now directs the men's and women's programs at Duke, was known to breathe audibly both for himself and his opponent! First, as the ball approached his point of impact, the inhalation occured followed by the audible exhalation as he struck his own shot. Then, as his ball neared the opponent's strike zone, anodier inhalation, followed by another audible exhalation as they hit theirs. Now, this isn't recommended for match play, but as a breathing exercise in a practice situation, this certainly has merit for those interested in becoming more aware of their breathing patterns... or lack thereof.

Jimmy Connors was the first tour player to bring attention to, and ultimately popularize with the advent of TV tennis, audibly exhaling on every shot.

Later on, Monica Seles, who clearly modeled her style of play after Jimbo, added her own innovation: the two-syllable exhalation, albeit considerably louder. The very first queen of scream. As she approached the top of the women's game in '92 it was a defining component of her game, that is until the player complaints grew and she became conflicted about it under heat from officials. That led to her underwhelming performance in a Wimbledon final where she lost lost badly to Steffi Graf, 6-1, 6-2, with her well over-the-top breathing habits completely disrupted.

Finally, who knows what the exact origination of the athletic term "choking" is. Most likely it's a reference to being so uptight and fearful that one has difficulty breathing normally.

The reality is that everyone chokes on occasion, but, yes, breathing absolutely does equal a better game and reduce its occurances.

Embracing
the Shot-Making Chain

Players serious about their games are absolutely correct when they tell me, with predictable frustration, that "there's too much to think about" when they first become exposed to mechanical ball-striking flaws and are motivated to improve. When recognizing the long-term limitations of sketchy technique, corrective fundamental information — even when offered in small doses — can be potentially overwhelming and result in shot-making paralysis through over-analysis.

Nonetheless, recognition remains the first step in game improvement. Yet many misperceive the improvement process. They think that since they made the effort to seek out professional help, and typically experienced an immediate improvement on the lesson court, they'll be able to jump right back into match play, with all its considerable pressures, and retain the new skills their muscles have not yet memorized. Hardly realistic.

World No. 1 golfer, Rory McIlroy, who struggled mightily early in the 2013 season, explained trying to right himself this way: "This year, we knew it was a little bit of a problem, and we were trying to find the balance between making a bit of a swing change and finding some payability in it so that I can actually go out there and play and not think about it. But we realized there are no quick fixes in golf."

Nor are there any in tennis either.

Players can become disappointed when they don't realize the miracle match-play transformation they expected following the quick success they had in that first session with their pro. When they return for a follow-up, it's not unusual for them to declare they're not playing at the level they expected, sometimes stating that they're "playing worse."

Unfortunately, an old, misleading adage is still around: "After a lesson, you get worse before you get better." Because, despite qualifiers from their pros regarding the necessity of non-match play practice repetition before jumping back in the fray, that's often what happens.

When you find yourself thinking about your new correctives in the middle of a match — precisely because you have not put in the necessary practice time to absorb a new motor skill into your random-access memory (e.g. getting your racket ready sooner or retaining your newly re-balanced position on your forehand follow through) — you'll become conflicted and won't be able to walk and chew gum.

Thinking about the "how-to's in the shot-making moment at 30-40 won't work. You can only monitor mechanics kinesthetically, maintaining a soft -grip tension, using a full range of motion backhand follow through or managing racket-head speed and the like for optimal results. Play by feel, if you will.

Conversely, left -brain analytical thinking about the mechanical necessities of the game in the midst of striking a ball makes it extremely difficult to keep your eyes fully focused on the ball — eye function is closely linked to which part of your brain you're accessing. And yes, this very possibly results in you playing worse.

It is, however, empowering to know that in live action, the very same kinetic sequence of events occurs every single time, which means getting into a groove is very doable when the process is understood physically, technically, mentally and emotionally.

Q: How many practice reps does it take to "own" a new or altered technique?

A: Unknown, but a lot. Not to mention the variable from player to player. But with sufficient practice, the shot-making chain can become second nature, a literal no-brainer while you, liberated from a ball-striking checklist, can focus on the ball and visualize instead. Note; daily rebooting in a diligent warm-up is always an absolute necessity.

Let's keep in mind that tour professionals practice hit — not play matches! — practically every single day to ensure playing freely and unconsciously...and to keep improving.

The sequential ball-striking process, work in progress or not, always begins with tracking your own ball's path into an opponent's racket. At their impact, you have landed your split step, and, upon recognizing their shot-response direction, you begin turning and preparing your racket simultaneously while initiating position for intercept.

In this first fractional moment — a 3.5 player has approximately .91 seconds to both assess and re-direct a 60 m.p.h. approaching ball — you "read" the speed, trajectory, spin (topspin, underspin, no spin), predict where it will touchdown and commit to how you're going to play it.

One of the three primary reads is realizing that the ball is approaching in a relatively low arc over the net and won't have an especially deep landing. Its resulting bounce won't be very high due to its low angle of descent, and you'll have plenty of longitudinal spacing to allow it to descend into your knee-to-thigh-high wheelhouse, everyone's favorite, most anatomically neutral hitting zone.

Another is noting an incoming ball's high rainbow trajectory well over the net (with or without topspin), but still with a landing point that's not particularly deep in the court. The steep angle of descent into the court will produce a high bounce that allows for an opportunity to play the shot at the ball's apex, or around shoulder high. Not only does this take time away from your opponent's positional recovery, it also eliminates the long-term, self-limiting habit of some players — especially in doubles — who choose to back up, often well beyond the baseline, to allow the ball to drop into that ideal low zone. Active net players love these easy to poach, one-dimensional ball strikers.

The other primary read is realizing that a shot is approaching very deep (with or without pace), necessitating that you're going to have to play the ball on-the-rise — still in front! — immediately after bouncing shin-to-knee high, at times a half-volley ground stroke if it's in very close proximity to the baseline or your position.

Once the read is made, visualization, or what you're going to do with your response, registers in a flash. This "flight plan" includes both direction and margin to the net, the latter being where the majority of unforced errors occur. This is the right brain thinking in pictures, which does not interfere with visual ball tracking.

Then, with two-thirds of that .91 second shot making time frame still unused, you arrive mentally clear and unhurried in position to breathe through the shot you've committed to make, unencumbered by over thinking and indecision, and recover into the next appropriate defending or attacking position while tracking your own ball out — not looking up at the opponent — into their racket. And so it goes. Over and over.

Dialing this sequence back-in from the first ball struck every single day will pay big dividends in not only calming and quieting your mind, but also putting an end to any hamstrung, reflexive, counterproductive over-thinking that's trying too hard to win, or afraid to lose, especially in those pivotal match moments when the pressure is on.

soft
POWER

It doesn't take immense physical effort to hit a heavy ball.

How can power be soft? Easily. Just think of those occasional moments — I know you've experienced them — when you're returning a first serve from a good server. After already launching your racket at the ball, you realize, a split second before making contact, that the ball, although close to the line, is actually out. Unable to stop your stroke, but fully aware that the pressure is off, you make the return anyway, producing a very penetrating shot with practically no effort at all. What happened? Soft power happened.

I've never seen virtuoso violinist Joshua Bell play tennis, but I know he does. I also know that he gets it. In comparing his artistry with striking a tennis ball, he observed, "Both require immense concentration and mental focus. Physically, when one draws a sound with the bow, relaxation is the key. Technique is more important than physical strength. Often, the harder you press, the less sound comes out."

And so it almost always is with the instantaneous, no consequences, loose-as-a-goose return. In a fractional moment, muscle tension plummets into an optimal range — substantially lower than your always well intentioned but often inefficient try harder, grip tighter mode — and a perfect kinetic chain is unleashed, producing a jaw-dropping would be winner or forced error.

Don Budge was the first player to win the Grand Slam, all four majors in the same year, way back in the day. Contemporary rival George Lott, commented on Budge's ball striking brilliance: "When you come in against Budge's backhand, he hit such a heavy ball, you'd swear you were volleying a piano." Well said.

The widely known formula $F = MA$ represents force (i.e. power) equals mass times acceleration. In the context of striking a tennis ball as cleanly as possible, it's relevant to how fast you swing the racket through the ball, in perfect synergy with the "swing weight" you allow the racket to have. This results in the racket easily dominating the collision with a ball that's designed to deform and store energy. Players employing this technique hit "heavy balls" with big "gas" off the bounce, even on clay.

Other players, those with excessively high grip tension, late take backs, ultra brief ball-on-string contact time and abrupt follow throughs, underachieve with shots produced through considerable physical effort that do not translate to effective power on the tennis court. And let us not forget the arm and shoulder injuries inherent in such an inefficient technique.

At his peak, Roger Federer's match play record was 315 wins and 24 losses (2004-2007), averaging out to 79-6 per year versus the world's best. In *Strokes of Genius*, Jon Wertheim describes the way in which Federer dominated: "He won not with unanswerable power, might-makes-right power, but with flourish and flair. His game relies on precision and nuance and talent. For all the modern touches, his style is mosdy a throwback, what with his one-handed backhand, his simple handshake grip, his fondness for net play."

On the women's side, the recendy retired Amelie Mauresmo, a former world #1 with Grand Slam titles and consistently high rankings, also displayed the Federer-type game with the same ball striking fluidity, lithe court coverage and ability to make all the shots look easy. She, too, played with soft power.

Just think of utilizing the racket — the hitting tool — much in the same way that a pendulum functions. The initial smooth, gradual acceleration from the beginning point of its arc, peaking in speed at the bottom of its range of motion, then gradually decelerating to its end. Or, with racket in hand, a smooth acceleration to peak racket speed through the point of impact from the take-back position, and then the methodical deceleration through one's full range of motion to the follow-through's completion.

Spectators don't always see it or fully appreciate it, but, like George Lott, opponents feel the "weight of shot," a phrase that the classic Wimbledon BBC broadcaster John Barrett is believed to have coined. Difficult to explain, it's a reference to a ball struck so perfectly that the energy produced at contact is maximized to the Nth degree, and the initial speed of the ball coming off the strings dissipates on the way to its target at a rate diat's considerably less than a shot produced with less efficiency.

Opponents, even experienced ones, also find it very difficult to anticipate, and are often surprised and rendered late to the ball since the stealth factor is very high in such a seemingly effortless stroke. Pete Sampras, unfairly regarded as just a big server, was that kind of player. He could dominate from the back of the court when he chose to, such as the '96 U.S. Open final when he made #2 Michael "Mr. Hustle" Chang look as if he wasn't even trying. Strangely, Pistol Pete never received any credit for his more nuanced skills.

So, in striving to achieve your personal best tennis day in and day out, and to continue to make very doable improvements in your game going forward, what is the more achievable model to aspire to, albeit not quite on the same scale? The silky smooth, clean-hitting, ball-striking machine standard displayed by Federer, current top 4 Andy Murray and the elegant Mauresmo, or the extreme gripped, concussive, brawling, physically demanding styles exhibited by the Rafael Nadals and Serena Williamses of today's game?

Go soft. Play big. Your call.

Playing
with a Live Arm

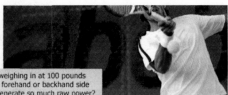

We've all seen it. Junior players barely over 5 feet tall, weighing in at 100 pounds with string bean arms and legs, launching shots off the forehand or backhand side with startling power. How do they do it? How do they generate so much raw power?

On occasion, even at the highest level, we see the same dynamic. Witness Alexandr Dolgopolov, the exciting young Ukrainian, all 5 feet 9 inches and 150 pounds of him, who has risen in the Association of Tennis Professionals rankings as high as top 20 in the world, competing against the game's very best, just about all of whom are mostly well over 6 feet tall and nearly 200 pounds of solid muscle. Just think of the recent best American men, all in or around the top 20: Mardy Fish and Andy Roddick, 6'3"; Sam Querry 6'5"; John Isner 6'10"; James Blake 6'2".

How does the comparative little guy hold his own with the big boys?

The answer lies, in great measure, in the ability to play with a very "live arm." For some, it's inherent in being gifted genetically, like Dolgopolov. As of late, the television commentators have been gushing over his special talents, particularly in light of his diminutive stature. Oh the women's side, there is no "livelier" player than the smallish 2010 French Open champion Francesca Schiavone. If size was a major part of the ranking equation, they would surely both be the world #1's.

But for the majority, at any level and of any physical stature, it's in the commitment to develop efficient ball-striking technique. Regarding the aforementioned youngsters, it's also found in their youthful fearlessness, often a product of not yet being intimidated by the possibility of negative consequences. "Losing Is not my enemy; fear of losing is my enemy" ~Rafael Nadal.

Pete Sampras, approaching 40 years of age, ancient by today's standards, can still bring heat on serve, the shot that catapulted him, as a slightly built youngster, to becoming U.S. Open champion at age 19. His legendary running forehand was, and remains, a weapon to be contended with as evidenced in his recent results versus current tour players on the exhibition circuit, including a win over #11 Fish in an exhibition prior to the French Open. How does he do it? It's the live arm that keeps on giving!

So what defines a live arm, and what do club players need to understand about motor skills in order to liven-up their arms to play bigger, and easier, at any age?

Live arms are, more than anything, loosey goosey. Relaxed muscles are smart. As a direct result, they are fast on call, explosive and free wheeling, which ultimately translates to being tennis powerful. They facilitate not only controllable, smart racket speed — essential in delivering shots with power and placement — but also allow a heavy racket "swing weight" that dominates the ball-racket collision to produce big shots that can be stunningly effortless. This is

34

why those 100-pound junior players can generate such unexpected "gas" with a racket in their hand.

How does one foster a relaxed hitting arm? Becoming cognizant of the fact that a human arm weighs approximately 6 percent of your total body weight is a good place to start. So use it! Let's say that the average man weighs approximately 175 pounds, and the average woman 135. That equates to fully juiced arms that weigh about 10 and 8 pounds, respectively. That limb weight, in unencumbered motion, can become a big part of the mix for striking tennis balls "big" with sticks that have scale weights of less than one pound.

This can only be achieved through a relatively low grip tension that's enabled by early preparation on all the shots, and in a nicely synchronized service motion. Note: none of this is going to be very doable, especially in warm, humid weather, if you complacently remain one of those players who neglect their hitting tool and seldom replace dirty, wet, slippery grips. The resulting low hand-on-racket friction coefficient absolutely will trigger racket strangulation. And tight muscles are dumb.

Gripping your racket in a relaxed fashion will allow you to generate a serious ball striking kinetic chain — a consistently sequential transfer of effective force from one body part and segment to another, culminating in a powerful but relatively effortless racket-on-ball moment — that's readily replicated. Your arm goes live!

Recognize that any shot really begins at the moment of impact as opposed to ending there. Question: In an ideal world, when do those balls that you've hit particularly well leave the racket face? Answer: When they're ready. Stay out of it. Stop muscling the ball. Once embraced, smoothly accelerating and decelerating strokes are born. Less becomes more.

It's impossible not to notice that there are individuals out there that drive with one foot on the gas and one foot on the brake at the same time, which exemplifies an obvious perfect storm of opposing forces. Forward movement is still possible, but impeded and slowed. Swinging a tennis racket is no different.

Former top 10 player Fernando Gonzalez once commented on the Tennis Channel regarding the way in which you always have to play in order to do your best: "You have to play freely." Learning to trust letting it go — the arm-racket connection — is the best chance for a positive outcome, and, more importantly for aspiring club players, to then be able to realize continuing ball striking improvement until the day arrives when the wheels fall off and you're forced into croquet.

Of course, arms can go "dead," too, almost always a result of long- term over use, even if your mechanics are stellar. Take U.S. Davis Cup Captain Jim Courier, for example, a finely tuned athlete, two-time French Open champion and perennial top 10 player. Towards the end of his career, he had to take months off from the game because of what he identified as a "dead arm." And dead arms happen in clubland more than is realized.

There are those individuals who love playing so much that it's not unusual for them to play 6-7 days a week. Since tennis is definitely a very physically cumulative activity, striking ball after ball after ball, days on end, can result in a dead arm sneaking up on you. Rushing out and getting a new racket when you're feeling flat is usually not the answer.

One day a week off is absolutely essential. Two is optimal. A good schedule, if possible, is three days of piay followed by a day off, then two more days of play followed by another day off, or any variation of that theme. Some maintain a routine of playing Monday-Friday and taking the weekends off. Fine.

So if you're going to make those feel good, effortless, penetrating shots more consistently, take a lesson from that Cuban friend of mine's absolute keeper comment mentioned earlier and worth repeating here: "First you relax; then you do nothing!"

Serving the
BOMB

Wouldn't it be nice to walk up to the tine, take that deep breath and reach into your serving back pocket to deliver a scorching heater, particularly when the score line is favorable to just go all out and go for it? No matter your physical stature — and yes, it really is all relative — you can bring it, especially if you're wielding one of today's turbo- powered rackets.

That stated, serving the bomb only plays a small role in club tennis, which mostly consists of doubles play in which first serve success is the real deal Making 60 percent-plus of well-placed first serves not only puts pressure on the receiver but also produces far more poaching opportunities for one's partner at the net.

Nonetheless, here are some key components that will allow you to maximize your physical potential when the time is right to strike, resulting in mph's you previously thought were beyond your reach.

Numero uno: you've got to be loose. Utilizing a serving motion that's robotic and looks suspiciously like an isometric exercise will negate any racket's inherent power. It also wreaks havoc on your body parts, especially the shoulder. So where does this looseness or, more specifically, low muscle tension begin? tt starts with gripping the racket loosely.

Relax! Strangling the handle, typically a product of the "try harder to do better" mind set, will severely limit any possibility of creating exceptional racket speed through the ball, and that's the bottom line.

Uninhibited racket speed converts to ball speed. You already know the physics: $F = MA$, or force equals mass times acceleration. The "mass" reference is about allowing the racket to have as much "swing weight" as possible, as opposed to its actual scale weight. I like the way former top 10 player, author and colorful television commentator Brad Gilbert puts it. "Get some stick on it!"

If you're one of those individuals who seldom replace their grip, you'll surely be one of the stranglers. Keeping your grip fresh and free of dirt, grease and grime — white grips are particularly desirable in that they clearly show the slime build-up — will facilitate the relaxation that's essential. The resulting high-friction coefficient will negate the urge to hold on too tight to prevent a slippery racket from being launched into the parking lot.

You also have to develop and embellish your ritual, a settle-to-the-task technique utilized in all sports. Think of the more obvious ones seen in golfers, baseball batters or free throw shooters in basketball where the action phase begins from a static start. Prior to serving, it's aimed at fostering a similar climate of total relaxation and rhythm creation by targeting one's entire body, including both the ball tossing arm and racket arm. This is particularly important when you're going to load up to really lay one in there and negative tension can easily creep in.

The toss itself plays an integral role in that your goal is for the racket to reach maximum speed at the moment of impact. This is achieved by keeping your toss well in front of your body, approximately an arm's length. Tosses drifting into the body reduce racket speed; tosses too far in front send balls into the net.

And let s not forget that the height of the toss is also very much a part of the bomb alchemy. Low tosses offer no advantage unless your rotator cuff is hanging by a thread. Creating enough time for a full, upward extension of one's hitting arm requires a toss that is approximately 6 inches higher than one's sweet spot reach — yes, big servers strike the ball as it is falling slightly — and also allows for an unhurried, "soft" coiling up movement that readily transitions into a full speed ahead hitting motion.

The racket's deceleration is also a factor. Some players attempt serving big the way I've noticed some people drive, one foot on the gas and one foot on the brake. Opposing forces create a muscular rigidity that prevents the racket from reaching maximum velocity. It's prudent to abandon any false sense of security you experience when over-controlling the racket by steering it. Allowing a free and easy deceleration into your follow-through zone, to its naturally occurring end, enables a hyper-charged, more coordinated racket dynamic.

Regarding the grip to rip, the old shake hands with the racket adage — the Continental grip — is a good place to start. You could also experiment with going a smidgeon towards the Eastern grip side in order to completely flatten the face of the racket if necessary. Unlessyou can bring 100+ mph heat, you won't need any appreciable spin to help bring your laser beam into the box. Go completely flat in order to get the biggest piece of the ball and longest possible impact time. And believe me, you'll feel and hear the difference when the ball, fully deformed, explodes off your racket.

By this time you're hopefully giddily anticipating the possibility of scrambling the electronics of your club's radar gun. So lets make sure that you know where you're hitting this bad boy. No, not the direction — up the T, out wide or into the body — but your intended margin of clearance over the net. That's the difference maker, and it cannot be much since this monster is laughing in gravity's face. Keep it close.

Last, and certainly not least, you gotta breathe! Holding your breath as you're unleashing a bomb, or any serve, actually triggers elevated muscle tension. Inhale as you toss, followed by a sustained exhalation as you're striking the ball for optimal loosey goosey relaxation.

The serve is undeniably the most mechanically demanding shot in tennis, with its nuanced kinetic chain or synchronization of myriad, accumulating moving parts. It would take a near tome to cover every single detail. Don't over think it. Just stay focused on these core essentials and let it happen.

Bob Brett, coach of the big-serving 2001 Wimbledon champion Goran

Ivanisevic — still the ace record holder at The Championships (not Pete Sampras) — described the Croat master blaster's huge but seemingly easy "cheese" this way: "At his best, he's a player who lets the racket do the work. He doesn't really swing or hit that hard. Goran is all about timing."

So, go ahead and light it up on occasion. It's empowering and fun too.

the joy of —————
——— PRACTICE

In this age of ever-expanding organized play — United States Tennis Association leagues, independent local leagues, regional K-Swiss competition, statewide National Tennis Rating Program events, Senior Olympics, regularly inked-in games at clubs and parks — the pure joy and satisfaction that can be experienced through practice, with a partner or completely by yourself, has an increasingly feint pulse. Even among aspiring players, it's in danger of flat lining in favor of playing match after match after match.

Even the pre-match warm-ups — tennis' unique dynamic of warming-up with the opponent — have been impacted in all this competition, in part, by television coverage that has really stepped up in the last few years. Viewers finally have the luxury of seeing the five-minute pro tour warm-up, including serves, that's beginning to be shown in more and more telecasts. Good for showing the cooperation between the players about to do battle; bad for subliminally indicating that it's all you need. The 45-minute to one-hour to one and a half hour warm-ups that are not shown —which are always utilized by professionals well before their actual match time — influence club players to embrace the express warm-up example.

Since convincing others to take the time to practice with you is challenging at best, practicing on your own is often the club players only option. And individual practice has evolved into being perceived as strictly limited to using pay-for-play ball machines, which feature an array of bells and whistles that are an operational mystery to most. It can be a tedious and often unsatisfying business that involves first getting it out onto a court and then tweaking the settings for speed, trajectory, spin, shot interval and direction to meet^our needs while occasionally having to deal with the dreaded jammed ball.

Unfortunately, the venerable backboard or hitting wall has become, as a direct result, an endangered species heading rapidly towards extinction. It's too bad really, because what could be more interactive in its cozy confines? Just walk up and play. It's user friendly and fast paced. And it's a great workout with the inherent development of ball watching, footwork, split stepping, racket preparation and margin to the net visualization skills.

More disturbing, the days of small children first embracing the game by gravitating to these backboards with a beat-up racket and one used ball are mostly gone. This is not a development that the stewards of the game, who constantly advance the rallying cry to "grow the game," appear to recognize. How many great champions of the past spent hour after hour banging away all by themselves? And how many older recreational adult players still playing today got their start on a wall? Simple was good.

The forgotten beauty and intrinsic value of solo practice, accommodated so perfectly by backboards then and by ball machines now (if accessible), remains just that: you can play by yourself. The hugely attractive appeal of the same dynamic in golf, and the insight by golf's stewards to offer designated practice areas and putting greens at just about all courses public and private, encourages solo practice and simultaneously promotes the game. Golf gets it.

If a backboard — think well-suited, threes-wall outdoor racquetball courts sometimes found at parks and colleges — or a ball machine are not readily available, no worries! Drop-hitting, or "dead ball" practice, along with practicing first and second serves, can absolutely represent some of the most rewarding, pleasurable and productive time spent refining your core strokes and an accompanying positive mind set. Calmly dropping balls in your forehand and backhand wheelhouse from different court positions will enhance that all-important feel-for-the-ball as well as open up pathways to experience a zen-like focus. Commonly regarded as "being in the zone," it's the end-all elusive state of mind that all players seek, but one that becomes increasingly difficult to experience when you've become relegated to just playing matches under pressure ad infinitum.

Even multimillion-dollar baseball players, when slumping at the plate, practice hitting off a tee, or enlist a kneeling hitting coach positioned in close proximity to gently toss up meatballs in their wheelhouse to get their hitting stroke back. Simple is still good.

If you do find a wall, know going in that they all have their own unique rebound quotient. Some, the ones typically constructed of concrete block, are so solid that you can approximate the normal baseline distance from the net — about 12 giant steps, or 36 feet, from the wall — and play the ball as usual on one bounce. Others, made of wood, often produce a shorter rebound requiring two bounces to simulate the same ideal hitting distance. Bring a yardstick or tape measure along with a piece of chalk to make a small but visible line on the wall representing the top of the net (3 feet) as a reference point.

When a ball machine is available and affordable, forget trying to sort out the multiple shot programs that might be featured. Stick with simple, one particular shot at a time. Thinking doubles for example, place the machine on the deuce side at the baseline, delivering cross court shots that you return back to the machine, deep. Then, by moving the unit slightly left or right, create balls coming in at sharper angles to practice hitting on the run out on the wing, or the inside out backhand or the run-around by jamming yourself. As an option, experiment with the topspin and underspin controls to become more adept at handling the bounce characteristics of those shots.

The serve, neglected despite being the most important shot in the game, typically becomes one's least-practiced shot. Regularly working on your serve in solitude will groove it and build confidence. When you do practice it, once you've warmed-up, go to the next step and effectively simulate real play pressure by playing one set against yourself. Alternating sides as usual, keep score by awarding yourself the point if you have placed a first or second serve into the service box quadrant that you visualized, or award your alter ego the point if you have failed to do so.

Yes, you're supposed to prevail over your other self 6-0. That's the joy of practice!

It's STILL
About the Warm-Up

How can so many players, players who love playing tennis, get this so wrong? The mutations that I regularly witness regarding the pre-match warm-up in both United States Tennis Association league play and in friendly matches — despite a universal protocol that has existed for eons — is disturbing and tarnishes the game.

Although players certainly have a responsibility to comport themselves in accordance with tennis' published guidelines when warming-up, how can they be solely blamed for being at odds with them if they've never been coached-up by their pros? Ignorance is no excuse, but it is the reason why they've made up their own rules.

Look no further than the United States Professional Tennis Association and the Professional Tennis Registry, the two main certifying professional organizations numbering 25,000 strong, who have done virtually nothing of any real consequence to promote the education of tennis-playing America on the warm-up protocol.

Just drop by any club or public park in the country and observe the dysfunctional chaos, often coupled with frustration that can become outright combativeness before the matches even begin. Everyone loses.

No wonder I hear players repeatedly saying non-sensible things, after only a couple of minutes into their versions of warming- up. "C'mon, let's get started. I'm not going to get any better." And, amazingly "Let's not waste any more time warming-up." Correct, they're not going to get any better with those warm-up habits, and, interestingly, their first set is typically marked by a deluge of unforced errors. Let's hurry up and play lousy.

First and foremost, as stewards of the sport, we tennis professionals should be held accountable. When was the last time you saw an article in *Tennis Magazine*, or anywhere else for that matter, shedding light on such an integral part of the game? Inexplicable, particularly since tennis is the only sport where opponents warm-up with each other (unfortunately that's often against).

In a seminar I presented not long ago at the USPTA-New England convention, I asked the pros in the audience, tongue-in-cheek, if they were aware of the pending class action law suit being brought against the USPTA for not teaching, and preserving, the long-standing proper pre-match warm-up routine. Both quizzical and guilty expressions appeared in the ensuing silence.

43

It's all right there, and has been all along, in the USTA's *The Code*, first written by Col. Nick Powell way back when, in the "Warm- Up" section, "*Warm-up is not practice*. A player should provide the opponent a 5-minute warm-up (10 minutes if there are no ballpersons). If a player refuses to warm up the opponent, the player forfeits the right to a warm-up. Some players confuse warm-up and practice. Each player should make a special effort to hit shots directly to the opponent. (If partners want to warm each other up while their opponents are warming up, they may do so.)"

Regarding serves: "*Warm-up serves and returns are taken before first serve of match*. A player should take all warm-up serves before the first serve of a match. A player who returns serves should return them at a moderate pace in a manner that does not disrupt the server".

So, for those of you currently practicing your winners in the warm- up while a more enlightened opponent hits right to you, and who immediately starts practicing their serve returns while announcing that they'll "take theirs later," let's get with the program!

For the more visual among us, I am now featuring a short video on my website (*www.JakBeardsworthTennis.com*) of Roger Federer and Novak Djokovic warming-up — note they are warming up at less than full power — prior to a tour match. And I'm told that the Tennis Channel, in its *Tennis Academy* series, has recently been airing top junior coach and former tour player, Nick Saviano, instructing viewers, with an added caveat for club players, in the very same cooperative give and take, universal warm-up technique demonstrated by none other than the world's two best players.

That caveat is where to first position oneself to begin rallying back and forth. Beginning in no man's land, as most often utilized by tour pros like Serena Williams, for practice sessions is commonplace, though not for match play (full court start) since pros always warm-up on a back court prior to their match. From there, you're far more able to dial-in your full stroking paths, albeit with minimal racket speed compared to match level (see video on my website). "This is in a positive, total contrast to those who, well intentioned no doubt, stand in close proximity to the net and initiate rapid fire volley exchanges to start the day. Rat-tat-tat. That's a practice drill, not a warm-up technique!

And there are those who choose "short court," or mini-tennis, right around the service line. Here, ball control is marginal at best and freely hitting through the ball is not very doable, resulting in inefficient, highly tensioned, truncated strokes.

At the three-quarter court position, initial ball control is maximized; one gets a better feel for the ball and playing the ball on the first, second, third bounce matters not. The warm-up is about finding your timing and creating the best possible shot-making rehearsal. It is not about immediately flying around the court with your hair on fire trying to get every ball on the first bounce. Wait, doesn't that just encourage those who practice winners?

Once players have hit 15-20 balls each, they should drift back for a seamless transition to the baseline. One player, after a number of full-court exchanges, then takes the initiative to move into the net for their volleys, always followed by a few overheads — after all, isn't that your answer to the ever popular lob? — prior to retreating back to allow opponents the same opportunity.

Once all players have had their turn at the net, it's on to serving, where one player serves the balls they have and the opponent gathers them and serves them back, from both the deuce and ad sides.

Question: How on earth do four club players expect that they can warm-up effectively with three balls?

Answer: They can't.

Shouldn't the four-ball can that the Europeans use be utilized in doubles? Yes, it *is* available in the US. And think about the fact that in professional doubles, players are provided six balls and a team of ball kids. And we're trying to warm-up with three, which always leaves two players with only one ball. C'mon folks, this game is already tough enough!

Going forward, let's all take a deep breath and get on the same page. Reduce the unnecessary testiness exhibited in too many warm- ups and show our opponents a little courtesy, not to mention good sportsmanship, with a truly cooperative warm-up.

Then, okay, it's time to rumble.

They are immediately recognizable. The thoroughbred movers of the game, flowing untethered from one ball to the next, seemingly playing above the court. Big and small, pros and clubbers, no matter — they motor light as feathers. Soft feet? Yes. And more.

Roger Federer, of course, heads the professional class. Athletically elegant, he appears to defy gravity when in full flight. Even in the midst of the directional changes tennis demands, he glides and reaccelerates invisibly. Martial art movies like *Crouching Tiger, Hidden Dragon* come to mind, but Federer is real and wireless.

In *Strokes of Genius*, John Wertheim's riveting deconstruction of the Swiss maestro's epic 2008 Wimbledon battle with the coming of age Rafael Nadal, the Federer anomaly is anointed: "Even in his warm-up, Federer is the picture of seamless efficiency. There's virtually no wasted movement. Like all great athletes, he has a natural mind-body connection."

Others have come before. Some well-known. Some obscure. John McEnroe, not normally mentioned as a great mover, along with Martina Navratolova, who single-handedly raised the women's fitness bar, and, yes, Pete Sampras, who too many, curiously, still think he only had a serve.

The lesser known in that era were no less impressive getting around the court. Miroslav "The Big Cat" Mecir, a US Open finalist and a big dude, whose sleepy, slow motion demeanor defied how he somehow managed to smother any fleeting opponent openings. Karol Kucera, doing the same, gave Andre Agassi absolute fits, appearing to be reading his mind. And let us not forget the silky Amelie Muresamo already mentioned earlier, the physically solid French woman that a young Lindsey Davenport, no petite damsel herself, accused of playing like a guy.

Today, Bernard Tomic, the underachieving, 6'5" Aussie bad boy, who best represents the illusion of laborless motoring, has emerged as a smooth mover with his Mecir-inspired gait. Still, he gets criticized in the press for his unique gift that's often wrongly construed as not giving his all, especially when he's compared to the hustling Jimmy Connors standard that endures.

The "Brash Basher" model, best exemplified today by Nadal, with its ballistic, court gripping, stutter-stepping, dogged ball pursuit, gets its due in Connors' new memoir, *The Outsider*, right alongside his primer on ball-stnking mechanics. "Now, here comes the second and most important part footwork. This is what made my game what it became. This was the hard part, and believe me, I worked on it every day," he writes.

For fans of brash, with a little gazelle sprinkled in, there's the enduring past TV commercial featuring fan favorite, Gael Monfils, hawking his KSwiss Big Shot pumps as he darts around the court from one end to the other, up and back in a blur, with his voice over proclaiming, "I am French. I am fast. Wherever you hit, I will be there." KSwiss made a bundle. Such is the tennis playing public's respect and admiration for the movement requirement of the game.

How do they do it? Is it self-taught, coached-up or inherently predisposed? Of course, one's genetics play no small part.

But anyone can, if motivated, make improvements in the way they move in and out of their shots while also defending the court in between them in a total synchronization. With understanding, and a work ethic for a little practice repetition, the core components of motoring can be advanced.

In his 1977 guide, *Quick Tennis*, two-time NCAA track champion and Olympian, Henry Hines, crossed his track skills over to tennis right in the midst of the tennis boom, and, unwittingly, took aim at some of the then still-existing country club conventions. I can recall one such purist, a stiff but appreciated regional steward of the game, telling me, right about the same time, that I "moved around the court like a monkey." Huh? Looking back, he was confusing a new age brand of tennis athleticism that was rapidly infiltrating the genteel Sunday afternoon mixed-doubles crowd on the grass of the most proper, and venerable, Longwood Cricket Clubs of the Northeast.

Other efforts have followed, but selections solely devoted to tennis movement are few in number and slow in coming. A good, all-encompassmg offering is *Complete Conditioning for Tennis*, a USTA publication by Paul Roetert and ATP trainer Todd Ellenbecker, whom you've seen on the Tennis Channel.

One DVD stands out, *Fast and Furious Tennis*, featuring University of Washington coach Chris Russell's program for movement excellence. If you're a cerebral type, check out David A. Rosenbaum's *Human Motor Control* with its motor neurophysiology, cognitive science themes.

Back in clubland, simply being cognizant of the active motion components is half the battle — quickness, speed, agility, balance and flexibility are all in the mix.

Quickness refers to how quickly you get off the mark in reacting to an opponents shot. Without a well-timed split-step, that little hop step that lands both feet lightly and precisely at their ball-on-string impact, you'll have no real hope of a quick start. Bodies in motion stay in motion. Standing motionless, poised but not a muscle stirring, is a delusionalist formula to be late to the party, particularly on the serve return.

The speed reference is with regard to, once you are in motion, shifting into whatever "gear" is necessary in a forward-leaning posture to intercept the ball at the right place and the right time. When top gear is required, arm movement, pumping if you will, plays a large part in being fast when working in perfect concert with one's leg action. Nonetheless, this is tennis, not a track meet, so you'll still need to prepare your racket on time.

Agility, more than anything, refers to an ability to change directions smoothly, without losing even a half-step going the wrong way. Once again, we're back to the all-important split step. Unless you're faced with an all-out sprint to a wide open court, a momentary split should occur, wherever you are on the court, at an opponent s contact point. Nothing is easier than hitting behind a runaway train opponent who is without one.

Maintaining body control in a multi-directional sport like tennis is what balance is all about. Being aware of keeping your head still at all times, in the midst of the shot making hip and shoulder rotations while also recognizing, and managing, your ideal center of gravity, are the most important ingredients. The head moves — bobble head, swivel head — the body follows and the accompanying unnecessary motion not only slows you down but also undermines your shot.

Since you will not be able to get every ball where you want it in your strike zone, *flexibility* is a must in adapting to mis-hits, bad bounces, when fooled, and when in full stretch. If you don't regularly work on your flexibility, especially if you're of an age where you can recall watching those aforementioned pro players examples, you'll be relegated to playing "tin-man" tennis.

Being kinesthetically cognizant of your body in motion can only lead to better and happier motoring. And better playing too.

Defending the
by _Reading_ Court
their Mail

The outcome of every single tennis point played is always the same: the last player or team to successfully hit the ball in the court wins the point every single time. No ifs, ands or buts about it. Also, it's best to also keep in mind that there are no extra points awarded for attempting difficult shots and no penalties for those who never attempt anything more than high flying floaters.

One needs only to flashback to a past US Open final between Rafael Nadal and Novak Djokovic, where there were several 30-stroke rallies and numerous can-you-match-this extended exchanges. Aggressive, all-out court defending — particularly when parrying opponent's more penetrating and well placed shots — becomes the name of the game at any level. Perseverance prevails.

In clubland, offensive skills develop far more slowly than defensive ones. Clearly there is a much higher difficulty factor involved in quick strike, thread-the-needle tennis to attempt an ambitious, outright win versus being mostly motivated to hit one more reasonably paced and placed ball than the other guy or team.

But I'm certainly not suggesting becoming a "pusher" — the dreaded P-word — or one who lobs incessantly and without ever revealing a hint of intentional, aggressive ball striking, even when an inviting opportunity presents itself. Commenting on these types of players in a Nike print ad campaign a few years ago, John McEnroe said, "If they arrested people for being annoying on the tennis court, they'd be looking at doing 15 to life."

Always play ggressively — by actually trying to play the game the way it was meant to be played — but well within your shot-making skill level, with safe and realistic margins to both the net and the lines.

Again noting the momentous Nadal-Djokovic encounter, the Serb, more than anything in the end, outlasted and wore down Nadal — previously thought impossible — in four grueling sets, prompting the Spaniard to say, "He's enough confident, is always thinking, one more ball, one more ball." Marian Vajda, Djokovic's coach, refers to this biow-for-blow tactic as utilizing "working shots" for as long as it takes until an opponent is worked out of position, then allowing a fairly routine placement to finish the job.

"Tennis is now all about defense," said Mark Kovacs, a United State Tennis Association sports scientist. Sam Tanenhaus, New York Times tennis columnist, had a similar take, "The dominant of the moment are not creative shot makers like McEnroe and Roger Federer, who end points quickly, but counterpunchers like Nadal and Djokovic, highly athletic versions of the 'grinders' from the past."

The advice I offer club players, those who tend to impatiently get out-on-the-jazz trying to be too offensive is to: a) expect the ball to come back; and b) and not even mind. How can you win the battle if you're unwilling to engage the enemy and make them play — heck, let them play — without flinching or panicking?

Of course clubbers are not as fit or fleet footed as tour professionals, so "reading" opponent's shots, or more specifically, predicting where the ball will be struck in relation to their body position, will create an all important jump-on-the-ball and compensate for being slower afoot than the big boys and girls.

In the accompanying image, although viewed from the side, one gets the concept of developing "triple-vision" the ability to focus directly on the ball while, through a layered periphery, still being able to "see" a player's stroke path and their court position simultaneously in order to read and better anticipate an opponent's shot direction as early as possible.

The first step in developing this shot-reading skill, very much a learned one, is to become very cognizant of consistently tracking the ball in both directions: into your point of impact and then, once the ball is struck, tracking it all the way to the opponent's impact point. Since the human eye isn't good enough to maintain a 100 percent connection completely through these ball flights, the brain joins in and taps into all, if you will, existing ball flight data on your inner hard drive to work in concert with the eyes to recognize and lock onto familiar flight patterns.

Unfortunately, too many are guilty of impulsively looking up at the court or opponent precisely at their moment of impact, which not only adversely alters their swing path — the head moves, the body follows — and the smoothness of the racket's acceleration- deceleration, but also disconnects them from both the opponent and the ball itself! Interestingly, the aforementioned "creative shot maker" Federer serves as an excellent model to aspire to in that he keeps his head still at impact well into the follow through and then looks up in plenty of time — even at the bullet speed of his groundies — to reconnect with the ball as it approaches the opponent's hitting zone.

Once reconnected and focused primarily on the ball — the opposing player "seen" only in his periphery — and after having seen his opponent previously play a number of forehands and backhands early on, he can anticipate with regularity approximately where the racket face will be positioned at impact.

That stated, forget about a well intentioned cue I hear among players periodically, "Watch their racket." There is no way the human eye can follow a racket speeding through an impact zone. But one can estimate, after a bit of trial and error observation, where the racket will meet the ball. It's all about the ball. And disregard those "guessing" comments constantly repeated by television announcers to describe how players successfully make great saves when in difficult, but doable, straits versus those when they actually are sitting ducks and do randomly guess to move to one side or the other with a hope and a prayer. Big difference.

Definitely not to be left out of the mix, the split-step becomes the necessary physical component if successful "reads" are going to be fully taken advantage of.

Landing your split-step at the precise moment of opponent's impact lends itself to quick, energized first steps that will pay huge dividends in covering more court more easily and also trigger better hitting positions for your own shot response!

The resulting movement fluidity, in synergy with maximized anticipation through highly evolved ball tracking, will serve to marshal your focusing skills by shutting off the completely ineffective thinking (guessing) where they're going to hit it syndrome, create a more relaxed perception of slowed action and result in greater court coverage with less wear and tear on the body, all while continually giving opponents one more opportunity to self-destruct.

And by the way, no worries, reading other people's mail, at least on the tennis court, is perfectly legal.

No Feet
No Game
No Future

"No feet, no game, no future." When I first heard L.T.A. British pro Steve Heron say exactly that to an obviously frustrated student who was unable to fathom why he was struggling despite Heron's repeated and crystal clear analysis, it immediately struck a chord for me.

I'd never heard that line before, and it was right on the money. The player in question appeared reasonably fit and owned a nice looking forehand and a reliable backhand, but still didn't get it. He was indeed misfiring and underachieving with an awkward, disconnected-to-the-ball movement that was not at all consistent with his racket skills.

So exactly what is good footwork? How do you define it? First, while being totally committed is a necessary component, it is much more than just that. If you don't welcome the idea of chasing a ball around 1,404 square feet of court, then I'd suggest concentrating on your golf game. Moving your feet non-stop in a completely unrelated time signature from the action at hand is certainly not going to cut it. The resulting out-of-sync state, one that's wholly at odds with the continually changing ball in flight dynamic, will make playing your A-game an impossibility.

Naturally, it's a bonus if you're blessed with a quick first step and speed to the ball. But in clubland, where players athletic abilities are often burdened with the realties of chronology — as compared to the young athletes we see on television — it is essential to understand the crucial relationship between eye-hand and eye-foot coordination. The great Bill Tilden — holder of the most consecutive U.S. Open wins — understood. "Speed and power are essential in the equipment of the great players, but they alone cannot suffice," he said.

What it is about is simply being at the perceived right place at the right time, to make your shot effortlessly with the kinetic chain firing on all eight cylinders. What this means is arriving at the optimal ball-striking moment and place, right on stride, open or closed stance. And then recovering to an ideal court-defending position at precisely the moment your opponent is striking their next shot. It's an ever expanding and contracting figure eight flow chart if you will.

Watching Roger Federer seemingly glide about the court with such relative ease is something to behold, win or lose. It's almost as if his shoes aren't even touching the court, reminiscent of Steffi Graf in her prime — that unearthly ability to move on top of the court, mostly up on the balls of the feet as opposed to pressing heavily into the court's surface with excessive, counter productive G-forces. Amazingly, Federer's shoes don't even squeak against the asphalt when changing directions or stutter-stepping those final little adjustment moves for a perfectly timed shot. He is the Baryshnikov of tennis. Everyone else, the world's best mind you, wearing the same Nikes, are often laying very audible rubber all over the court.

Right now you're most likely beginning to think that moving like Federer and Graf isn't an option for you. Well, certainly not to the extent that he does and she did, but, yes, it is doable to some degree. And it is certainly an improvement, and far better than the alternative of moving in a comparatively ungainly manner with an inefficient, injury prone gait.

Think back to your youth, those days when you had to get across a scorching-hot street to reach the beach or lake in the dead of summer. Without any contemplation, you instinctively became as light and quick on your feet as you possibly could, springing from one step to another, on the balls of your feet, until you safely reached the other side.

Way back in 1984, biomedical designer Van Phillips created a stateof-the-art prosdietic for amputee runners. In order to replicate the action of the human leg at its optimal performance, Phillips cleverly omitted any semblance of a heel since the heel exists — as both evolutionary history and modern biomechanical research has unanimously concluded — only for standing, not for running.

It all begins with that consistently produced "split-step" — the ultimate trigger to better movement already noted — occurring right at the opponent's point of contact. It's a simple, easy to execute, hop-like step wherein both feet landing precisely as the ball is struck from across the net. You've seen it on television thousands of times, yet, like so many club players, fail to employ during your own game.

Now you're already naturally up on the balls of your feet, possessing a far quicker and lighter first step, and a physically less stressful one compared to the undermining delay experienced without a split-step — flat footed, disengaged and not a muscle stirring.

However, in the end, none of this will be possible if you just stand around doing nothing in between points, which is where more match time is spent than actually playing points! Bodies at rest stay at rest. You must continually pace back in forth — be the tiger in the cage — in your own mini-quadrant until the next point is about to begin. Then, slightly before the serve, ramp up your energy level with some quick, bouncy foot-to-foot shuffling for a couple of seconds before settling into your ready position. Once there, continue swaying your torso, racket included, side-to-side along with a subtle shifting from foot-to-foot, leading up to that all-important split-step.

Bodies in motion, stay in motion.

The Club Doubles Game
MATRIX

When I see all four players standing well inside the service box sharing a single ball to "warm-up" with no apparent rhyme or reason in sight, I know the sign post just ahead says: "Doubles Troubles in Clubland."

Dysfunctional warm-up habits notwithstanding, the fact remains that the vast majority of league players here in Charlotte County, Florida — well over 1,500 strong — or anywhere in the US for that matter, play doubles almost exclusively. Yet, strikingly, many of these devoted players — including some 4.0s and even a few 4.5s — have not fully grasped the fundamentals of net positioning, strategy, tactics and shot selection.

That reminds me of doubles mensa Martina Navratolova's comments about Venus and Serena Williams' doubles play earlier in their careers, alluding to their consistently out of synch court positioning that was completely overcome by overwhelming power. Shock and awe trumps all.

Unfortunately since you're not partnering with them, or the Bryan twins who play text book doubles, playing smart, efficient doubles becomes a necessity in your world.

Unlike pros, club players are especially prone to unforced error, low percentage, overly ambitious quick strike tactics or a somewhat unwillingness to methodically engage the opposition, often impatiently perceiving imminent failure at the third or fourth ball struck.

Still, at any level, the bottom line remains being the last team to successfully hit the ball in the court, which wins the point every single time.

Keep remembering how Zen master Shunru Suzuki put it: "In the beginners' mind there are many possibilities; in the expert's mind there are few." Okay, so you're not a beginner, but take heed anyway.

Make them play. Heck, let them play. Put the onus on them to blink first and adopt an undermining, panicked mind set. Matches that are among relative equals — 3.5s playing against other 3.5s — are, at the end of the day, almost never won. They are lost. Gifts.

Once the afraid-to-lose mind set takes hold — didn't Rafael Nadal himself say, "I do not fear losing, I only fear the fear of losing." — it's not unusual to witness moon ball play, complete net avoidance and no- man's land court positioning that's somewhere between the middle of nowhere and the end of the line. Four players playing singles.

John McEnroe's already mentioned one-time take on the ugliness of non-engaging, pitter patter doubles players in that Nike print ad remains an all-time classic.

An old friend, a nationally ranked super senior doubles player, once became so seriously irritated at the play of four of his not so nationally ranked buddies — all of whom were playing at the baseline launching lob after lob after lob — he stood up and very colorfully exhorted in their direction, "For blank's sake, hit the blank, blank ball. That's what they make 'em for!"

The core of successful club doubles development can be distilled into four axioms:

1. Acquire the ability to consistently deliver deep, cross-court groundies with enough pace to be unpoachable.

2. Maintain a high first-serve percentage rate (60-70 percent) by taking some pace off with effective placement.

3. Continually shift back and forth at the net from an offensive position to a defensive position.

4. Visualize every shot struck from the first ball in the warm-up.

Deep penetrating groundstrokes rule the day, including negating effective lobbing! Determined by a combination of ball speed, spin and, most important of all, the margin to the net clearance that is mostly responsible for depth of shot They handcuff opponents, leading to either short ball responses that one can come in and munch on, low risk poaching opportunities for net partners to take full advantage of and salavating lobs in your wheelhouse.

In a recent doubles friendly with three 4.0s, I challenged the opponents with consistent, deep, penetrating forehands and backhands directly at their back court position. My partner at the net had a field day poaching practically at will and thanking me for setting him up and making his day. Match over.

Low first-serve percentage (30-40 percent) results in both a proven statistical disadvantage and a less obvious but equally demoralizing psychological impediment. Advantage receiver. Hall of Fame golfer Jack Nicklaus used to say, "If you're putting badly it goes through your whole bag." It then follows, if you're serving badly, it adversely affects your entire game.

One of the revealing and match-determining stats on the pro tour, along with the obvious unforced errors, is percentage of second serves won. Better to not place yourself in repeated second serve situations by consistently going for too much on the first. The results won't be pretty.

A prudent approach to bumping up your first serve success and reducing your second serve liability is to adopt the "2 to make 1" tactic. Instead of going big on the first, then tapping in a Great Aunt Agatha second serve, dial-in a three-quarter speed delivery that's still good enough and manageable.

If you can't consistently make one out of two at three- quarters, without backing off on the second when needed, then it's time to spend some time actually practicing the most important shot in the game.

Maintaining an offensive net position in the middle of the service box when the opposing back courter has the ball, or when they're returning a serve, provides viable opportunities to cut the ball off. But then, when unable to poach, immediately shift to a defensive position by going back on the diagonal within close proximity of the service line near the "T" to defend the middle of the court from a net opponent's possible cross on your partner. This is an absolute positional necessity.

Back and forth all day long. Offense to defense, defense to offense. After all, isn't playing the net — half the time spent on court — what distinguishes doubles from singles?

Just being in constant motion in and around the net will not only make you a better volleyer, it will also create a net presence that will absolutely impact the opposing team in a big way. Points for free.

Last, but by no means least, visualization is an immensely powerful tool in tennis. All professional and accomplished players visualize. They "see" task success in their minds-eye, versus thinking about, fretting about, the possibility of failure or being afraid of making errors. Picturing a successful shot — both directionally and marginally over the net — immediately upon recognizing your opponent's shot will not only make your existing game considerably better, it will also make you a better ball striker by always having crystal clear shot making goals.

Over there somewhere, hoping, is a performance disaster in the making.

I'm forever bringing up Rod Laver on my lesson court to continually remind sometimes frustrated students of his right-on-the-mark analysis of the challenge: "It's a simple game; it's just not easy."

So keep your doubles game simple. Forget the high difficulty, low risk "glory shots," an apropos label I've heard club members using in good natured ribbing after an opponent attempted a delusional down-the-line, running backhand passing shot, off-balance in full stretch, with the net man waiting.

Doubles can be tricky, and certainly there's more to playing it well than I have offered here. But adopting these four core principles will both shore up your game and open other doors you didn't know were there.

What We Have Here is a Failure to Communicate

It's not unusual for me to comment supportively to doubles' players - those especially befuddled by the constantly changing positional responsibilities unique to the doubles game - that, in marked contrast, "a chimpanzee could play singles" considering the devolvement of tennis from the more tactically complex and nuanced game that preceded the arrival of today's big bang, slam bam equipment.

Look no further than the extraordinary success of the Williams sisters, whose doubles play is often characterized by an out-of- position ball-bludgeoning style that so few pairs on the women's tour — even those who do utilize text book teamwork and court sense — can stand up to.

Yet, with inter-club league play now in full swing in our area - that's approximately 1,500 players - doubles play in men's, women's and mixed takes center stage, but the brand of play brandished by the Williams is not a doable option for most by a long shot.

Clubbers, from 2.5 up to even a 4.0 rating, are, despite their own hopped-up rackets and strings, typically still dependent on out- smarting and out-flanking opponents who might be the better shot makers, albeit with equal-on-paper NTRP ratings.

But, on their own, ball-striking skills coupled with text-book positioning are not necessarily the holy grail of success in team play despite being an essential part of the mix.

This article's title, borrowed from a line in the classic movie *Cool Hand Luke*, just might strike a chord for tennis players who have experienced playing with an unsupportive, bossy partner — one whom you'd think by their behavior never makes errors —who has yet to discover that there is no "I" in team. The eye rolling and the negative body language at your errors - who misses on purpose? - plus the barked commands to do this or that without your input are debilitating to any partner at any level.

Not to be underestimated, the lack of positive dialogue and encouragement in between points or on changeovers, especially when the score line is going south, contribute mightily to a self- fulfilling losing chemistry.

The great Rod Laver's now dated, but still relevant, hilarious assessment of husband-wife play in particular covers double's troubles this way, "An otherwise happily married couple may turn a mixed doubles game into a scene from, *Who's Afraid of Virginia Wolf*." Long before Laver's time, and tennis itself for that matter, another legend, Plato, personified the trials and tribulations of today's doubles this way: "You can discover more about a person in an hour of play, than in a year of conversation."

Today's professional players, unlike some of our league player friends, are the epitome of unconditional partner support. It is a rare day that you see one partner overtly communicating to those in attendance that they are in no way responsible for the losing effort being put forth.

Truth be told, I do remember witnessing a Davis Cup rubber at the Jimmy Connors Tennis Center in the early '90s. It was US versus Czechoslovakia. The Americans teamed John McEnroe with Rick Leach in the crucial middle day doubles. Leach got off to a terrible start that didn't improve much throughout the first two losing sets. Mac, not exactly known for his tolerance at the time for anyone underperforming, slowly but surely went on the boil with some world class shoulder shrugging, eye rolling and even the throwing up of the hands. Leach, a seasoned pro and doubles specialist, desperately trying to find his form, ultimately succumbed to the two-pronged pressure of the opponents stellar play, and his own partner's abandonment, and folded like a deck chair.

Game, set, match.

Which brings to mind former US Davis Cup Captain, and current USTA player development coach, Tom Gullikson, who typically led off his clinics and exhibitions - including one here in Punta Gorda, Florida a few years back - with a keen observation, one that always led to audience laughter, by noting that the most important element in doubles is choosing a good partner.

Intangibles.

In today's professional game we witness most team's high fiving or fist bumping encouragement after every point, win or lose. They overtly practice tennis amnesia, a trait consistently exhibited by the great Pete Sampras, who was always about playing the next point positively no matter what the difficulty he might be experiencing.

Be like Pete.

Along with the ritualistic fives and bumps, there is now also the quick chat. The old hand signals by the net man to the server – the net player dictating to the server in clubland was never a good idea - have, thankfully, lost favor.

On the professional doubles tour, a typical huddle after a point might go like one between recent US Open semi-finalists Raven Klaasen and Eric Butorac, with the server doing the quarterbacking: "High kick T left second serve high cutter body right"

Relax, it's okay if you're not exactly sure what that means. Create your own jargon.

Players are careful not to project their voices though. Don't think the opponents aren't eavesdropping if possible. It's "hearing gate" if you can get away with it, but unlike pro football's infamous illegal video-taping (Spy Gate) of an opposing team, it's all good in tennis.

Tim Smyczek, who partners with Bradley Kahn, is one of many promoting another come lately adaptation for tactical stealth that's quickly becoming the norm: covering one's mouth with the balls when convening. "You don't want the other guys reading your lips" Smyczek said during this past year's Flushing Meadows. Really, Tim?

The Bryan brothers, who celebrated their 100th career victory at this years New York slam, are practically frenetic in their huddles - much like their play - and critical of those who take too long. "A few teams talk for, like, 30 seconds, and it just gets kind of boring" Mike Bryan said. "There's no need to go out there and have a conversation. You have a two second serve, and they miss the return, and their back at the drawing board again?"

Some see an opportunity for a little levity in the heat of serious battle. Rajeev Ram and Scott Lipsky shared this exchange at a winning press conference: "I told him not to hit any more lobs, and then 1 hit a lob the next point" Ram said, and he then told Lipsky, "Except for that."

Of course, there's always going to be some no nonsense, back in the day old-schoolers like Paul McNamee, who are not enamored with all this huddling and talking in today's game. The former Aussie doubles wizard believes that professional players should be readily able to read the situation in an instant - poach, close, return placement, etc. - and just react spontaneously if they truly know the game. And he makes no bones about it when he says, "At the end of the day, the best communication is unspoken."

In any event, club players who have solid shot-making skills and know their way around a doubles court can, like their professional models - McNarnee's comment notwithstanding - make good use of in-between-point communicating, even if it turns out to be, more often than not at the club level, offering partner support and encouragement versus the x's and o's.

A good place to start.

How to make the
most of team tennis

I've been maintaining for years that a chimpanzee could be trained to play singles. Doubles, however, is an entirely different animal, to say the very least.

Doubles is, simply put, complicated. Getting two players to work in perfect harmony offensively and defensively, and even in neutral rally situations, is a daunting task. Factor in styles of play, shot- making strengths and weaknesses, personalities, partner support issues, positioning and the myriad misperceptions regarding strategy and tactics and you have a Rubik's Cube on your hands.

One particular component of club doubles play consistently reveals itself as the #1 pitfall: the inability to play the net position fluidly, or continuously shifting back and forth between offensive and defensive court positions touched upon earlier..

By isolating the net player on the serving team, an understanding of this dynamic can be fully appreciated. Initially, they are positioned offensively in the approximate middle of their service box, not hugging the singles sideline! From there they are well prepared to poach into the center of the court, on a forward diagonal, to intercept and wreak havoc with any cross court return that's vulnerable and reachable.

This position is also equally predisposed to both protecting against any down-the-line intrusions — you must slide towards the alley if the action is forced out wide — and moving back to comfortably handle all but the very best lob attempts as well.

However, when a successful cross court return is made by the receiver, the norm for a solid opponent, the netman is then required to abandon the offensive position and retreat back towards the "T" on a slight diagonal — approximately two feet off the center service line — and square off to the opposing net player, now in a defensive position to defend the middle against their possible poach. Role reversal accomplished in a fleeting moment.

In the usual one-up, one-back point starting alignment, switching from offense to defense, then defense to offense, is a never-ending constant. Done well, formidable court positioning around the net is achieved, maximizing both attacking opportunities and defending necessities as partners in the backcourt engage in dueling ground stroke exchanges.

Another common failing is found in the often heard "switch" command, when the net player is lobbed over and the partner in back has to come to the rescue. Typically, the net player switches sides while remaining at the net, fully exposed, while their partner, also switching sides, attempts to run down the lob and extricate the team from the predicament. Not a good idea if the lob is a good one and difficult to handle, unless of course your partner is one of the Bryan brothers.

If the effectiveness of the lob is marginal, then the parallel-to-the-net switch is appropriate since the partner should be able to take care of business. Conversely, when the lob is immediately judged by the netman as representing real trouble for their partner — a quick glance back to evaluate is okay — they should then move back towards the baseline area vacated by their partner as quickly as possible. If the response is indeed a weak one, with the opposing netman lurking and salivating, at least you and your partner are now both in a hack defensive posture, eliminating an easy chance for the opponent to transform a doddering "parallel switcher" into Swiss cheese.

While we're on the subject of lobbers, they are not uncommon, and typically, they are particularly adept at their "craft." This results in thwarting attacking styles of play — coming in behind short balls or serving and volleying — and causes those who attempt to play "proper" traditional and aggressive doubles to mumble to each other in total frustration: "How could we lose to them?"

So, short of calling the sheriff, what can be done, strategically and tactically, to take these sorts out of their counter punching game? Bring them in! These folks are practically never a threat when at the net, and often find ways, either right at the start of a point or even in mid-point, to assume a totally defensive alignment with both players in the backcourt. A well executed drop shot, or even a mundane short chip forces them off the baseline and into the forecourt, thus eliminating the lob from the back and forcing them into an unwelcome shootout in and around the net.

Finally, when in the back of the court and faced with an opponent who is on their way in to the net, visualize going low and right at their feet, handcuffing them in transition, forcing them into a weak volley and allowing for an alert partner at the net to move in quickly and pick off the weak response for an easy winner. Unfortunately, all goes wrong when the back courter does just that but the net partner hangs back at the service line, foolishly worrying about perfect lobs off of opponent's shoe laces. With that maddeningly glass half-empty mindset, the opportunity to capitalize in a team effort is quickly lost, often repeatedly, and so is the match in a close encounter.

Okay, sure, the doubles game can be a dizzying experience. But two on two tennis becomes less frustrating — and more fun — with these few simple adjustments that, ideally, should be universal to all partners.

PLAYING

Local tennis expert stresses the
importance of playing well with **nice**
others, *especially* your spouse!

Always encourage your
partners to get into the
act, to be a part of the
"T" in team, win or lose.

With over 50 years in the game, I've witnessed some harrowing encounters and can recall displaying some very boorish and unfortunate behavior myself, directed at my former spouse in a USTA husband-wife tournament. Many years later I still have a stinging Kodak moment taken immediately after she had blown an "easy" put away at a pivotal juncture in a tight match. There I am, glaring in her direction; there she is, feeling horrible about her missed opportunity. Not nice.

In retrospect, my goal was to win at all costs, short of tubing anyone in a totally defenseless position. Her goal was to enjoy playing doubles with her husband and have some fun while sharing the great sport of tennis together. My actions and negative vibe ensured that she would now play tentatively, afraid to miss, creating a strained climate for the remainder of the match, which we lost... not to mention the long ride home. How could I have strayed down the path of creating completely unrealistic performance expectations of the person I cared for the most? After all, I was making errors, too.

A lesson for all partners, married or not, is to never, ever, to unconditionally support a struggling partner, especially one who isn't your equal in skill, experience or both. I have yet to ever play with, or observe, anyone participating in a tournament or competitive club encounter making errors on purpose.

The game is difficult enough without rolling your eyes in disgust, shrugging your shoulders in resignation, barking accusingly loud instructions, turning your back and not talking on the changeovers and generally communicating to your opponents and anyone else in proximity to your court that your partner is dragging your otherwise wonderful game down.

In reality, influencing the best doubles partnerships, whether partners in life or not and whether there's a clear disparity in playing skills or not, is so easy even I learned do it. First and foremost, adhere to a fail safe prime directive, which is the acceptance of the "anything you can comfortably reach and hit is yours" contract. After all, this is doubles.

Avoidance items include darting in front of your partner to take a shot that is clearly their ball, even if their backhand is a bit dodgy. Don't incessantly tell your partner to watch their alley to, in effect, get them hugging the singles sideline to create more balls for you giving nothing more than the appearance of playing in tandem. And please, unless a family member has received a death threat if you lose, don't tell partners, "I'll take all the volleys in the middle," or especially, "I'll take all the overheads." If any of these examples is striking a chord, you might reconsider your take on doubles play and think about playing mostly singles.

For better or worse, it takes two to tango. Always encourage your partners to get into the act, to be a part of the "T" in team, win or lose. Be continually positive with any partner making inadvertent unforced errors with supportive comments like, "No problem!", "Keep going for it!", "Good effort!", "Almost!", "It's okay; no worries!" or "It's alright, let's go!" You can be instrumental in helping them to relax, regain their focus and composure, diffuse over trying and, ultimately, right their game to influence the result in a positive way. Or, you can literally join forces with the other team and add to the adversity that they already experience. You choose.

When communicating with a sputtering partner, never use the "you" word even when offering positive advise. "You've got to do this." "You've got to do that." Always, even if you aren't experiencing the same difficulties, use the "we" word. "If we can avoid lobbing the opponent in the blue cap, I think we'll be better off." Or, "Let's both go crosscourt on the return and keep it away from him if we can." You'll find that partners are much more accepting of the types of exchanges that indicate you're in it with them, not against them.

Besides the psychological aspect addressed thus far, along with underdeveloped mechanics, keep in mind that the two biggest liabilities in doubles play are playing out of position, especially ar the net, and poor, low percentage shot selection. Make it a point to continually improve these areas of your game. The demand for your doubles services will continually improve as well, and all will be well in your tennis world.

Prior to his untimely death, two-time Kentucky Derby winner Chris Atley explained his widely recognized ability at getting the most out of his mounts, even ones he had never ridden before. "To make the horse my friend by the time I get to the starting gate," he said. If he could successfully communicate that with an animal, shouldn't it be a given for all of us to coax the best out of another human being?

That Plato sage advice about play deportment remains. So just be the best you can be and allow your hour to be one filled with shared fun.

MAXIMIZING
the Health Benefits of
Tennis

I can't think of another activity that can keep you fit, from head- to-toe, in your post-school years like tennis. Frequent tennis players of all ages, including those playing mostly doubles but playing it dynamically, enjoy a unique health advantage over their sedentary peers.

Despite the obvious benefits inherent in the sport — cardiovascular, cardiorespiratory improvement, enhanced muscle tone, increased stamina, bone mass enhancement, flexibility, agility, balance and even brain function — there are a number of all too common pitfalls that can seriously undermine these gains.

The most serious of these is the near epidemic of breath holding as one is in the act of striking their shot. I regularly explain to clients who have improved enough to engage in long, physically demanding exchanges, "If you're going to play that well, you're going to have to breathe!"

Grunting, as in audibly exhaling through the ball-racket collision, is often negatively viewed by the unenlightened, but is absolutely necessary in warding off the onset of oxygen debt and the resulting premature fatigue. Repeatedly holding one's breath on every shot leads to unnecessarily elevated and potentially dangerous heart rates, not to mention the ill effects on physical play performance and the poor decision making that's a byproduct of the diminished brain function that goes along with it.

Lack of quality footwear is another example of where devoted, well intentioned players put themselves at risk unnecessarily. Inadequate or worn-out tennis shoes will ultimately take a toll, possibly a severe one if left unattended, on ankles, knees, hips and the lower back.

In evaluating your current shoes, it isn't how long you've been wearing them, it's how many hours you've played in them. Once the insoles are compressed to the point where they've lost their cushioning – replacements are readily available versus a new pair of shoes - you begin to pay a price. It's a slow process, and it will sneak up on you. I urge you to pay close attention and notice when the smooth, comfortable ride you once enjoyed is no more.

Then, of course, there's the physically self-destructing warm-up habits of so many otherwise intelligent individuals who start their day positioned at full-court, immediately hitting balls at match speed while simultaneously sprinting for every ball in order to play it on one bounce. There is no "warm-up." People treat their automobiles better than that! Starting up slowly, deliberately and methodically positioned in no-man's land, choosing to not chase errant balls and even playing warm-up balls on the second or third bounce will collectively allow your hitting machine to comfortably ease into the task at hand without experiencing the always lurking negative physical consequences.

Many players greatly underestimate the importance of an inexpensive, fresh over grip, at least every other time you play, but ideally every time out, to contribute to a relatively relaxed upper body. Clean grips, especially in warm weather, create optimal hand- on-racket friction that allows for low grip muscle tension resulting in improved shot making and reduced hand, wrist, elbow and shoulder injuries. Old, dirty, greasy grips encourage handle strangling and inefficient muscling of the ball. I prefer the white rubbery type that clearly show the fast dirt build-up and signal a change.

Monitoring one's pulse rate during play represents yet another tool in maximizing both your heath and your performance. Starting points prematurely while experiencing a highly elevated heart rate, or beginning a point with an under stimulated rate, will both work against your success. If, after a long and grueling exchange, you find your heart jumping out of your chest, use all of the 25 seconds allotted in between points for recovery. Go to the towel like the pros do; they're not doing it for effect. Additionally, breathe in through your nose and out through your mouth to optimize that recovery before starting the point.

Conversely, if you're involved in a match that's slow going with quick points and very few extended rallies, and your heart rate is at the low end of the spectrum — less than 100 bpm — you'll find yourself in an under-aroused athletic state. This results in sufficiently sluggish and lackluster play, especially in terms of footwork and focus. When this is the case, energize your feet while shuffling in place just as you see the pros doing so often. This will elevate your pulse up to a more optimal 110-115-120 bpm in order to begin the next point more physically engaged. A pulse monitor is an ideal way to quickly get in tune with your actual status while playing.

Now a word on stretching. Cold muscles are not stretchable! It's not uncommon to witness players walking on the court, stone cold, and immediately launching into a ballistic stretching routine. Wrong! Your muscles have to be warmed-up before stretching or you can actually do damage. Try jogging very slowly around the court or parking lot for 2-3 minutes to elevate your core body temperature before doing any static stretching exercises. And don't over stretch. Work well within your range of motion at that specific time, not what you would like your range of motion to be, or what it was yesterday. Stretching should be comfortable and enjoyable, just observe your cat or dog stretching. Clearly it feels very good to them, and it should to you as well.

Stretching after play is also important, if not more important, in order to reduce the degree of any stiffness experienced later in the day or the next day.

If you do injure yourself during play, typically a pulled muscle or a back gone into spasm, stop immediately and ice the affected area. Continue icing as often as possible for the remainder of the day.

Sure, you're a fighter and you're going to want to push on and not "ruin the match" for everyone else. But true friends and teammates will understand, accept your predicament and offer encouragement to stop play and begin treatment immediately in order to minimize the seriousness of the injury. Continuing to play will most certainly exacerbate the injury and extend your time away from the game for longer than you thought possible at the time.

Battling the
3-Headed
How to survive Monster
the hot summer heat on the court

It comes as no surprise to anyone who lives in Florida that the men's and women's professional tours do not schedule tournaments here during the summer months — too hot, too humid, too sunny! Only the January conditions in Melbourne, Australia (Australian Open) — summer down under — occasionally replicate, much to the chagrin of the players, the same suffocating conditions that can adversely affect performance in a big way.

Yet here in Florida, or any other warm climate place, the beat goes on after the snowbirds have departed for cooler climes up north. A still large contingent of year-round, frequent players brave the oppressive heat in league tennis, tournaments and friendly intra-club play. Naturally, adjustments must be made from the idyllic winter conditions — hydration, attire, nutrition and even accessories — in order to maintain one's level of play without, hopefully, experiencing any negative physical consequences.

Since approximately 65 percent of your body weight is fluid — about 15 percent less in women because of their higher fat tissue content — let's start there. Core body temperature can rise a significant one degree and heart rates can jump 10-20 beats per minute at the same work rate when the body isn't fully hydrated.

In 90-plus-degree heat with extremely high humidity under a blazing sun, a head start in hydration is absolutely necessary before play. Drinking up to two 8-ounce glasses of cold water at least two hours before play is necessary to pre-hydrate. Waiting until you're on court, warmed-up and into the match before beginning to drink will predispose you to the onset of dehydration coupled with the inability to catch-up no matter how much you ingest. Worse yet, if you don't bother drinking until you actually become thirsty, you're already toast — an irreversible loss of conditioning has already begun, ultimately leading to a possible cessation of sweating, the body's cooling, heat-loss mechanism, and possible cramping or even heat stroke.

Even with proper pre-match or practice preparation, you'll still need to take in fluids during every single changeover, thirsty or not. This is where an electrolyte-enhanced carbohydrate beverage featuring sodium and potassium becomes prudent, since water alone cannot replenish lost nutrients. However, sports drinks that contain too high a percentage of carbohydrates can slow the rate of fluid absorption, so stay with recognized brands like Gatorade and keep the water electrolyte mix to 50/50 just like the pros whom you can observe with two bottles of liquid by their chairs, one water the other an electrolyte which they take equal drinks from.

The year-round Florida player, especially more fit individuals, can and do develop a respectable tolerance to heat and humidity, but the penetrating sun bearing down on them represents another challenge. A lack of protection from the sun will bring even a well- conditioned player to their knees, reasonably hydrated or not. White hats — white to reduce radiative heat gain — are a must. Whether a baseball cap or some variation on the theme, the protection offered pays big dividends versus a dark colored hat, or, especially, no hat at all. Visors do not get the job done! Soaking these hats in cold water on every changeover, and even wearing an equally soaked bandana around one's neck, will provide a very effective moisture barrier, creating a considerable cooling effect in particularly tough conditions.

Regarding apparel, the lightweight, breathable fabrics of today's tennis clothing manufacturers are designed to allow sweat to evaporate easily. Shirts and tops — white or a light color — should be loosely fitted and untucked to maximize ventilation. The old school expectation of tucking one's shirt or top in as proper is antiquated at best. I believe that Todd Martin was the last man on tour to tuck his shirt in.

Sunscreen's role in reducing skin cancer is obvious to all when applied liberally and reapplied as necessary when perspiring heavily, especially for those with fair skin and light colored eyes. Its sunburn prevention properties also regulate skin temperature, which can contribute to heat-related problems. I forgot to apply my 75 SPF sunscreen to my face one morning and then proceeded to complete five hours of lessons facing the sun without a hat. Idiot! It took me one week to completely recover. Don't tell my dermatologist.

Of course, not being able to grip your racket properly because of the perspiration running down your arms and into your hands makes for an exercise in complete frustration. Wrist bands, along with daily over grip replacement, are a necessity in hot weather. The bands also come in handy to wipe the sweat off your brow if a ball kid isn't available to dutifully deliver your towel to you after every point on your tour. Having a plentiful supply in your racket bag will allow for frequent replacing as they become soaked in sweat.

Eating right will also help in preventing nutrition-related problems in the heat. Here's some trade-offs you can consider. Lose the sodas, fake fruit juice, french fries, white bread, processed foods, frosted flakes, donuts, fried chicken, hamburgers, canned fruit and vegetables and ice cream, just to name a few. Instead choose water, 100 percent orange juice, baked potatoes, whole wheat bread, shredded wheat and bran, bagels, skinless chicken breast, lean steak, fresh fruit and vegetables and fat-free yogurt. Naturally, don't wolf down even a healthy meal immediately before play. Give yourself a couple of hours to allow for digestion.

Finally, as an active regular player battling the ever present "3- headed monster," keep an eye on the color of your urine as an indicator of possible dehydration. Proper and consistent hydration leads to nearly colorless urine. The onset of darker colors is a warning that you are not drinking enough fluid and are at greater risk for heat illness.

Stay cool to be calm and collected to perform your best and be healthy as well.

Tennis Wellness Life

The examples of professional athlete's dedication to their overall well being, physically and mentally are brought to our collective attention at every turn. No, not the ones who've been convicted of illegal performance enhancing drug use and stripped of their medals, trophies and prize money or the ones under constant surveillance who employ private chemists to remain one step ahead of the enforcement agencies and beat their drug tests. Not that.

I am referring to the trendsetters who have embraced legitimate, above board regimens and protocols, off the playing field, which have steadily mainstreamed in the past few years. Not only into the lifestyles of motivated weekday and weekend warriors, but also into the lives of those who might be without a particular sport but are committed to their head-to-toe health, fitness and longevity.

Tennis players in particular, of any age, are a very physical, dedicated and in tune with their bodies bunch due to the obvious demands of the game. Nancy Stout, 84 years young, has been ranked in the top 10 internationally (ITF) in the women's over 80 singles category She periodically treks down from Sarasota to Punta Gorda for on-court training sessions to help keep her edge. But, regarding her off-court cross training, she said, "It's the regular Pilates that really keeps my tennis going." And she is amazingly injury free despite a demanding year-round schedule of national and international events along with constant practice.

Yoga, much like Pilates, has also found its way out of the studios and into the lifestyles of tennis players looking to enhance the physicality of their games. Punta Gorda based USPTA tennis pro Margit Bannon, who is also a certified yoga instructor, has uniquely merged the two in her coaching with glowing testimonials from local players.

Tennis itself has been on the cutting edge of human performance development for some time. Tennis legend Martina Navratolova, once a chubby, mercurial tour rookie, albeit with immense talent, fully realized her potential only after adopting a holistic, far ahead of its time approach to excellence back in the early 1980s. Team Navratolova included a fitness trainer for speed, flexibility and endurance, a dietician to properly fuel herself, a coach to fine tune her skills and strategies, and a sports psychologist to foster a new mental toughness component. The rest is history

Along with Ivan Lendl on the men's side, she influenced an entire generation of tennis players at all levels, exemplified in spades by pros Novak Djokovic and

Mardy Fish in 2011. The "Djoker," who finished the year as the best player on the planet, achieved as much notoriety for his gluten-free diet as he did for his stellar play. A previously often-injured Fish, a good but not elite player, became a top 10 player in one season at age 30, old for a tour pro, as a result of better fitness and diet. Relatively same playing skills, very different results.

In today's increasingly health minded, aging boomer society, the term "holistic" has given way to "wellness," a lifestyle trend that has become far more reaching.

The Starwoods Hotel chain broke new ground at recent U.S. Open by awarding rewards program members with free lessons with former top 5 touring pro James Blake right at Flushing Meadows. That beats a free room any day if you're into improving your game.

And large metro area client service movers and shakers are now foregoing the traditional schmoozing tactic of lunches, dinners and cocktails in an increasingly more health conscious marketplace. "People are tired of boozing it up with clients," according to New York City's SoulCycle founder Julie Rice. "Businesses are looking to engage their clients in new and healthy ways." Working out with clients is now referred to as "sweatworking." Keith Ferazzi, a how-to-book author on networking, believes workouts in any venue are ideal for closing deals and winning new accounts by "accelerating personal relationships" while becoming healthier at the same time.

It's all changing and simultaneously becoming both more sophisticated and diverse. In their book *Mindset: The New Psychology of Success,* Stanford psychologists Carol Dweck and Greg Walton argue that willpower is not, as previously thought, solely dependent on biological factors, mainly glucose depletion. Their control group studies, with fellow psychologist Veronika Job, indicate that willpower is self-renewing; when "you work hard, you're energized to work more." Proper food and rest are a given, but now willpower is being recognized as being mostly in your head That reminds me of the old adage: "If you want to get something done, give it to a busy person."

Another side of the emerging multi-sided wellness coin is a heightened biochemical interest among researchers and wellness doctors in how aging individuals deficient in vitamin B12 may exhibit slowly entrenching symptoms aside from an obvious anemia diagnosis that any blood test will flag. "Muscle weakness, fatigue, shakiness, unsteady gait, mood disorders, low blood pressure and cognitive problems" are being recognized as related. This deficiency — our body's ability to absorb vitamin B12 from food is severely diminished as we age — could seriously affect anyone, particularly a tennis player's longevity and effectiveness above and below the neck.

Thankfully, what has, in part, conversely emerged from the win-at- all-costs pro sports drug culture, where large amounts of money and personal cache are at stake and cheating by injection and ingestion has been perceived by some as a necessity to be competitive, are above-board programs developed and administered by forward thinking doctors focused on prevention and promoting a physical and mental enhancement that best represents "wellness" as we know it today.

One of those innovators is Dr. Grant Mansell, founder of Life Logic Wellness for Life. Since aging systematically reduces hormone levels, a foundation of his program is the restoration of those hormones to ones previous more beneficial levels. Complete resignation to "normal aging" is no more. It can be successfully treated through not only hormone therapy, but diet, exercise and effective supplementation collectively aimed at checking one's advancing chronological clock in order to maintain a "vigorous, healthy and youthful lifestyle" for men and women.

As a still effectively functioning career tennis pro — one with a Medicare card in my back pocket I might add — I thankfully continue to be mostly able to physically outperform my peers, thanks in large measure to embracing a wellness program. By maintaining good muscle tone, keeping the energy up, watching the body fat, staying sharp and paying attention to reducing the risk of age related disease, I'm cognizant of striving to stay ahead of the aging curve.

Whatever you do, whoever you are — tennis player, golfer, runner, swimmer, walker, bridge player — it makes sense that going the extra mile will make a difference in your body-mind self. A wellness lifestyle is the new countermeasure to old-aging versus succumbing to what senior care specialists now refer to as becoming "the old old."

Is Tennis Elbow Passé?

When Novak Djokovic, well known for his Gumby-like flexibility, once walked onto the famed Monte Carlo Masters center court for a semi-final with a mummified-looking right wrist taped all the way up his forearm, it registered as the tipping point for the epidemic of wrist injuries on today's pro tour.

Obviously hampered, the Serb would not have nearly enough to overcome a resurgent Roger Federer, a tour elder who had fallen to #2 incredulously in tiny Switzerland, losing in straights on the majestic red brick dust. He then was forced to withdraw from the weeks following event, the Madrid Open, as the 2014 French Open loomed.

Another one bites the dust. Hopefully in his case it's only a small taste of the wrist malaise that has steadily crept into the so-called "modern era" of professional tennis, particularly on, but not limited to, the men's side.

Back in the day it used to be about elbows when players, sans the off-court trainers, massage therapists, and nutritionists employed by today's big budget players, wielded heavy chunks of small-headed wood and metal sticks pitted against slower, heavier balls compared to todays lightweight cannons and juiced balls. No wonder.

Tony Roche, one of the world's best in Rod Laver's time, who eventually became one of Federers early mentors, once famously sought out a Filipino faith healer to rid him of a debilitating tennis elbow that was threatening his game. Such was the quixotic state of solutions — surgery could be career-ending at that time — for the affliction of the day.

Of course backs and shoulders are, and have always been, at risk as well for anyone playing tennis. Maria Sharapovas comeback from what was thought to be career-ending shoulder surgery astonished both her peers and the pundits. And the new Swiss #1, Stan Wawrinka, took full advantage of Rafael Nadai's ailing back — the same infirmity that derailed Federers entire 2013 campaign — in the down under slam final in Melbourne.

Hip problems have not been absent from the mix when it comes to ending great runs and even careers. Both Guga Kuerten, the ever smiling Brazilian of French Open fame, and Magnus Norman, a stoic Swede who is now Wawrinka's brain trust, fell from world #1 rankings as the open stance, drive-off-the-back-leg forehand came of age, putting undue loads on the right hip, which is mostly solved today by more sophisticated training methods.

Nonetheless, the pervasiveness of the current wrist outbreak is attention-getting and of great concern on both tours.

The first big hint of trouble came in 2010, right after Juan Martin del Potro broke through the Federer-Nadal-Djokovic triumvirate to win the 2009 US Open title. He then missed an entire year recovering from right wrist surgery. Now, after clawing his way back to the top echelon of the game, he is facing surgery again, this time the left one, the driving force on his two-handed backhand.

The women have not been immune. The big-serving, young British lefty Laura Robson recently went under the knife on her dominant wrist and will miss her hometown slam in London. Conversely, like del Potro, former #1 Caroline Wozniacki, and # 17 Sloane Stephens, one of America's top prospect, have either withdrawn from events or played hurt with two-handed backhand, top-hand wrist problems.

Enter Dr. Richard Berger an orthopedic surgeon at the Mayo Clinic in Rochester, Minn., who has emerged as the pros' wrist surgeon of choice, having previously operated on del Potro and now Robson.

Berger's take on the physical stress of the game being played today is revealing: "Tennis is one of those sports that, honestly, the wrist is one of the structures at most risk because the force of contact with the ball is transmitted directly through the wrist, and very often, with an element of torque as the player attempts to place higher and higher degrees of spin on the ball."

He goes on, "There's such a tremendous transfer of total body energy. This energy springs from the legs, up through the spine, down the arm to the forearm and across the wrist to the racket. At some point, either through genetics or the playing style, the structural integrity of any of those structures is exceeded. For any given individual, the force is greater than the structures are capable of withstanding."

Berger's real kicker comes with this realization: "I think that with the technology available for training, the regimens that these players go through in their daily routines for fitness, you're getting close to superhuman capacity. Again, the ligaments aren't really able to keep up with that because they don't change."

Okay, so you are not a finely tuned professional player, but, nonetheless, it's all still relative. Most club players stress their bodies not through high intensity, off-court daily training programs, or through match play, mano-a-mano, 25 shot singles rallies. Their physical stress is a by-product of poor technique, mainly preparing the racket repeatedly late for ground strokes.

Couple that with their penchant for playing with oversized, head-heavy, thick-beamed war clubs - a non-solution for inefficient mechanics - which are unwieldy, lack maneuverability, and have grips that are often dangerously too small, and you have a game that puts wrists, elbows, shoulders and backs all at risk, not to mention the resulting out-of-control shot making.

As a senior player still competing - #3 nationally in 2014 USPTA 65 clay court singles - I'm playing with a lightweight, 9.2-ounce mid-plus 98, a fairly stiff, medium-beamed frame that's evenly balanced. Just hit the "easy" button. It's easy to control and readily maneuverable, especially when jammed or at full stretch. No pain and plenty of gain. No chronic upper body injuries, and that's factoring in the gazillion balls I've struck over the past 55 years.

Early on I was lucky in that I was taught an essential core fundamental of striving to never be late preparing for shots, and it has paid big dividends over decades.

Here's a few recommendations, especially for the 2.0, 2.5, 3.0, 3.5 crowd, and even some 4.0s: Consider at least trying a few demos that are more user friendly, ones that will stress your body and appendages far less. Start monitoring the timing of your forehand and backhand take backs - ideally fully loaded by the approaching ball's bounce, or even earlier (Serena and Venus).

And realistically assess your playing style. Trying to emulate the degree of topspin that today's pros put on the ball — Nadal leads the league with up to 50 revolutions per second on his lasso forehand — with their extreme grips and roll over follow through, makes this sling shot wrist action unrealistic for the masses.

Comfortable grip positions that generate moderate topspin off both wings, or a bit of underspin on one-handed backhands, can still get the job done very nicely in Clubland, and be far kinder and gentler along with a lowered difficulty factor for anyone, especially those who actually remember Tony Roche.

Something to think about.

the racket Evolution ...or Revolution?

In Lydia Netzer's recent New York Times Op-Ed piece on the history of space flight technology, "The Man tn the Moon," she reasons. "Most technological advances are actually just improvements. First you had a carriage, then a car, and then an airplane; now you have a jet."

French monks in the 12lh century, responsible for tennis' first incarnation, used gloves to hit hand-made balls against walls. Then they had wooden paddles. By the 1500s, it's believed the Italians came up with what could be considered the first wooden racket with strings in a game that could be characterized as squash in a courtyard. In 1874, British Major Walter C. Wtngfield registered a patent not only for the rules of "lawn tennis" - the true forerunner of the game we play today - but also its racket, which remained virtually unchanged in concept for nearly 100 years.

Beginning around 1970, the metals came into being. Jimmy Connors with his steel alloy Wilson T-2000 along with the aluminum Prince Classic, the first oversized racket, used very successfully by a 16-year-old Pam Shriver. Then the first composite followed, the Head Comp popularized by Arthur Ashe, inspired by ski "sandwich" technology, all of which ultimately led to the graphite-carbon fiber sticks that completely took racket construction to another level in the early '80s, and still keep on ticking right along with every possible new space-age material in the mix.

My own first top-of-the-line racket in 1960 was not the popular, now iconic, Wilson Jack Kramer Autograph, or the flashier Dunlop Maxply Fort with its exceptional feel and craftsmanship. It was the Pancho Gonzales Autograph by Spalding (which actually produced the Kramer for Wilson), a Kramer identical twin, strung with blood red Victor Rob Roy gut. No, not "cat gut," as it was commonly referred to by non-players back then. In reality gut string was, and still is, processed lamb or calf intestines, which you could not get wet, or its many wound strands will first fray and then completely unravel before you can finish your match. Nylon, or "synthetic gut" as it eventually became generically known (first introduced in the '60s by a fishing line company in Rhode Island), was far less expensive, did not play nearly as well, and was not looked upon favorably.

Some look back nostalgically at the woodies, like a classic wire- wheeled roadster in the garage. Truth be told, these rackets were Neanderthal "clubs" compared to the magic wands that we whip around today They were very heavy and unwieldy, with slippery leather grips and tiny 68-square-inch heads. Mere four-cylinders next to today's enabling, turbo-charged V12s - shot-making on steroids.

In a preview of the 2012 U.S. Open, renowned sports writer Harvey Araton noted not only the "enhanced physicality of the sport since the days when shorts were really short," but also that back then "the rackets did not pulse with power." An understatement at the very least.

Ball striking was more massaging than bashing, which required highly developed finite motor skills. Those little 68-square-inch heads demanded impeccable technique along with "good hands" in every phase of the game. You had to have all the shots, because those rackets could not cover up mechanical inefficiencies.

Today's hopped-up, hi-tech weapons, with their dramatically larger heads and more forgiving string beds of super-playing synthetics, have not only made the game lethal in the hands of today's tour pros, but also less difficult and more appealing for recreational players at public parks and clubs. That's been a very good thing for the club game, and especially for its older players.

The mood in today's battle-of-the-rackets among the big three manufacturers - Head, Wilson, and Babolat - is one of a dead serious corporate cold war for market share. "There is an arms race," according to Wilson Racquet Sports' Jon Muir. "If we don't continue to innovate, we are going to fall behind."

That sentiment is nothing new, and just about everything has been tinkered with in the past in seeking to hyper-jump the competition. Rackets with two handles attached to a single shaft. Ones with heads tilted at 45 degrees (the same angle at which ocean waves break - something about universal physics?), models with interchangeable screw-on heads at different string tensions, and even one with a feature to lengthen the shaft another inch, if desired, from its standard 27 inches. The list goes on.

Manufacturers pitch the catchy names of their latest concepts and newest materials – always lighter with breakthrough strength-to-weight ratios - predictably promoted as providing, like never before, the ultimate balance of power, control, and maneuverability with a more forgiving sweet spot. There's Hybrid Beam technology, Organix carbon nanotubes, MicroCore, Cortex, and Adaptive YouTek, just to name a few.

Since topspin has become the hallmark of the game at the highest level, Wilson built its Innovation Center outside the O'Hare Airport in Chicago to measure, in addition to spin revolutions per second, ball speed and flight patterns - based on both new string patterns and tweaks in racket frame design - on a special court with live players, versus laboratory-only results, for the first time with a goal of enhanced spin without the necessity of stroke changes. A January release date has been announced for rackets with this new technology Still, its still just an airplane.

Wilson's business director for rackets, Cory Springer, acknowledged as much. "Instead of revolutionary" he said, "it's been more evolutionary. Is there another revolutionary advance in our future? I'm sure there is, but those things don't come along every day"

Not so fast.

Netzer's theory of methodical next-step improvement just might be in question - hearkening back to Thunderclap Newman's '60s anthem lyric, "Call out the instigators, the revolution is here." With Babolat boldly doing the instigating, looking to turn racket technology on its head, well beyond the airplane becomes the jet - the revolution is here.

Where else but at Roland Garros would the French company introduce and demonstrate a prototype that looks and feels like a normal racket, but it's far, very far from it. The "Play & Connect" did not become available until 2013, and reportedly only Rafa Nadal, Kim Clijsters and Li Na, Babolat elite players all, had hit with it prior to then.

So what's the big deal? It houses a computer chip in the handle that records biomechanical information - spin, swing speed, impact points, shots struck, actual playing time, and more still in development. It will wirelessly link to your computer, smartphone or tablet for post-play analysis and the establishment of a playing profile that, down the road, can be compared to both peers' and professional player's data. Now that's revolutionary.

Locally, we're fortunate to have two excellent tennis specialty shops, long standing Wrigley's Tennis and newcomer Grand Slam Tennis Company, led by racket tech heads Will Wrigley and Matt Protz respectively. Both are also accomplished players whom you can talk to in order to insure that you are currently playing with a racket that's well suited to your game and your physicality - which makes all the difference - without having to rely solely on all the manufacturers' repetitive, promise-you-everything marketing hype.

Although I haven't made a racket change in 10 years - my trusty old Head Intelligence iS2 Mid has remained a perfect fit for me despite trying the latest and greatest periodically. I haven't yet tried a "chip stick" myself to compare my data with Rafa's.

On second thought, maybe that's not such a great idea.

It's Now All About the Strings

It's not so much about the racket anymore- Sure, it's still very important to have a stick that matches your swing speed, swing length and fitness profile. Nonetheless, it's really difficult in 2016 to find a badly designed one. The research and development money spent by today's leading manufacturers is unsurpassed. Couple that with some clandestine reverse engineering by competing but undercapitalized rivals, and

you have dozens and dozens of frames with excellent playability across the spectrum.

With such a level playing field, it reasons why top pros are being paid enormous amounts of money to play with this brand or that since players drive sales. It's also why club pros and journeymen tour players receive theirs for free.

So, when I heard '87 Wimbledon champion Pat Cash, no spring chicken at this juncture, say, when asked about the "new strings" in an interview at the 2013 Championships, "I can hit shots now that I couldn't hit when I won here" it really got my attention.

These polyesters, versus the more traditional nylons and natural gut, have been in the tour headlines for a few years now. Just visit your local pro shops and check out the dizzying array of choices.

This past summer, in a surprising convergence, a very good college player I knew, now in his 40s, arrived in Lake Placid looking to hit. We sparred from the back of the court for longer than my body wanted, just trading but doing so pedal to the metal. A fit lefty, he always played big topspin off his forehand, but what I experienced that day, 25 years since our last hit, was something else entirely.

Although no Nadal in stature, he was bending in look-alike forehands, sharply descending rainbow rockets that were exploding off the court, pushing me back off the baseline even when they weren't that deep in the court! I was having to take most everything aggressively on the rise, or back up way off the baseline to buy space and time, something my player ego was not about to allow.

"David, you're crushing the ball," I told him during a break. "Are you living at the gym these days?"

He laughed, "No, it's these strings. They don't move," referencing the amount of ball rotation he was generating off his mains. He handed me a set of his polys out of his bag, one of the multi-sided, sharp edged ones that don't move but also, apparently, gripped the ball far more than the David I remembered ever did.

The jury had been out for me since the early polys, which had become generically known as Luxilon — even though that was really just one of the brand names — and had a reputation for stringing up very tight and being tough on the arm. With decades on the court and counting, I think it prudent to always err on the side of caution.

But, first Pat Cash and now David.

I'd been playing the same hybrid nylons for years - slightly textured Head Intellistring 16g mains with Head Power Gel 16g crosses in that dated Head Intelligent iS2 previously mentioned. Although at times important to vary tensions 2-3 pounds based on temperature, humidity, court surface, altitude and current physicality, I stay mostly at 65 mains, 62 crosses.

Having started playing tennis as a youngster with a heavy wooden racket in the late 50s, my game does not exactly resemble Nadal's in any way, shape or form. But, if the polys could enhance my moderate topspin forehand, my skidding backhand slice, and bend my second serve in at an even steeper arc and angle of descent, I'd be all for that.

Since they do indeed string tighter, but now also come in slightly softer versions — easier on the arm — I chose the newer, more forgiving Babolat RPM Team 125mm/16gl and Luxilon Savage 127mm/16g mains at 60 to go along with my usual Gel crosses in my other two frames, and headed out for a playtest. (I took particular notice of the near disclaimer on the Lux packaging: "Savage strings are for powerful players who take big cuts and want to hit a heavy ball. The unique six-sided shape provides 'savage' amounts of spin and kick for all shots.")

Switching back and forth between my norm and the polys, I found that although the Gel crosses still retained some of the softer, bigger ball pocket feel that I prefer, even with the poly mains, I also noticed a stiffer overall sensation, even at their recommended lower tensions (approximately 10 percent) compared to my usual nylon mains.

The question came soon enough: Can I up my typical sv/ing speeds, firmly entrenched on my hard drive, to sufficiently take advantage of the edged, tighter playing polys to get more ball r.p.s. (revolutions per second) — Nadal currently leads the tour with about 50 on his battering ram mega topspin forehand, compared to Pete Sampras' more laser-like, somewhat flatter 25 — without changing my grip and normal stroke paths?

Not really as it turned out. Nor, I ultimately realized, after a solid hour of hitting against a good player, did I want to. But experimentation typically yields a pearl. I also realized I should at least go ahead and try replacing my regular 16g mains with the thinner 17g version to get a bit more bite on the ball without reinventing my game.

Curious, I decided to ask my area's stringing gurus, Will Wrigley and Matt Protz, along with pro friend Margit Bannon (www.facebook.com/playtennispracticeyoga), all excellent players in their own right, what racket they played and what strings they preferred.

Wrigley wields a Babolat Aero Pro Drive 100 (think Rafa), strung with Babolat NVy 16g, his favorite, at 62/62, which he described as a "soft nylon synthetic gut that reduces ball load and shoulder, elbow stress." He also uses Technifibre X-One Bi-Phase 16g, a polyurethane similar in construction to natural gut, but at 55/55 for the same feel.

The Head Radical Mid-Plus 98 (Andy Murray) is Protz's stick of choice. He's used every version of that frame since Andre Agassi first put it – the Bumblebee because of its black and yellow graphics - on the map. He's also stayed with the same Head string all along, Head Rip Control nylon 16g at 55/55. He commented, "strings don't create topspin; they can only enhance it" recalling customers seeking instant mechanical fixes through polys.

Bannon's preferences were not dissimilar. She plays with the Wilson Blade 104 (Serena) with Wilson 17g Pro nylon at 55/55. "I haven't changed tension or gauge in about 20 years," she told me. "The low tension with 17g gives me a nice power-spin combination... and I rarely change rackets."

These folks know their games, know what they like and tend to stick with it.

Today's pro players are the fastest, quickest, strongest, fittest ever, men and women alike. They swing through the ball at Mach 1 racket speeds to take full advantage of the polys unique ball gripping characteristics. Their extreme forehand grips, triggering open-stances and exaggerated over-the-ball stroking techniques with new follow through paths — like Nadal's lasso — have evolved in lock step with the string technology.

The game's always naturally evolving and improving, as an excellent TV feature during last year's US Open so aptly illustrated, in marked contrast to the constant, annoying announcer references to the "modern game," with their subtle, sometimes overt, discrediting connotations towards all that preceded it. More on that later in the book.

Being willing to experiment with your string set-up can potentially maximize your current ball striking skills, but it won't change your mechanics.

So, as the long standing axiom goes, restring as many times per year as you play on average per week for your personal best, day in and out.

NTRP
and the Health of the Game

The National Tennis Rating Program, formally launched by the United States Tennis Association in 1980, and now an integral component of both inter-club team play and individual tournament competition, is not without its flaws. Although well-intentioned, in certain instances it has, unfortunately, been allowed to evolve onto a slippery slope.

Motivated by golf's long standing handicap system, tennis attempted to follow suit in order to better level its competitive playing field, particularly with regard to league doubles play, which represents the heart and soul of USTA membership with nearly 350,000 participants nationwide. It replaced the long standing A, B, C rating system for team play — any given club's best players were designated as As, their second tier were B's and third tier were Cs — along with specific age group differentiations for individual play. Unfortunately, tennis skills and levels of play — with 13 different NTRP rating levels — are far more difficult to compartmentalize and do not lend themselves well to handicapping.

For those unfamiliar with the current system, a beginner is designated a 1.0 player, while the big boys and girls on the professional tours are at the very top of the spectrum at 7.0. In clubland, the most populated divisions are 3.0, 3.5 and 4.0, with a 3.0 rating being a first modicum of skill and earned success and a 4.0 being a very well-rounded player.

Official match results are regularly entered into the USTA computer to maintain a player's status quo, advancement or even rating demotion. This is a never-ending topic of player conversations, and it often becomes, rightly and wrongly, a source of frustration and dissatisfaction among many.

You would think that players would be continually striving to improve their games and results in order to play at "the next level," a phrase commonly cliched by athletes in all sports. Not always so in the NTRP scheme of things. Why not?

Some express dissatisfaction, once their rating has been elevated because of their success, over then not being able to win matches as easily and regularly. Winning, albeit at a level they no longer belong in, trumps the sense of personal achievement that one would think would be embraced in being "bumped-up" to play against better competition.

Others decry their upward ascent because they won't be able to play with their friends anymore — players whose match records happen to not warrant promotion — prompting some to formally file protests with, would you believe, made up excuses about physical limitations they don't really have or have embellished, and even ghost operations that never took place in order to maintain their status quo.

I also know of a league match in which one of the doubles partners, a good player who worried about being recognized as belonging at a higher level, queried their partner about easing up in a match where a lopsided victory was probable in order to avoid triggering a rating red flag.

Early on, one had to attend an NTRP rating session in order to be evaluated and rated by one of the attending pros before they could participate in league play. I recall volunteering for one of these sessions and remember it as, shall I say, a very interesting experience. Lower players, typically 2.5's, perceiving themselves as better and better players requesting in earnest that I not rate them "too high," again apprehensive about taking on better opponents.

Currently, first time players are allowed to rate themselves — pros eventually shunned the process en masse — with their submitted results regularly computer crunched to make any necessary adjustments if they were too modest in evaluating their games, or, as is more often the case, willingly "sandbagging," not unusually at the urging of a team captain looking to gain an unfair advantage.

"Everyone else is doing it," is the party line rationale among players and their captains seeking an edge to win, whether it's men's, women's or mixed-doubles. And therein lies a problem. And yes, they are all doing it.

An instance of this occurred not long ago in which a 50-year-old relative rookie and newcomer to USTA league tennis participated on a team that won their local 6.5 Combo league (a 3.0 and 3.5 player partnering-up) and qualified for the state finals at the USTA tennis center in Daytona. Early in his first match against two allegedly equally skilled twenty-something players, both of whom exhibited big topspin forehand weapons and kick serve skills that normally don't exist in a 6.5 combo league, he sarcastically asked them, "So which one of you is the 3.0?" They laughed nervously, yet unapologetically regarding their obvious scam.

A post-match protest was filed against their participation at that level — officials were not on site to monitor any clear violations that slipped through the cracks at the local level — but the powers that be gave these guys a pass with a full plate of blue blazered mumbo jumbo despite the indisputable match-up discrepancies. Not a good message to the perpetrators. And then the word gets out.

Of equal concern, if not more so, is that it's not uncommon for club pros, some of whom are not that far removed from playing college tennis or stints in tennis' minor leagues, or even veteran pros who have decades of playing savvy, to participate in USTA league play. I thought that these leagues were aimed specifically at promoting participation among club and public park players, i.e. the "growing the game" slogan, not at individuals earning their living in tennis?

I know of a very good woman player, a solid 4.0 player with 4.5+ talent, who told me about playing against a young "ex-Gator player" in a 9.0 combo mixed league whose serve was so overwhelming she "couldn't even return it into play".

Additionally, it has actually become acceptable, represented as "strategic" to alter a team's actual line-up strength as if all the players involved are perfectly interchangeable parts, which they are not. Example: placing a teams top doubles team in the #2 or #3 position to get a sure win and sacrifice the #1 position since it's being projected as a sure loss. That's not strategy; that's poor sportsmanship. "But we're all 3.5's and that's what we've been rated, so why shouldn't we be able to do that?" is a common rationale. "Besides," they say "everyone else is doing it." And, truth be told, they are.

This state of affairs reminds me of something I read recently about the way in which today's society has evolved in general: "We used to devote ourselves to doing things right. Now we're more interested in how we can sell it."

Over the years, the sporting challenge of pure club-to-club, head-to-head, strength-to-strength, let the chips fall where they may competition has fallen victim to an increasingly accepted culture of circumventing tennis' long standing tradition of fair play This development should be alarming to all who love the game and its integrity.

It's up to the USTAs national leadership, and those in the trenches of its 13 sections, to step-up and reset the current culture with an updated mandate, a League Tennis Code of Conduct if you will, hopefully one backed-up by a no-nonsense monitoring and enforcement system to penalize those individuals and teams guilty of egregious manipulation of NTRP's original intent.

BAD CALLS
MISPERCEPTION OR CHEATING?

It's a heated USTA match in clubland. After battling on all cylinders in the hot sun for more than two hours, a point here or there could mean the difference in experiencing, as ABC's Wide World of Sports would say, "The thrill of victory, or the agony of defeat." Then, always at the most inopportune time, it happens.

Your shot lands squarely on the line, predictably skidding away at a speed considerably greater than a ball bouncing off the clay alone while simultaneously emitting that distinct "splat" sound of ball-on- plastic that's completely at odds with the usual ball-on-clay noise.

The opponent, with no chance of making a play immediately calls the ball out. There is no ball mark on the court on either side of the line, and there are no tour umpires climbing down from their chairs to overrule and reverse the call. And their doubles partner has conveniently recused themselves both in their body language and silence. The call stands.

Where's Hawkeye when you need it?

In my early tennis life I was quickly introduced to what I thought was a curious attempt at levity that club players constantly, half-jokingly used to banter about regarding any questionable line calling of the day, "When in doubt, call it out." Ha ha. It wasn't funny then, and it's not funny now because, in reality, it actually happens far too often.

Later, as a teenager taking it to the long-reigning city champ, when big city championships were a big part of the national tennis fabric in the "shamateur" days before the arrival of open tennis, I experienced it firsthand.

My opponent, 20 years my senior, began making bad calls. Lots of them. Years later, it begs the question: Was it willful, overt cheating, or was he so repelled by the prospect of losing his title, to a kid no less, that he was victimized by his subconscious mind distorting what he was actually seeing, seamlessly deferring to his less virtuous self?

This was in complete contrast to the player morals of the day at the elite level, long before the advent of professional officials and hi-tech line calling wizardry. Pre-open era piayers, often faced with coping with untrained spectators coerced into sitting on a line, routinely overruled bad calls that went against their opponents. Such was the state of fair play among the very best in more genteel times. Accepting unearned points was unacceptable and considered very bad form.

In the big money tennis of today, when was the last time you saw a player, even a multiple Stephan Edberg ATP Sportsmanship Award winner like Roger Federer, approach an umpire and insist that a point be awarded to an opponent after a particularly egregious missed call that the other player failed to challenge?

Overt cheating, if you can get away with it, has always been in the human nature mix, and it's not unique to tennis. Baseball has always had the spitball. Jersey holding to inhibit an opponent in contact sports like basketball, football and soccer remains commonplace. A world class speed skater was recently caught tampering with a rival's blades. Fishermen are being busted for smuggling in prize winning fish not hooked during the tournament. A marathoner hacked into his event's computer timing system to digitally fabricate a terrific run that never took place.

Worse yet is the doping phenomena rampant in all sports. Outside of sports we have, among myriad examples, the Bernie Madoffs of investing, scientific researchers fudging findings for recognition, and even cheating scandals in Ivy League institutions and our service academies.

Amazingly, all this boldly occurs right smack in the face of the very regulatory officials and agencies in place to specifically prevent an unleveling of any and all of society's playing fields.

So, is it an epidemic? A sign of societal decline? Or is it that the 24/7 news cycle, along with the explosion of social media, that has resulted in such an information overload that it only appears that way and, in reality, the level of cheating has changed little over time?

In *The Honest Truth About Dishonesty*, Dan Ariely tells us that cheating is contagious. The more we see, and the more that goes on unbridled and unpunished, the more we begin to methodically, unconsciously con ourselves into thinking that it's okay.

Where does this behavior begin? In his article, "The Competing Views on Competition," Matt Richtel shares his concern when his 4-year old son, on the way to the bathroom with his little sister to brush their teeth before bedtime, exclaimed, "I'm going to win. I'm going to win!" Young Milo, figuratively fist-pumping with his toothbrush in hand, is a scary thought going forward.

The psychology of cheating is stripped down in David DeSteno and Piercarb Valdesoios new book, *Out of Character; Surprising Truths about the Liar, Cheat Sinner (and Saint) Lurking in All of Us*. The often depicted cartoon angel on one shoulder and devil on the other is concluded as not exactly right. Character is instead viewed as the always fluctuating result of warring impulses in the brain that focus on either immediate rewards or long-term benefit.

Of course, line calling in tennis by club players officiating their own matches encompasses both subconscious brain impulsing and one's visual acuity. Enter renowned tennis authority Vic Braden and biomechanist Dr. Gideon Ariel, who once spent $50,000 of their own money to study the visual aspect of line calling, and its inherent fallibility, back when only the service line was called electronically while all others were called by trained lines people and pro players would regularly go ballistic over perceived missed calls.

In a control group of eight veteran officials and 12 former player teaching pros, it turned out that it was the players who were the least accurate, a surprise since players had always maintained that they knew best. And they admitted that 40 percent of the time their calls were really educated guesses; getting a stationary fix on a fast traveling ball is extremely difficult when in motion with a jiggling head. Try reading a book while jogging.

The seated lines people fared far better precisely because of their advantage in having a still head while sighting down a single line, interestingly the very same dynamic employed by players to strike a ball cleanly and eliminate miss-hits.

Those in the umpire's chair, although scoring belter than the players, were not as good as those sitting on the line because of their in-point head movement following the ball back and forth, which will undermine even 20/20 vision in a big way

Today's tour players benefit from a computerized line calling system, the aforementioned Hawkeye, that interfaces with strategically placed multiple cameras and boasts to have a miniscule margin for error. Have you noticed that player challenges to a suspected bad call are incorrect far more often than not.

So it appears that when there is doubt, there is a good chance that the ball is *not* necessarily out. Your call.

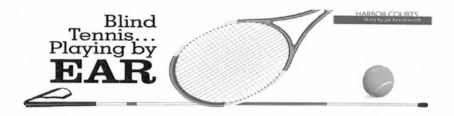

Blind Tennis... Playing by EAR

HARBOR COURTS
Story by Jak Beardsworth

Sooner or later, just about everyone who plays the game realizes that watching the ball is absolutely the holy grail of tennis – the difference maker, if you're going to have any shot at playing your A-game.

Ed Rice, an older gentleman I knew in Lake Placid, NY, who played well for years with a patch over his glass eye, was a master at it. What he could do on the court was both amazing and something to admire since without one's normal binocular vision - both eyes working in concert - depth perception, a hugely important component in tracking flying tennis balls, was completely undermined.

I make it a point to never stop trying to get aspiring tennis players to fully understand the difference between completely ineffective peripheral ball sighting and direct tracking - only-the-ball both incoming and outgoing. On occasion, for more years than I now care to admit, I would offer up to those frustrated with their up and down play mostly due to complacent focus on the ball, "Hey, c'mon, there aren't any blind people playing tennis."

Turns out I've been dead wrong all along.

Blind individuals have been playing tennis, albeit adapted, since 1984. And if you watch Miyoshi Takei - the so-called Roger Federer of blind tennis - on the internet (*www.hanno.jp/matsui*) versus another excellent player, you will not believe your eyes. His performances have been referred to as "transcendent" by able-bodied journalist Thomas Lin (who tried, repeatedly whiffing, playing with a blindfold on), which may not even do them justice. Takei, still just a teenager, designed the very first "sound-adapted" tennis ball. By 1990 he organized the first national tournament for the blind in his homeland of Japan.

Photos courtesy of Ayoko Motsui

Miyoshi Takei - the inventor of blind tennis, sits with the sound-adapted foam balls he created.

So., you're wondering exactly how is this even possible - blind individuals participating in a sport with visually following a fast-flying, small yellow sphere at its core.

The human brain's extraordinary visual cortex not only processes what you're seeing, but also what you're hearing (auditory) and what you're feeling (tactile). According to

88

Dr. Robert Cotlin, Director of Orthopedic and Sports Rehabilitation at Beth Israel Medical Center in New York, the visually impaired "can also perceive objects in space using other senses," which have always entered into the able-bodied tennis sensory mix as well.

Remember all the commotion back in the mid-1980s at the US Open, when the world's best, with razor sharp vision and highly evolved ball-tracking skills, complained vociferously that the deafening jet noise directly overhead was adversely affecting play by eliminating the auditory informational cues of the ball being struck?

Try playing with noise canceling headphones on sometime and you'll immediately experience what those players did - that all the senses are indeed in play. Or, conversely, play past dusk and you'll become aware of a heightened auditory awareness as the light fades and vision becomes severely compromised.

Takei's prototype, a sound-adapted, low-bouncing foam ball impregnated with tiny noise producing ball bearings rattling around at its core was the first step in making tennis doable for the visually impaired. A smaller than normal court with raised lines, a lower net, shorter rackets, and up to three bounces - wheelchair players are allowed, too were collectively added to the format to make blind tennis doable for those motivated to learn.

Because of the obvious, players cooperatively announce before serving, "You ready?" Receivers respond, "Yes," and the points begin.

When Takei tragically lost his life in a train accident at 42, Ayako Matsui, a special education teacher, took up his cause: "He wanted to make society better with able-bodied and disabled playing tennis together and understanding each other."

Blind tennis is now played worldwide not only in Japan, but also in China, the Philippines, Singapore, Australia, Canada, Spain, Italy, Argentina, South Africa and the Bahamas, and it has recently gamed traction in the US.

Institutions such as Lighthouse international in NYC, the Perkins School for the Blind in Boston and the California School for the Blind in Freemont, Calif, are leading the way for volunteer sighted players to be paired with visually impaired students - just as Takei had hoped to facilitate and advance learning the game.

When Dan Guilbeault, an upbeat participating teenage student at the Perkins School says with sincere incredulousness, "I never thought I'd be able to play tennis," you cannot help but take that to heart. After treatment for a brain tumor at the tender age of 3, he was left with seeing steadily increasing faint shadows at best.

Yet, despite the adversity he has been dealt, he keeps moving forward with an expansive mind-set that's expressed when he wishes out loud that "they had this [program] for public school kids who are blind all across the country."

The very first blind tennis tournament in the US was held this past January at a Boys and Girls Club in Mission, Texas, where traditional spectator silence during the points, as one might envision, was an absolute necessity. Martha Rodriguez and relatives traveled three hours from Laredo to watch her son Cruz, whose special school in Austin brought him to the event, participate. She noted that he has become generally more independent since he began playing tennis, and, "He's more confident in the things he does now."

Matsui, who regularly witnesses the accompanying emotional frustration that often includes tears of frustration for the beginning younger players, sums up the end game perfectly: "I love their smiles when they can finally hit a ball and it flies over the net."

Try imagining what that must be like.

On a personal note, I experienced a retinal hemorrhage last season, ultimately leaving a blob of dried blood over one eye for some time - Ed Rice came immediately to mind - which made tracking the ball effectively, something I would normally take completely for granted, far more demanding and not even close to my norm. A mere hiccup in the world of the seriously visually impaired or especially those without any vision at all, but enough of a wake-up call with regard to my own gift of sight

Make the most of yours on court; be grateful for it, and then enjoy your best tennis.

The
New Ball
Kids

I fondly recall training and coordinating the ball kids for two ATP Paine Webber Super Series tournaments at the Jimmy Connors Tennis Center back in Jimmy's time in Southwest Florida.

They had to try out, with the average age of both boys and girls - the politically correct tournament director insisted that we refer to them as "ball-persons" – being approximately 14. They dreamed of the chance of being on court right next to their idols. Great kids all, aspiring players, and hilariously mischievous despite my apparently transparent attempt at a John Wayne leadership style, or maybe because of it.

They were hard-working, dedicated to serving the players correctly, on-time, well behaved and generally responsible. And the free uniforms and shoes didn't hurt - a badge of honor and achievement.

But...

There were other volunteers, mostly handling the usher duties in the stadium. "Their motivations were very different. They wanted the accompanying free ticket along with the uniform shirt, shoes, cap or visor, so they could take in the matches when not on duty. But, I soon learned, never underestimate free lunch with a retired person who's entitled to it.

The kids co-mingled with them in the volunteer food tent for lunch and dinner. The kids quickly figured out the delivery times and orchestrated covert tactics to relieve the tent, and the ushers, offer more than their fair share of the desserts. That's when the trouble started.

They were "stealing" the desserts before the ushers could get back to the tent from their assignments, according to a number of the very distressed adults. I told them I didn't know anything about it "Are you sure?" I asked them. They angrily accused me of covering up for "my kids" And I happily was. Desserts - really?

But that was trivial to the tournament brass - more desserts would be provided and we got our own tent. However, stuffing tennis balls into some of the public toilets during one night session was an entirely different matter. The finger was pointing straight at them. This time I took the heat, and, in turn, so did they, although the culprits were, amusingly too scared to fess up, my John Wayne act having gained credibility.

It never came up again. That's when we really became a team. A solidly functioning unit to the satisfaction of all concerned, especially the players themselves. I could see some of the older kids, cognizant of the big picture, now taking leadership roles voluntarily

Early on in training, I had the kids throwing the ball back and forth, as was the custom on US soil. They were good tennis players. They were American. They were accustomed to throwing and catching. A total no-brainer for me. That is until a USTA official ball-kid trainer and entourage was brought in to evaluate our progress as the event loomed.

"No, no, no, they have to roll the ball back and forth," the consulting Blue Blazers informed me. What? I explained that these are not eye-foot kids from futbol nations who can't catch or throw. These kids grew up polishing their hand-eye skills from the time they were tots. They could do it; they were doing it, and doing it well.

But it was a losing battle. I was outranked and not amused. Neither were the kids who, you could see it in their eyes, felt demeaned and underestimated. One of the new leaders came to me and said passionately, "Coach, we don't need to roll the ball."

Rolling had started becoming the ever-increasing norm. We might have been some of the last of the throwers at that time who didn't get to throw.

Thirty years later, ball kids are still a welcome necessity on the court, but ball-kid organization and training has taken on new dimensions, led by, who else, the predictably romantic French. You will not see 250 ball kids, arm and arm, singing and chanting their way down a wide walkway prior to the start of the early matches anywhere but in Paris. "The positive vibe it transmits to the people, a welcome in the stadium, [creates] a good feeling in the morning," according to their coordinator, David Portier. Classic old school charm building esprit de corps.

It all began more than 40 years ago at Roland Garros, when a Tunisian-born tennis pro, Ridha Bensalha, devised a program to organize and train ball kids uniformly - all for one, one for all. Although it was successful, Portier, ironically, replaced him in 2010 when Bensalha's long-standing old school manner - not so charming - was judged too harsh despite all his success.

Conditioning and physical balance became the hallmark of the French training, in which only 250 kids would be chosen among 3,000 applicants each year.

They begin each day by stretching, followed by running, hopping, skipping sideways, practicing rolling the ball and finishing with five minutes of meditation while lying prone en masse, all aimed at systematically preparing them for the challenges of the day ahead. Although Portier plays down their collective confidence evident in their post-meditative singing - "We are the ball kids; we are the best in the world." - many would judge they are second to none. Not so fast.

Enter our own local ball-kid star, 40-year-old Terry Yonker. A solid tennis player in his own right who, sitting in the nose bleed section of the Sony Ericson Miami event a few years ago, decided it would be far better to be down on the court with the players up close and personal. Over five consecutive weekends the following year, he got through the extensive tryout period that had a very strict "militant," as he put it, flavor. He counterintuitively knew how to properly roll balls, and how to, in a somewhat sarcastic tone, "field ground balls."

With his Sony experience, he recently assisted officials with the ball kids at the annual Sarasota Open, a minor league tournament held every April. Yonker told me that there was a startling contrast to the median age of the ball kids in Miami - approximately 16 - and the 60 something Sarasota club member ball "kids."

In one match he was working, the time between points was really slow-rolling...confused with bocce ball? He suggested to the umpire, a paid regular tour umpire, "I think we'd better start trying to throw the ball or we're going to be here all day with this group."

The ump concurred. Even old Americans can throw.

Yes! Throwing however and whenever we can get it.

Yonker did remind me that the US Open, which he also hopes to work someday, does indeed utilize the good old American standard of throwing and catching with mostly late teen crews.

So, all is not lost after all! Although I did notice that the USTA did note "ball-person" information on the current website.

Then, right after Wimbledon's completion, and already looking forward to the real ball-kid deal going on right now at Flushing Meadows, it happened. I tuned into the Mercedes Cup on the Tennis Channel. I couldn't believe what I was seeing. It was rolling as usual, but "fielding ground balls" was clearly verboten in Stuttgart. Each ball kid, except those working at the net, were equipped with fish nets that were approximately 12 inches in diameter mounted on a 2-foot handle to catch the rolling balls.

Ground control to Stuttgart. Come in, please!

Apprehensive
Breaths

The usually gregarious Cyndi Mehl was uncharacteristically introspective, and clearly nervous, too. Fair enough. It was her debut match in the United States Tennis Association's 2.5 rookie doubles league this past fall and eons away from her first apprehensive breaths on a tennis court in April 2009. It was also a culmination of her courage — and faith — in her on-going battle to overcome a disastrous meeting with a cruel fate some 14 years earlier.

The Surflight Playhouse in Beachaven, N.J., a seemingly safe haven if there ever was one, was presenting a Summer Stock Theater production of Evita. Mehl, a volunteer costume designer, had logged countless hours of work into an elaborate wedding dress to be worn by the actress playing the Argentine diva, Eva Peron. She was excited and looking forward to seeing how it appeared on stage during the final dress rehearsal on an idyllic Jersey Shore August evening.

A fog dispersing machine, on loan from a playhouse in Southern California, was primed to create the desired ethereal backdrop for the wedding scene. Sitting up close to best critique her work, and in close proximity to the descending fog, she was, ironically, concerned about the climatic haze possibly effecting the delicacy of her dress. As the scene began, she almost immediately began feeling a strange burning sensation in her throat, followed by equally puzzling blurred vision.

As the symptoms seemed to worsen, she retreated backstage with her thoughts shifting from the preservation of the dress to her suddenly not feeling well. Perhaps it was just time to call it a day, she thought. She'd been at her typical daily routine since 5 a.m., and it was now 10 p.m. She assumed she was simply exhausted, arranged a ride home for her daughter Jennifer, who was in the production, and began the 30 minute drive home.

The ride home became ominous. Still not completely cognizant of the urgency of her situation, which was exacerbated by a searing headache triggered by the oncoming headlights of other vehicles, the trip morphed into an hour-plus ordeal.

Husband, Kurt, a police officer on patrol at the time, had run home after receiving her distressed call. He helped her into bed to get a good night's sleep, which they both thought would do the trick.

But concerns heightened in the morning. Despite her streak of not missing a day of work in 10 years, Kurt insisted his wife call in sick to the orthopedic group where she coordinated surgery. Her symptoms — repeated coughing, shortness of breath, excruciating headache — only intensified as the day wore on.

Even then, it was not fathomable that three bedridden weeks in the hospital would follow, with the worst to come. Oxygen deprivation became a constant, a pulmonary nightmare. Since she could barely talk and breathe simultaneously; a full oxygen face mask became her constant companion. Tests were conducted. More tests were conducted. Multiple medication combinations were tried and re-tried in various configurations by a team of frustrated doctors.

They had been able to connect the dots, but were stymied in that both the fog machine and its paperwork had mysteriously disappeared. Others in the company had experienced similar symptoms, but none nearly as debilitating as Mehl's. As such, their treatment protocol necessitated some educated guesswork, since they didn't have the benefit of analyzing the fog machine's contents.

Although the machine was never located, it was suspected that the mineral oil typically used to create fog was not a pharmaceutical grade as required. And the pneumatic functioning components were believed to be otherwise contaminated by a previous usage. In retrospect, its use, unknowingly precipitated an inevitable incident of serious airborne toxicity.

Mehl slowly experienced some pulmonary improvement, although she said she spent that first year "at home doing nothing, existing but not living." Being mostly confined to a wheelchair, with an eventual "graduation" to an electric scooter, would be her lot for the next 10 years. Her prognosis was that any progress she might experience in the 18 or so months immediately after the incident would most likely be the extent of any healing. After that there would be no further expectation of improvement in her condition. Faced with being carried up and downstairs, or worse, Mehl said she suffered a shattering "loss of pride and dignity," all while maintaining a facade of normalcy as best she could.

Although always vigilant, she is by no means out of the air quality woods today, 14 years later. She is still vulnerable — even outdoors — by any sudden inhalation of gasoline, perfume, bleach, black topping, you name it. But through it all, her improvement, particularly in the last year, has been remarkable. Yet right in the midst of our interview, she experienced a significant episode of airway blockage, right in front of me. A diesel truck's exhaust briefly wafted by our downwind location, which then required her emergency inhaler. She also carries an EpiPen intramuscular injector, which delivers a dose of epinephrine to buy time to even use the inhaler in the very worst scenarios.

Nonetheless, Mehl's ever present positive mind set is that as long as she "avoids being in the wrong place at the wrong time" her respiratory function remains mostly on the upper end of her qualified 1-10 scale.

Moving to Punta Gorda, Florida more than five years ago now has been, as she puts it, a "user friendly blessing." Her very first time on a tennis court — she would not be dissuaded from trying after watching Kurt enthusiastically embrace the game — was, as you can imagine, approached with extreme caution.

Early on, it was an exercise in stationary, easy-does-it drop-hitting, along with constant reminders to breathe — to inhale before each swing and then exhale while striking the ball every time. And relax. Breath holding and excessive muscle tension, common failings among club players, was not an option for Mehl.

From there it has amazingly evolved into her incredible tennis journey, one that includes full-on running, jumping and aggressive ball striking. Occasionally, we enjoy one of those "I know what you're thinking moments" by declaring, "It's a long way from Tipperary!"

Now, completely immersed in playing on two USTA teams,, she recently shared this after winning a league match: "Can you believe I'm really playing tennis! I don't even think about the consequences of moving anymore. My muscle tone is coming back. My breathing is better than I ever thought it could ever be. And, you know, I'm just now realizing, because of the tennis, how much of me had been kinda buried in my past limitations. I'm having so much fun."

A brief moment later, she turned, beaming, and added, "Oh, and this smile you're looking at [the Tipperary one] is the real thing."

A STAR IS BORN FAR AWAY:
Now a *Gem* in our Midst

HARBOR COURTS | Story by Jak Beardsworth

Thein Phyu Stadium in Rangoon, a remnant of the 122- year British colonization of Burma - now Myanmar - was filled to capacity on May 9, 1988. Nang Ngwe Lin, "the queen" as she was respectfully known, was defending her national women's singles title for the 9th time. Most were there to both support her and see her rout her latest challenger, 18-year-old Julie Biak Cin.

They would be disappointed.

The young girl who once brought a tattered, feltless ball to a backboard on a court in disrepair to practice her tennis pro father's instructions for the day - "1,000 times" - would prevail. Surprisingly, as she remembers today, to the delight of the partisan crowd she had won over with her stellar play.

At the end of the day, after a three-hour battle, Biak Cin, battling nerves as she edged closer, would craft the upset in the deciding third set. The queen, in the British tradition, was dead, and the genesis of the Burmese Scorpion, aka Julie Heitman as she is known today, had begun.

As transformational as that day was for Julie, another day just three months later overshadowed even her great triumph, a day that she can still recall today like it was yesterday.

Burma, no longer subject to British rule, had devolved into a socialist dictatorship. The Burmese Socialist Program Party, led by one Ne Win, was the country's only legal party. Love it or leave it. But leaving it was no easy matter.

Julie's parents were university professors and had suffered financially under the BSPP's rule, especially when Rangoon University was shuttered due to rising student unrest. It also cut short her pursuit of a college diploma at RU, studies she began at 15 in a five-year honors program.

When asked today what motivated her to leave all that she knew and loved for the unknown, she responds in earnest, "I wanted a better life both on and off the court. There was no future for me there." She was not buying into the accepted Burmese norm: being a married mom at an early age, never to venture out of the homeland.

Her father's tennis coaching did afford him some cache among the foreign diplomatic core that sought him out for lessons. Robert Biak On was once the best player in Burma. Coupled with the feat that he had a tennis superstar daughter - who ultimately caught the altruistic eye of more than one politically connected foreign service officer - it went a long way in raising both his and her profile.

Enter diplomat Robin McIntosh, whose parents lived in Gainesville, Fla., and knew Andy Brandi, the highly successful coach of the Gators men's team. Julie's adventure was on, but many hurdles needed to be cleared.

First, no one outside of Burma had ever seen her play. So, Mac, as she soon began to refer to him, organized a videotaping to showcase her prodigious talent, which is still evident today among those in Charlotte County's tennis community - and beyond - who have watched her classic game and explosive ball striking in both exhibition and charity tournament play. Anyone who has played against her, including myself, fully comprehends the Scorpion reference.

Additionally, she was literally studying day and night for the required SAT and TOEFL (Test of English as a Foreign Language) that were administered in English! Spoken English was uncommon in 1988 Burma, a residual of resentment towards the previous British rule.

McIntosh's parents, with Brandi's crucial endorsement, sent out the video to numerous Florida and Georgia schools, but timing was not on Julie's side since available scholarships had, by early summer, already been awarded.

The dream and hope of "getting out" was fading fast until a tragic accident intervened. Mandy Stoll, the #1 player at Stetson University in Deland, Florida, died in an automobile accident. Her scholarship was given to Julie. Troubled and conflicted with being the beneficiary of Stoll's fate, she then managed to dodge more bullets with the help of sympathetic university officials after her test scores arrived late.

Then, on August 8, 1988, the very day that Julie was scheduled to depart Rangoon to attend Stetson, hard-earned Burmese passport and American student visa in hand - completely unheard of in a country that routinely subjugated women, especially those of Chinese decent - a military coup, engineered by General Saw Maung, previously a close associate of Ne Win, overthrew the BSPP and immediately established martial law.

Her father procured a UNICEF van through his part-time position and, with her mother and two sisters, gathered as many relatives and friends as possible to accompany her to the airport. There was an atmosphere of great joy and best wishes for her. Yet, at the same time there was a heavy, underlying sadness among them, realizing that it was very possibly the last time they would ever see their Julie again.

Meanwhile, all hell was breaking loose in Rangoon as the military junta was asserting control over the government, its people and its infrastructure. Roadblocks and armed checkpoints were being quickly established all throughout the city just as the van was making its way to the airport for her flight to San Francisco.

Freedom, opportunity and dreams were in serious jeopardy, just as the starting line for her new life was so close and after so many seemingly insurmountable hoops had been negotiated.

Robert Biak Cin, knowing his way around Rangoon, managed to avoid some of the obvious checkpoints all together, and somehow talk his way through others while those in charge were still, thankfully, unclear about who gets through and who doesn't.

Within hours, the airport would be closed down completely and occupied by the military, but not before Julie made it onto her flight. Once on the plane and in the air, knowing all too well that she also may not see her family and friends ever again, the tears that she stoically held back earlier came streaming out.

While playing mostly #1 in singles and doubles at Stetson, and adapting to a new culture, she earned a degree in accounting and math. She also met fellow student Gene Heitman, whom she eventually married and with whom she had three beautiful children

Many years later, she did happily reunite with her family, who followed her courageous path and settled in the Bay Area.

During the day, indefatigable Julie teaches pre-primary (ages 3-6) at Charlotte Academy in Port Charlotte, a Montessori school. After school and on weekends she shares her considerable knowledge of the game with both juniors and adults at her tennis workshop at the Twin Isles Country Club Punta Gorda.

But don't let that beautiful, warm, endearing smile completely fool you if you find yourself on the other side of the net from her. There's a scorpion lying in wait, a Burmese one, with a game that will sting you in a heartbeat if you're not paying attention.

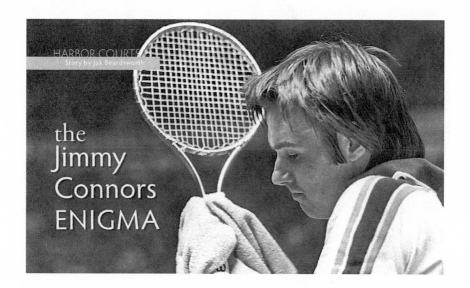

the
Jimmy
Connors
ENIGMA

Like him or not, Jimmy Connors was instrumental in taking the country club out of tennis in the 70s, plain and simple. Important stuff. Nonetheless, just as he was back then, he remains a polarizing figure. Those who jumped onto that decade's tennis boom bandwagon loved what he represented, and still do. The patrician crowd, tennis' hierarchy at that time, not so much. A residual of that sentiment, it seems, remains.

Just when Connors was seemingly fading into the sunset after coaching Andy Roddick a few years ago, he's back stirring the pot with his recently released book, *The Outsider*, and, kind of a shocker, by, at the time, signing on as Maria Sharapova's coach after she suffered an early round loss at Wimbledon.

Before his arrival on a finally genuine pro tour — after winning the NCAA title as a freshmen at UCLA in 71 when college tennis was a common path to one's development as a player — tennis, still in the early stages of the "open era," continued to be stifled by the stodgy, blue-blazered shamateurists with their holier than thou trappings of elitism and exclusivity.

I remember the period well. My own big break — a coveted invitation (the wild card of the day) to the Newport grass court lead- up to Forest Hills (then the US Championships) — came in 1964 as a 17-year-old, well before Connors' rise and before tennis did open up in 1968.

The player's bold boycott of the '68 Wimbledon Championships succeeded in putting an end to the International Tennis Federation's draconian policy of banning players from all tour events who "turned pro" and accepted above the table pay for play.

Connors himself was particularly singled out and denied a chance to capture the '74 Grand Slam — all four majors in the same calendar year — when the ITF ruled him ineligible for the French Open because he had signed to play in Billie Jean King's upstart World Team Tennis league.

In his revealing memoir, Connors traces his evolution from the rough and tumble public park courts of blue collar East St. Louis, Ill., to becoming the #1 player in the world, a position he held for five straight years, 268 weeks total.

Its candidness has stirred controversy, just as Connors did as a young player and even well into in his prime. Much of the feedback I've received towards it and him personally — I was on staff at the Jimmy Connors Tennis Center at Sanibel Harbour back in the '80s — surprisingly negative.

Yes, he was brash and in your face if he thought he was being wronged. He was not one to ever back down, especially from anyone in authority wearing the blazer uniform of the day. He was not representative of the gentlemanly sportsman demeanor that was expected at that time, best personified by earlier champions like Rod Laver. And hooking-up with savvy tour promoter, Bill Riordan, who became Jimmy's point man, didn't help with tennis' cognoscenti.

It took years for Connors to win the public over — the arrival of a younger, untamed rival, John McEnroe, set the wheels in motion — culminating in his spectacular last hurrah at the 1991 US Open where, at 39, he staged repeated improbable, dramatic comebacks over much younger men to reach the semi-finals with frenzied, unanimous crowd support.

The public backlash, especially about his books outing of Chris Evert's career "decision" regarding their early-on courtship, a private matter for all these years and opportunistically represented by the media in the worst possible light, was not surprising. Other issues have, unexpectedly, triggered a piling-on, such as when Arthur Ashe and company formed the ATP, a first-ever player's union to finally give them a voice in their own careers; Connors was the only player in the top 100 not to join.

And there's more in the book that has been viewed as loutish behavior by those who will not be dissuaded by the many more touching, heart-warming revelations and regrets that are also openly shared.

Prior to my time at the JCTC, my view of Connors was, like most, from a distance. Once there, I saw first-hand something wasn't necessarily anticipating. Promotional events were first class and often. One such event, a cocktail reception being held in the lobby of the luxury spa built into the stadium, was crowded with VIPs. A lone young lady was manning the reception desk. As Connors made his way through the crowd to the desk, she looked up and asked, "Can I help you?" clearly not having any idea whom she was talking to! Oh, this is going to be interesting I thought, standing in close proximity. It didn't disappoint. Jimmy politely said, "I'd like to sign for my massage." "Name please," she replied.

No, no, no. I couldn't believe what I was hearing, "Connors," he said.

Still nothing. Finally, mercifully, she sorts out his chit. He signed, thanked her and went on his way No one ever knew that she had dissed the very one whose name was on the facility. It never came up.

But that was the Connors we came to expect: Unassuming tennis royalty down to earth with the rank and file, in complete contradiction to the in-your-face, competitive, completely self-absorbed image perceived by those on the outside.

On another occasion, I saw him going out of his way to stop and engage a landscaper who — again clueless as to Connors' identity — was trimming the hedges, telling him what a good job he was doing and how he appreciated it.

And how about asking me, practically apologetically, if I could keep restringing his trusty T-2000s with his favorite 17g gut until "we" got the tension just right.

Then there was the long ago forgotten Frying Pan Challenge. A character named Jim Barker, the self-proclaimed Florida frying pan champion, showed up with a camera crew from the local CBS affiliate along with a racket bag filled with the Head, Wilson and Prince pans of the culinary world. Connors, going right along with the gag chose, if memory serves, an aluminum Teflon model for, one could only surmise, its lightness and maneuverability.

A brazenly overconfident Barker got quickly deep fried with Connors instantly adapting to his pan of choice, his flat strokes predisposed to the task, Barker's jaw dropping. Connors could play metal.

The crowd delighted in him laughing, joking and trash talking his way through the match with the same humor he displayed, still just a kid practicing at the Jack Kramer Club in LA, where he played good club players right-handed to hustle some spending money well before the big paydays to come.

What you think you see is, still, not always what you get.

Sharapova knows.

A Kris Kristofferson lyric from his song *"Pilgrim, Chapter 33"* just might be apropos for the James Scott Connors' paradox: "He's a walkin' contradiction, partly truth, party fiction, takin' every wrong direction on his lonely way back home."

Sugar Daddy

and the Match that Changed the World

During a recent visit to the Tennis Hall of Fame in Newport, R.I., I came upon a very prominent display featuring a cheesy yellow windbreaker boldly emblazoned with "Sugar Daddy" and it all came rushing back.

Bobby Riggs, aka the Sugar Daddy was widely known for his unapologetic self-promotion, a willingness to place a bet on almost anything, but, most of all, for his historic role in the famous, or infamous depending on your perspective, Battle of The Sexes singles match versus Billie Jean King — promoted as "The Lib vs. The Lob" — at the Houston Astrodome in 1973 in front of 30,000+ spectators.

It was a 3 out of 5 set winner-take-all format with $100,000 to the victor. But, with the exception of Riggs, his faux male chauvinist persona fully embellished, the money was not the issue in a match that would air on worldwide television and attract more than 50 million viewers, shattering any previous TV ratings for any event of any kind. French Open champion Li Na had similar numbers on Chinese television alone at the height of her popularity, albeit the beneficiary of a 38-year technological revolution. Such was the magnitude of the '73 Battle.

King rebutted Riggs' initial challenge, so, cleverly enlisting Sugar Daddy candy as his sponsor, he convinced the top-ranked woman, to play him instead — on Mother's Day naturally — to prove to the world that a 55-year-old man could beat any of the top players on the then financially struggling women's professional tour. The timing was compelling since the Women's Liberation Movement had been steadily gaining traction, and there was much to lose and little to gain from the women's perspective.

Whatever his eccentricities, this was not your average over 50 male tennis player. Riggs had been a Wimbledon champion, where he not only placed a $500 bet on himself to win the singles one year, but on the men's doubles and mixed doubles as well. And he did just that, earning himself, by today's standards, a cool $1.5 million. He had also been the world #1 and a member of a winning U.S. Davis Cup team.

Court, a tall, rangy Australian, and the big women's hitter of the day had cavalierly accepted the challenge without sufficient preparation or, as some would say later, a fitting appreciation of what was at stake. The Sugar Daddy, always the calculating showman, lowered her guard further by lovingly presenting her with a dozen red roses prior to the warm-up.

The cagey Riggs dropped her, lobbed her, off-speeded her and completely

103

took her out of her power game to win, unexpectedly and easily, 6-2, 6-1, turning the fledgling women's game on its head and simultaneously igniting women's lib groups around the country seeking redemption.

Riggs, who claimed he took 450 vitamin and mineral supplements a day to "stay young," and the Sugar Daddy candy people, were wide eyed at the marketing possibilities going forward after the Mother's Day Massacre, as it came to be known.

At the urging of everyone and anyone with a stake in the future of the women's tennis and women's rights, Billie Jean King stepped up and agreed to The Battle, to be played four months later in front of, as it turned out, the largest live single tennis audience ever.

The magic was gone this time, and Riggs lost, 6-4, 6-3, 6-3. The women's game was saved, the tennis boom of the 1970's was off and running, Billie Jean was $100,000 richer and the women's movement breathed a sigh of relief. Most believe that the Sugar Daddy was also handsomely rewarded — no doubt negotiated prior to the match by the calculating Riggs — for hatching the promotional tennis event of the century.

I first met Bobby Riggs in the mid-eighties at a celebrity event hosted by the Jimmy Connors Tennis Center at Sanibel Harbour. He was still getting mileage out of his now iconic Sugar Daddy jacket with his mouth going, in good fun, a mile-a-minute. I also recall him talking more trash that evening over a couple of beers with his buddy jimmy — who also liked a friendly wager to make things interesting — about that night's poker game before they departed for an undisclosed location.

I didn't see him again until the following year when he was, would you believe, headlining the Marco Island Seafood Festival. Such was his enduring across-the-board promotional currency more than a decade since playing in the match heard 'round the world.

I was helping fellow pro Doug Browne move into his new gig Marco when, nearing the club entrance, we spotted what appeared to be, and quickly realized was, a bale of marijuana that had apparently washed ashore. Something along the lines of, "No, don't even think about it," occurred to both of us, thankfully, simultaneously. We later learned that a major bust had taken place somewhere in the Ten Thousand island maze the night before, which was widely known as a popular off-load destination from down south.

With absolutely no idea that the master tennis hustler himself was on island, we couldn't possibly have imagined what other bizarre circumstance would transpire in the next few hours.

While glancing over a local ad rag at lunch, I saw it, "Bobby Riggs, the Sugar Daddy, appearing today and signing autographs from 1:00- 4:00." What?

"Doug," I blurted out, "Riggs is here. Let's get over there and talk him into an exhibition match with you tomorrow." This was too good to be true. Could we pull it off? After all, how amazing would it be for the Hideaway Beach Club's new pro to stage an Exo and meet-and-greet with Bobby Riggs himself on his first day on the job!

His autograph not being what we were interested in, getting an audience with Riggs was a challenge. Passing muster with his considerably younger, totally loyal, bodyguard girlfriend — a one woman phalanx bent on making damn sure we sincerely had Bobby's best interests in mind, which we would soon learn were indeed *his* interests — took some time.

After dutifully establishing our respect and sincerity, Riggs agreed to a one-set match with the following provisos, which he presented to us one-by-one, each requiring agreement before he would proceed with the next. "First, it'll cost you $500 cash. Okay? Second, you only get one serve. Okay? Third, I get to hit into the alleys. Okay? Fourth, I win. Okay?" We nodded and okay'd our way through each. Riggs now warming up to us and his fee, shook our hands as we all laughed together at the frivolity of it all. The match was on.

Doug, true to his word, made sure that Bobby, now 67 years young, won but only after slipping him five obligatory C-notes before they even stepped on the court. Despite no promotional opportunity at all, Riggs was immediately recognized, sporting his jacket, on that sleepy Sunday morning. It didn't take long for him to have a sizeable audience to banter with, which he did happily while good naturedly harassing Doug from across the net at every opportunity. Doug informed me recently that those early Hideaway members still remember that day fondly and boast that they were there.

Bobby Riggs passed away in 1997. He was a world class tennis player, once a world #1, a record-breaking Wimbledon betting shop beneficiary, a seminal figure in the tennis boom of the 70s, and, ultimately and ironically, a positive element in the advancement of the women's rights movement. He was a one-of-a-kind, fun, all- around good guy and it was an absolute pleasure to have briefly crossed his path.

PART TWO:
Newspaper Columns

The Elusive
SERVICE TOSS

The service toss is not to be taken for granted. It's very much a triggering element in achieving a fluid service motion, and managing it is trickier than it looks.

Even the pros struggle with it - exclusively nerves at that level - occasionally aborting serves at the last moment, catching the toss and starting over. "Sorry mate."

Yet, consciously embracing last moment toss reads - dictating whether or not you'll pull the trigger - is a guaranteed rhythm buster and an all-around bad idea. To be an effective server you must be fully committed to completely letting go once the service motion has begun.

Only the very worst, completely unhittable tosses should be caught, and then only on a spontaneous basis. Small in-serve adjustments are still more than doable on slightly errant tosses. Plus, playing in the wind often makes that a necessity.

Note: Incessant toss catching invites legitimate protests from annoyed, rightly so, receivers.

But club player tossing yips are mostly because of poor technique.

Tossing technique? Yes, there's even technique on the toss itself, paramount in setting the table for an effective serve.

In the accompanying image you can see that I've fully extended my tossing arm up-and-out through its full range of motion - versus the sudden alligator arm quick flips exhibited by too many - before releasing the ball open handed.

In the serve ready position, and into the ritual stage as well, the tossing arm should be bent at the elbow or in close proximity to the body - with the ball resting against the strings at the racket's throat, not ram rod straight already extending well in front

Hold the ball lightly, finger tips only - not completely enveloped in your hand - in a neutral anatomical position that replicates the way your arm would naturally hang by your side. Definitely not palm up.

Using your arm's own swing weight inertia, nothing more, the ball is placed high enough to accommodate a fully extended racket reach. That up and outward toss motion that's produced, away from the body, insures that inviting in front toss.

At the release point, the trick is to open your hand, versus rolling the ball off your fingertips. This eliminates any complicating spin, resulting in a knuckleball consistently right where you want it.

Serve 'em up.

Maximizing on the *Serve* **Leg Drive**

The serve, like every other shot to one degree or another, is a whole body effort - that kinetic chain again. On the serve in particular, leg drive is a key component in maximizing that chain.

Above you can see that I've engaged my legs. As the ball-tossing arm begins to move upward, the upper body begins coiling, and the knees simultaneously bend. Arm up, legs down.

Note that I'm in the process of dropping the racket head into the full back-scratch position from the loading stage where the racket is initially cocked up. And my tossing arm is still extended. Up on the ball of my lead foot, I'm readying myself to jump up and into the ball-striking moment. That's effortless power in contrast with the "arm serve" we see all too often in club and rec tennis.

My head is up and my eyes are plotting the optimal moment of racket-on-ball impact - an effective cue, versus the usual "watch the ball." Avoid pulling your head down prematurely at all costs - perhaps the biggest challenge in serving which always leads to dysfunctional trunk flexing and tosses invariably dropping too low.

Even if you're an old-schooler and not a jump server - as all of today's pro players are and have been for years - at least rising up onto the ball of your front foot during and through the hitting zone will only make you a better server.

Way back when, jumping was not permitted, yet the very best in the game still served effectively with even limited upward movement into the ball, although with predictably lower tosses than today's pros. Some might be able to remember huge-serving Roscoe Tanner's "low" toss which some mistakenly thought he struck on the way up.

My head is up and my eyes are plotting the optimal moment of racket-on-ball impact - an effective cue, versus the usual "watch the ball." Avoid pulling your head down prematurely at all costs -perhaps the biggest challenge in serving which always leads to dysfunctional trunk flexing and tosses invariably dropping too low.

Even if you're an old-schooler and not a jump server - as all of today's pro players are and have been for years - at least rising up onto the ball of your front foot during and through the hitting zone will only make you a better server.

If you are a modern day leg-drive jumper, maintain your balance through the follow through by kicking your trailing leg back while landing on your front foot. Since you've landed well into the court with your toss in front, remember to recover your defending position fairly quickly back behind the baseline, but without rushing the serve's finish.

If you find – no, when you find - that you're now getting a little more pop on your first serve delivery, and you're drawing shorter responses, then okay, remain inside the baseline to begin taking advantage.

In the end keep remembering to "take care of your serve" as television commentator Mary Carillo likes to say.

Stick with it. It's *always* a work in progress for everyone at every level.

Serving TALL

Serving is both the most difficult and most important shot in the game. Here are a few key components to get the most out of your serve.

Being fully extended at the moment of ball contact is paramount if you're going to enjoy a high percentage of successful serves. In the above image, you can see that I'm at full stretch at impact.

Taller servers are always at an advantage in creating a more acute downward ball trajectory that's safely over the net — greater margin for error — and yet still lands in the relatively small service box. Be as tall as you can be.

By making better use of your legs to drive up into the ball you'll facilitate your maximum reach. Note I have jumped off, and into, the court with my lead foot to insure an unencumbered, upward moving kinetic chain. This is not a foot fault, in that the ball has been struck prior to touchdown.

An inline body alignment is also ideal at the strike point to allow for the greatest racket head acceleration through the ball. This is fostered by a toss that's both as high, and in front, as you can comfortably reach with the racket.

A relatively low grip position on the handle is recommended to create wrist involvement, and, of course, is applied with minimal tension — a 5 on a scale of 1 to 10 — versus the all too common undermining death grip approach.

Finally, note that my head remains up momentarily even after the ball has exploded off the racket face. Club players are often guilty of pulling their head down prior to impact causing premature trunk flexing and blind, poorly-timed ball striking.

Have you ever noticed that at times you serve well in the pre-match warm-up only to then serve inconsistently once the match begins? There's a reason.

As tennis pro/humorist Vic Braden used to preach: "There's only one ball and you have it, so what's the big hurry in looking across the net for the return before you've struck the serve?"

Be acutely aware of avoiding that possible undermining hiccup during the serve practice. Never take it for granted.

Finishing the SERVE

Photo by Shaun Cedak

There are five distinct stages to the serve, the most intricate shot in the game: 1) visualization, 2) ritual, 3) racket loading/toss, 4) impact and 5) follow-through. In the accompanying image you can see that I am well past the ball striking moment and in the process of finishing my service motion.

My follow-through, or more precisely, the all-important deceleration of the racket, is near its ending point on the left side of my body. I have allowed it to arrive there with a fully relaxed "brakeless" technique by hitting through the ball completely unencumbered of any counterproductive, trying-too-hard, excessive, inefficient muscle tension.

To promote this swing freedom you can also see that I'm gripping the racket down low — which I also employ on all my shots — with the butt cap fitting neatly into the concave palm of my hand. This position contributes to the kinetic chain connection of the hips, shoulder, arm and wrist to generate easy racket speed, equaling power.

None other than Pete Sampras — whom I saw recently on the Tennis Channel still serving bombs with, would you believe, a puny wooden racket (Donnay Borg model) in a bring-the-wood-back chanty event staged by, who else but John McEnroe — is the best example of this all-time.

I've also jumped off my front foot up into the ball striking moment, and then have landed in the court. To maintain balance I have "kicked" my right leg back which also contributes to a biomechanically smooth hitting action.

No worries, this is not a foot fault. Nor is yours if you're not a "jumper," and it's your back leg that lands in the court. In either instance, the ball is being struck prior to touchdown. Many older players — myself included — first learned this latter technique even before there was a Donnay Borg model. Would you believe that leaving the ground was against the rules back in the day? The front foot had to remain on terra firma, so players used the front foot as a pivot to accommodate the back leg swinging around and into the court, and that technique remains.

So, whether you're an old-schooler or you've embraced today's approach doesn't matter, you'll still need a sustained freewheeling, full range of motion follow-through to fully maximize your serve.

Whether swinging fast or slow (typical of many clubber second serves), avoid slamming the "arm brakes" on after you've struck the ball. Understand that it actually takes 3 to 4 feet of the swing path for the human body to bring the racket to a sudden stop which, unfortunately, is not uncommon, and results in swinging and braking beginning at the racket-on-ball moment. Not good.

Try being more like Pistol Pete.

Embracing the

Spin Serve

If your arm-racket start position on serve doesn't look something like the one I'm getting ready to serve with in the photo you're probably serving a spin-less, flat serve with long-term limitations.

You cannot easily impart serve-enhancing spin with the same grip you're using on forehand. Yet, that's precisely the reason why so many players get stuck, too often seldom graduating to "bending" - yes, like Beckham - their serves in, and plateau with their strictly flat deliveries, their Wimbledon dreams permanently dashed.

In the image you can see that I'm not remotely close to a forehand grip position. Since I am about to bend one in - also loosely referred to as a topspin serve - note the backhand grip and the aforementioned arm-racket configuration (a version of which you typically see on TV) with the resulting "closed" racket face. A less exaggerated continental position, with the racket head right on edge, can work just as well.

Keeping in mind that since the service box - only 18 feet long and 13.5 feet wide - accounts for a mere 17 percent of the in-point whole court (doubles), aggressively clearing the net safely without being long is challenging. That's why you get two.

Plus, never lose sight of the fact that serves in the net have zero chance for success. So when you miss, miss long. It's okay; that's a good miss.

So what is the magic elixir of spin on serve? Enhancing gravity. When the ball is traveling through the air with rapid forward rotation – let's say 20 rotations per second - the ensuing air pressure on top of the ball becomes greater than the pressure below the ball, making it descend at a faster rate than a ball struck flat.

Up, safely over, and still in.

The resulting looping trajectory, versus the laser beam of flat delivery, allows for a far greater and forgiving margin to the net - a bigger vertical space above the net to pass the ball through while still dropping it in. Because of the accompanying steeper angle of descent, the ball will bounce considerably higher and out of the returners preferred knee-to-thigh-high "wheelhouse" power zone. Advantage you.

Now, how do you hit it? No worries, you already know how.

Initially, now that you've altered the face of the racket at impact because of the grip change - at first only an extremely small change from your flat grip (1/16-of-an inch max) is necessary - the ball will not be struck head-on (flat), but instead will be, ideally with unrestrained racket speed, brushed up, over and around the 1 o'clock side of the ball creating an effective combination of both forward and side spin.

You'll immediately produce a more rainbow like trajectory, including a bit of right-to-left ball movement as well. You'll most likely have to adjust your previous serve flight plan and visualize a bit higher and more to the right than you're accustomed to until your brain wires it in.

It's recommended that you put in some individual practice before unveiling it even in friendly play - using it exclusively in first-serve situations only at first - until you own it and it becomes, ultimately, a reliable solid second-serve "bender."

Now you really can be like Beckham.

Loading the STICK

Preparing one's racket to make a ground stroke sounds like a cinch. It's not. Yet it's crucial to your success.

Racket preparation is a whole body movement known for eons as the "unit turn." Common misperceptions of preparation mostly lead to players flinging the racket back randomly or, worse yet, a last second tin-man effort - all arm no body - eliminating any hope of an integrated hip, shoulder, trunk turn. Tennis elbow anyone?

In the accompanying image you can see that, from an initial ready position, I've recognized a forehand opportunity and have initiated this hip-shoulder turn while simultaneously pivoting my lower body. It's all connected.

With my left hand releasing the racket for the take back, my off-arm (left) begins assuming a position of balance that's maintained throughout preparation, continued through the ball striking moment and into the follow through where the racket is literally caught at rotation's end, then seamlessly dropped back into a ready position in recovery.

As the racket continues to fully load in the shown sequence I'm retaining the ready position's initial forward, over-the-ball forward leaning posture to insure a leveraged point of impact well in front. You can also notice that I'm unweighting my left foot to push off with the right in pursuit of the ball.

In an ideal world, my racket will reach full prep at precisely the time the approaching ball bounces - the rate of the take-back matches the speed of the incoming ball - no matter my court position at that moment, a valuable and underestimated timing device.

Note: I am not suggesting "running with the racket back," a tired old misnomer that's a close second to the trite "bend your knees, $5 please."

Now, with the arm, racket, hips and shoulders fully coiled one is able to generate a considerable amount of racket "swing-weight" (versus scale weight) resulting in a powerful kinetic storm with minimal effort that moves the ball quickly through the court without hitting "hard."

Timing The Take-Back

The synchronization of the mechanics necessary to be solid from the back of the court, and on short ball opportunities as well, starts with the all-important timing of the "take-back."

As you can see in the accompanying image, I have finished preparing my racket — note my compact prep — precisely at the moment my opponent's shot has landed on my side of the court.

I have accomplished this in a singular, unhurried motion that is always linked to the speed of the approaching ball, and is in concert with the hip and shoulder turn. This creates a connected sense of rhythm, and initiates a positive sequence of events regardless of whether the pace of the incoming shot is fast, slow, or somewhere in between.

Notice that my left arm is simultaneously in a balanced position — appearing as if I'm going to catch the ball — along with a slightly forward trunk posture and a lowered center of gravity compared to my normal standing height. In short, I'm coiled-up and primed to then take the necessary adjustment steps in order to position myself both laterally and longitudinally (forward-back) as necessary according to how I intend to play the ball.

Club players are notoriously guilty of preparing the racket late, often finishing well after the ball has already bounced. In some instances there are well intentioned individuals who unknowingly bring it back to their preferred position in two separate motions, first approximately three-quarters the way back, then, at the very last moment, back again. This better known as a "hitch" and leads to difficult-to-manage, late racket-on-ball impact points, quick hitting, short follow-throughs that brake to a sudden stop — the primary cause of tennis elbow — and diminished power.

Start monitoring a timely take-back in each and every warm-up, day in and day out — that's assuming you're not initially standing in such close proximity to your warm-up partner that it becomes impossible to utilize the intended full range stroking motion. Improving this component will set the tone for consistently smooth ball striking off either wing right out of the box, and in time become a positive muscle memory conditioned response.

# On The Rise

There are fundamentally three immediately recognizable incoming shots that require a specific positioning - both laterally and longitudinally - for an ideal ball-striking opportunity when in the back of the court.

Everyone's most preferred ball of the three, including pros, is the one that has a relatively small incoming rainbow arc, doesn't clear the net by a large amount and bounces not especially deep in your court. With well-spaced forward-back positioning, it can be played in its descending arc right into that knee high, "wheelhouse" power zone. Anatomically just right.

A less compatible dynamic involves the underwhelming, problematic, high-looping trajectory, high bouncing half-lob. Although extremely annoying, it can be effective in club play since players typically fail to play this shot aggressively, meaning well in front, and "up" at its highest post bounce point moment. Instead they spontaneously choose to retreat, often motoring well past the baseline trying to allow these balls to also drop down into their preferred knee high zone. One dimensional "track meet" play.

The final recognizable incoming shot is the one that has to be played on-the-rise: the biggest difference maker of all. It's coming fast. It has a laser like flight path. And it's landing in very close proximity to your court position with very little time to adjust. There is no escaping by running backward and away from it as so many attempt. Playing it at the bounce's peak or as it descends is now not an option.

Holding your ground, feet still moving - stutter-stepping a bit to stay connected, getting low and staying low, and connecting with it out in front just off the bounce at about shin to knee high at most, is your only out. The goal is to smother it, absorb it, redirect it back over with minimal pace and ride out the storm to just stay in the point.

A quick take-back is obviously required to, ideally, swing as slowly through contact as possible - staying under control to put the fire out.

Once you've acquired this shot, you'll find that you not only can handle your peer's occasional $100 balls, but comfortably stay in back court rallies with more experienced players as well.

And, after diffusing their best stuff, you'll also experience the satisfaction of a certain message sent: "Is that all you've got?"

# Half-Volley Groundstroke

No one ever played closer to the baseline in the "Open era" than Andre Agassi. Why was he able to play so close?

Because his half-volley groundstrokes - off either wing - were the game's best at not only handling opponents' deep, heavy, penetrating shots, but doing something offensive with them as well.

Rare.

He was the pro's pro at the short-hop on-the-rise. As a result he was able to take time away from big-hitting opponents recovering to defend their court, and suddenly turn the tables by transitioning from what appeared to be a defensive position to offense in a moment.

Here, with the ball already struck and in full flight, you can see my head is still down - as close as I'll ever get to being reminiscent of Roger Federer - and that I'm finishing the shot with an open stance. It's the Nadal-inspired "lasso" with the follow-through back over my hitting shoulder behind my head. This is typically out of necessity in fending off quick-strike, deep bombs, especially when on the run.

A similar technique used to be called the "buggy whip," but the game's lexicon is constantly being updated and rewritten, and the current version of the shot is definitely more extreme in today's faster game with 90 mph groundies.

The lasso enables an acute brushing up behind the ball that produces considerable topspin with "safe air" over the net. A quick flick when there's no time for a full swing that bends the shot back into the court.

Since there's almost no time for repositioning when opponents play shots this deep - backing up trying to buy space and time as many attempt - don't try to. Hold your ground, tower your center of gravity with a still head to stay visually connected to the ball, and stay down to prevent last-moment stroking path deviation - the head moves, the trunk follows, the arm is connected to trunk, the racket is connected to arm. Mishit.

This shot comes in handy for club players who get caught in no man's land - often after they had properly positioned themselves there to return a weak second serve - and become victimized by a server's response, now able to place it well past the service box.

Don't the majority of in-point ground strokes land, on average, halfway between the service line and the baseline?

So do not hang out there unless your opponent hasn't hit a deep ball since Billie Jean King won her last US Open.

But since it's not uncommon to face less than lethal second serves in club level tennis, it's important then to either follow the return into the net and create pressure, or retreat to a safer baseline position.

Yet, on occasion, even the game's best movers get caught in between by opponent's smart shots. So you'd better have the half-volley groundstroke in your tool box.

As is often the case, you can practice this shot by yourself. Take a position at the baseline, best with the previously noted open stance.

Then drop-hit low bouncing balls, about shin high, with a contact point that replicates the less in front one that you'll have to deal with in live play. Aggressively lay on the extra topspin with the lasso. Nothing to it with a bit of practice.

Since it's never too late to improve your ball striking skills, you'll hopefully continue to believe in the possibility.

 # Handling High Bouncing Balls

Club players, even good ones, all too often play one dimensionally from the back of the court – they never seem to like hearing that - which also happens to raise the difficulty factor. By attempting to allow every incoming shot, regardless of its trajectory, bounce point, or bounce height, to descend into their preferred low, knee-to- thigh-high power zone they reduce their options dramatically. And, that's a lot of no reward extra footwork.

In club land, it's not unusual for balls to pass over the net with high clearance, or steep, rainbow like trajectories — topspin or no topspin. Operating well behind the baseline is not only physically impractical, but also eliminates possibilities to dictate play.

As you can see in the accompanying image, I have selected a court position that allows me to strike a high bouncing ball at its apex after it has bounced. This cancels the need to back up, which often ends up being well behind the baseline, rendering it impossible to play offensively and simultaneously empowers the opposing net man. Is there anything worse than witnessing a doubles match where two opposing back courters are pinned back passively trading moon balls they consistently allow to fall into their low zone? No proactivity. Just defense, defense, defense. This is not the way the game was meant to be played.

Playing the ball in front at its high point, versus this powder puff facsimile of multi-dimensional play, will not only take recovery time away from opponents, but also, when these loopy balls land a bit short, predispose you to getting a jump on moving into the net from the resulting closer positions versus always being resigned to playing back.

Feel free to jump up into this shot, triggering a clean, athletic, kinetic chain that dumbs down any mechanical overthinking. Per usual, you'll still have to finish your racket prep — a little higher than your norm to get behind the ball — by the approaching ball's bounce point. Don't think about your stroking path. No need. You already know how — it's on your hard drive. And yes, the follow through will naturally finish at a lower position compared to your finish after striking those wheelhouse balls when you get them.

So take initiative. Broaden your strike zone. Start taking advantage of these floaters. It's a lot more fun.

The One-Handed Backhand: Alive and Well?

At last year's French Open men's round of 16 half the players sported one-handed backhands. Does this mean it's still alive and well in today's pro game? Has it managed to survive the four decade long two-handed onslaught initiated by Jimmy, Chrissie, and Bjorn way back when?

Not really.

Even the one-handed maestro himself, Roger Federer, agrees, albeit with a hint of reluctance, probably not wanting to think about the fact that he was ultimately supplanted as the world No. 1 by Rafael Nadal, specifically because of Nadal's lethal lefty topspin forehand cross court up high to the Fed one-hander.

The USTA's scaled down mandate for kid's tennis - smartly modeled after little league baseball with its smaller fields, lighter bats and softer balls - is fully supported by its industry partners including club pros. This means, the one-hander really should be alive and well with the super lightweight mini-rackets and the age varying low bounce spongy balls that eliminate the previously demanding physical task of the one-hander. Regulation heavier balls bounce unforgivingly up and right through kids' strike zones.

Previously, as children began playing at a younger and younger age, a 26-inch racket (27 inches is the standard length) was the only alternative. It was a marginally scaled down version of a conventional stick. Although somewhat more maneuverable, it was still an unwieldy club for still developing, smaller youngsters compared to what's available today.

No wonder an entire generation, spurred on by its coaches, embraced the two-hander to offset the more physically challenging and longer learning curve one-hander.

But the Nadal forehand ferocity won't be at a club near you anytime soon. So, with today's lightweight, powerful equipment, the challenge of the one-hander is no longer daunting for any age. Now it's just a matter of committing, for both those new to the game and its long termers - who have mostly favored the one-hander for years - to really learn its nuanced technique for it not to be a liability as is too often the case.

In the photo you can see that I've already changed my grip and have coiled-up in one motion preparing to take an aggressive one-handed backhand cut. My right shoulder and chin are in close proximity to insure a sideways, fully turned hitting position, while the left hand - the "off-hand" - has drawn the racket back positioned around its throat. Yes, it takes two hands to hit an effective one-handed backhand.

The racket face is slightly open since I'm going to drive the ball with considerable underspin pace that will skid the ball quickly through the court upon bouncing - otherwise known as "the knife." Opponents do not like this in club land and on tour as well at times. It's a rhythm buster, especially disrupting since it's in such marked contrast to the higher bouncing topspin typically generated off the forehand wing.

To maintain balance and facilitate racket speed through the impact zone, the left hand remains back as an anchor and stays back during the follow through – picture Federer. Because you're reaching across your body, the trunk rotation so prevalent on any forehand or two-handed backhand is a no-no. That difference is defining.

More than anything, staying sideways through the shot, and keeping the ball in front, will make you and your improved one-hander famous by next Thursday.

Racket Head Up

Club play worldwide is predominantly doubles. That fact immediately, and continuously, begs the question: Why do so very, very few televised tour matches feature doubles?

Curious since the overwhelming TV audience is made up of clubbers. But let's be thankful that the Bryan brothers - the most successful doubles team of all-time - are Americans, or we could very well be seeing zero doubles.

Nonetheless, another axiom is that approximately half the time that's spent playing doubles is at the net - one player aggressively occupying a threatening position and wanting the ball. In an ideal doubles world, the ball is played in the air whenever possible to take time away from opponents, to try and get on top of the point, and even end it outright on occassion.

When already positioned at the net, as seen in the accompanying image, and also when in transition and approaching the net from the back court, it's important to keep the racket head elevated above the wrist.

Too many players unknowingly allow their racket ready position to consistently be mostly parallel to the court surface - a placement more suitable for preparing to hit groundies - which typically leads to unwieldy, ill-timed swing volleys that often end up being mishit or in the windscreen on the fly.

Racket-up triggers a smaller more compact prep - a take back path that saves time, enables a more easily maintained and better leveraged arm-racket shot making configuration, and allows for a better opportunity to keep the racket-on-ball impact well in front of one's body.

Simple. Better volleying 101.

Do your best. Always aspire higher. Love the game.

The Tricky Forehand Volley

So what's so tricky about it? When you turn into a one-handed backhand volley - most two-handed back courters go to one hand at the net - the hitting shoulder is naturally positioned in front, versus the forehand where the shoulder initially moves away from the net while preparing, making striking the ball in front more challenging.

There's more.

The first thing to notice about the forehand volley technique pictured above is that I'm playing the shot eye-high with the racket elevated from my wrist at about a 45 degree angle. This, coupled with the accompanying lowered center of gravity and the resulting forward posture, equals textbook stuff.

Since backcourt opponents are geared to keeping the ball low to the net when you're positioned there, or when moving in, keeping the racket head up is essential when getting down for the ball to avoid dumping it into the net. Dropped racket heads spell trouble.

Perhaps that's where that old saying, "bend your knees, $5 please," comes from, back when far more balls were taken in the air.

The eye-high cue also leads to better ball-tracking - can't succeed without that. What better way to see the ball clearly, and keep it in front, than keeping your eyes on the plane of the approaching ball?

With those approaching balls varying in height, keeping them "high" in the strike zone will produce opportunities to be more aggressive and do damage - a much less likely outcome if one is playing the net "tall."

Now what about the wrist action, or no action as the popular misperception endures?

Yes, there is some subtle wrist on the forehand volley, which is exactly what provides that extra pop and control. Keeping a "stiff wrist" is analogous to trying to volley with a surgically fused one - the Frankenstein volley. Not good.

"Winning ugly" - think Brad Gilbert - isn't going to work this time.

In the preparation stage, just lay-it-back a bit but avoid getting the racket head much past your ear. The forward wrist flexion then occurs as the racket meets the ball. That's when the racket wins the collision handily. You'll feel the effortless power. But absolutely keep in mind that it doesn't "break" loosely through the hitting zone, although there is some limited follow through. Just no wavy gravy, please.

Then it's just a matter of recovering for the next ball - that is if there is one.

The Backhand Volley

The overwhelming majority of tour players today (yes, even the many using the two- hander off the ground) choose the one-hander when volleying. The inherent considerable increase in reach and versatility is a necessity when at the net, or in transition, where reaction time is at a premium.

But do not be misled - it takes two hands to execute a solid one-handed backhand volley just like the one-hander from the back.

In the ready position, with the racket head slightly elevated by a cocked wrist just below one's sight line, the left hand of the right-handed player cradles the racket's throat and, in terms of hand tension, is always the dominant hand at this juncture.

Once a backhand volley opportunity is recognized, the left hand, already engaged, draws the racket generously back with a slightly elevated elbow in order to fully load the racket.

Simultaneously, a shoe-on-court pivot should occur resulting first in both a hip-shoulder turn into the shot, and then an accompanying crossover hitting step.

Much confusion forever reigns over whether or not there is a slight grip change when at the net. Of course there is! However, it's much more of a subtle arm-racket reconfiguration initiated from the forehand position that exists when poised and ready to a very different leveraged alignment for the backhand, an absolute necessity unless you possess the uncanny, funky, one of a kind ball striking mechanics, back then and now, of the no-grip-change representation perpetuated in the TV booth by none other than John McEnroe.

Finally, as the racket head moves to the ball, the off-arm simultaneously snaps back to foster both balance and surprising power. This action also eliminates counterproductive trunk rotation and maintains a sideways to the net hitting position. Note also that I've lowered my center of gravity in order to make contact with the ball eye-high, and, as a direct result, well in front where the ball can be clearly tracked.

Remember, it takes two hands to hit a one-handed backhand volley, that is if you're interested in hitting it well.

The Smash

At times I wonder if using the traditional "smash" reference is a good idea in describing the overhead since the connotation among club players is that they should crush them. The motivation is certainly there to aggressively answer Jobber's avoidance to get-it-on.

Yet, in many instances, a really good hitting position - absolutely essential in going big - is challenging. When it often cannot be achieved backing off the gas pedal and simply making a good placement to stay in the point is prudent.

Fundamentally, the overhead is nothing more than a serve off of a very high toss. So what's the real difficulty? It's that the vast majority of mid-level clubbers don't even ask for any "up" in the warm-up, and, as a direct result, not only generally fear the shot, but precisely because of this omission, are not very good at it as well.

Consider the overall ratio of forehands hit versus overheads in your lifetime tennis experience. Twenty to one? Maybe greater than that.

And it's being neglected in the warm-up? A bad idea that leaves a big hole in your game - especially your doubles game. Once exposed, it becomes an embossed invitation for opponents to lob you, and often.

Positioning, in relation to the always angled downward trajectory of the lob, is the overhead's core building block. Maneuvering yourself into a perfect position, one that allows the ball to descend into an ideal in-front strike zone, does indeed represent the smash opportunity.

But the mistake commonly made is positioning directly underneath the downward flight of a lob - good for a header in soccer – making both watching it and getting on top of the ball very challenging unless you have a very flexible neck, a strong, whippy wrist, and you play on the ATP or WTA tour.

Lobs, by their very nature, are seldom right into your wheelhouse, never mind the effect that even a slight breeze, or a bright sun, has on them. Moving backward or forward to achieve a good hitting position, often on a diagonal simultaneously, requires an energized brand of non-stop footwork to get the ball where you want it.

In the accompanying image you can see that I'm in a balanced, ready to fire, sideways to the net position. My head is up tracking the ball, my racket is loaded in concert with my left arm, and I'm moving laterally - my back foot is leading stepping back - in pursuit of a lob that's going past the service line in order to try and keep the ball invitingly in front.

Caution: Never, ever chase deep lobs by back pedaling in a facing- the-net position. I've witnessed some nasty falls - triggered by a loss of balance or a caught heel - sometimes with even worse consequences like broken wrists and arms trying to break the fall, and concussions from unimpeded head plants. Move laterally!

"Grounded overheads" are just that - hit off the forward left foot (righties) while connected to the court, or while moving forward with the ball nicely in front

"Jump overheads" - referred to as the "scissor kick" back in the day - require jumping both up and backwards to intercept a good, deep lob.

Either way, stay aggressive. Attack the ball. That doesn't mean kill it. It means go up and get it whether jumping or not. Do not wait too long to pull the trigger as so many do. Choose a manageable swing speed - only as fast as you can control - along with always visualizing where you're going to place the shot.

Now go make those lobbers pay the frustroball price!

Getting Out of Trouble

You're on the dead run in pursuit of a very possibly out of reach ball. You know early on you're not going to be able to get this ball where you want it.

In short, you have no offensive or even neutral shot, and attempting one would be delusional. So what to do?

Lob now, and lob high!

Lobbing, defensive lobbing, is a last ditch effort to stay in the point for one more shot. It's buying time to recover court position and challenge an opponent to close the point out with a not-so-easy overhead in the air or off the bounce - definitely not a gimme.

In the accompanying image I have barely caught up to the ball and am coming up underneath it with an open racket face. Striking it softly, almost "carrying" it, with a very low to very high stroking path, will get this ball on a welcome steep upward trajectory.

The goal is to get the defensive lob a minimum of 40 feet up with touchdown in the middle of no-man's land, preferably cross court where the court is forgivingly four-and-a-half feet longer on the diagonal.

How many opponents relish the sight of this response to their near winner? I'm thinking very, very few.

Keep in mind that the motor skill component of ball striking mechanics is highly influenced by pre-Shot visualization. What you "see" - your intended shot flight plan in your mind's eye - is then more readily realized by triggering the appropriate neurological pathways to your existing "hard-drive" racket skills. The mind-body connection at work.

If it is doubles you're mostly playing, and you do have the ball right where you like it, then definitely and aggressively go for your shot. That's the essence of the game.

Other options include, when in good position, offensively lobbing over a net player crowding the net, or one who is adept at poaching. Mixing in the occasional lob will keep them honest and off balance, and, hopefully, keep you on top of the point.

Versus these same net opponents you also can attack their position by going right at them – short of head hunting! - when you get that inviting, short second serve that is if they're in a position to ably defend themselves. Otherwise go for the pass. Don't forget the hand-wave apology if they're offended.

Lobbing is a necessary defensive measure, and as noted, can be an effective offensive tactic as well, but it should never be the mainstay of anyone's game.

If it is stick with backyard badminton.

In the adjacent image the "backfire" looks a bit tricky. Perhaps a little. No matter, I'm betting that Houdini himself would have liked it since it's the best answer to retrieving a lob that's sailed over you and, at first glance, appears to be a complete impossibility.

In singles it comes in very handy since you're on your own. In doubles, where you're expecting a bit of help, it's especially useful when playing with spectating backcourt partners particularly those not so fleet-of-foot - who fail to cross and cover for you.

Once you've realized that you have no play with an overhead, and your partner's out to lunch, don't concede the point since the backfire offers a very viable option to make the opposition hit one more shot always the last resort goal.

You can see that I have successfully caught up to, and already made a play on - note the ball in its upward trajectory - a perfect lob that had initially passed over me at the net, bounced, and began tailing away. I have made contact up high over my left shoulder with my back to the net. Pretty cool.

Striking the outside of the ball - carving around it at approximately the 8:00 locale - requires changing your grip to, minimally, a "continental," commonly related to by many as the traditional "handshake" grip, or even a little more to an "eastern" topspin backhand grip to adjust, close the racket face more (my visible grip of choice).

You'll then have the best chance to generate enough power and spin to both elevate and bend the ball successfully back into the court with a save-the-day defensive lob of your own.

Hustling, well intentioned club players typically fail to make any grip change from their "eastern/western" forehand grips in their attempts at this shot. Big problem. Upon running the lob down, they position themselves squarely to the escaping ball - lining it up equidistant between their shoulders - resulting in a directly over the head attempt, often with, amusingly, two hands on the racket. This always strikes me as strangely reminiscent of an ancient Scottish field game's backwards small boulder toss over a football like goal post, with a result that veers far off outside of the court.

Ugly.

As always, "flight plan" visualization, along with court positioning awareness while in pursuit plays an important role in pulling the shot off - what you "see" is what you get. Picturing its intended curving, rainbow trajectory, and direction, pays particularly big dividends on the sparingly called on backfire.

Definitely one of the most fun shots in the game, you'll love using it once you get the hang of it. But you're going to have to practice it first. No problem since you can do it alone before your foursome arrives.

While standing on the service line with your back already to the net, toss a simulated lob - underhanded with your non-racket hand up high (approximately 20') that lands a few feet inside the baseline in the middle of the court. Take off after it, catch up to it, stay a bit to the right of its path, and give it a shot. Make that a few tries since beginner's luck is usually not applicable. Even Houdini worked out his escapes before performing them on his court.

Once unveiled, your playing partners will no doubt be wondering what tennis school you snuck off to over the weekend.

The Great Escape

Again, getting lobbed over is not an unusual occurrence, particularly in club play.

You've rushed the net behind, as it turns out, an approach shot lacking depth, resulting in your opponent having their lobbing way with you. Not one to fold your tent, you wheel in full pursuit, afterburners on, to run the ball down and maybe make that backfire mentioned previously.

Arriving in striking distance, albeit just a bit late as it nears a second bounce, you have only one option left: the "tweener" of course.

Relax. It's all about positioning and the grip. Another tricky one, but not as big a problem as you might think.

You can see that I have caught up to the ball in a last ditch effort to stay in the point, and have positioned myself directly over it to take the shot. On the way, I changed my grip to an extreme topspin backhand grip to open up the racket face at impact.

The stroke, with a fully loaded wrist, initiates from a high position and sweeps downward through the legs to the ball. An aggressive wrist snap will be necessary - made possible by the grip change - and substitute for the lack of follow through for all the obvious reasons.

To create needed additional spacing club mortals need, the outside leg - the left for right handers - can elevate slightly right at the ball-striking moment.

Since it takes some drop-hit practice to gauge and feel the degree of wrist flexion necessary to get sufficient air from such a low, deep position with your back to the net, visualizing a very high over the net shot trajectory will be initially useful in getting your shot over the net and back in play one more time.

Getting Set vs. Setting Up

There are two systems of coordination at work in tennis: the obvious eye-hand and the not-so-obvious eye-foot. The latter, much to the surprise of most, is the far more difficult and important of the two.

It's not at all uncommon to hear club players mumbling to themselves to "get set," after missing a so-called easy forehand or backhand that's right in their zone. Dead wrong.

Good players do not get set, or planted, to make their shots. They instead utilize an energized brand of footwork in these instances to create an optimal, right place-right time position by "setting-up." A major difference in approach and results.

In the adjacent image you can see that I am taking my final ball-striking step right as I'm about to launch the racket — slice backhand — into and through the ball. I like to refer to this footwork management as "step and strike."

Tennis is a differential relaxation sport requiring the lower body to remain very active, to continually adjust to the ball in order to allow the upper body to then be flowing smoothly and effortlessly. This is exactly why the game, as played by professionals and accomplished club players, can appear to be easy to the uninitiated.

Achieving good footwork consistently is especially challenging with regard to those aforementioned balls coming right to you — so typical of doubles play since you're hemmed in defending a relatively small area of the court compared to singles. There's a tendency to become footwork complacent, especially among those who stand around like cigar store Indians, instead of setting the bar by pacing back and forth in between points to keep their feet stimulated.

When on the run to cover wide balls, you're automatically predisposed to athletically making your shots non-stride." Those are the "easy ones." It's literally a no-brainer.

However, the lack of physicality that results from planting and standing comparatively motionless while waiting for approaching shots coming to you typically leads to over consciousness (time to think), disrupts rhythm and makes tracking the ball a more difficult task since the eyes and the brain work in concert.

So, when there is little or no running to the ball necessary, the trick is to employ numerous adjustment steps, those commonly known "stutter steps." The physicality of this "setting-up" for your shot technique will keep you connected (unconscious) and in sync with the ball right up to the moment where you take the last shot-making step.

In the end, British pro and friend Steve Heron still had it right all along with his persisting dictum: "No feet, no game, no future."

Right Place, Right Time

Now that the peak outdoor season is well under way, and the optimal playing conditions afforded by indoor hard surface play are no more for our Northern friends, increased footwork becomes paramount with the wind and clay courts in the mix affecting both the flight and the bounce of the ball.

Here's more on that to consider.

Striking one's shots in balance with the ball right where you want it in relation to your body require, simply, being in the right place at the right time. This holds true for groundies, volleys, overheads, and even lobs.

With two systems of coordination working in concert — the obvious eye-hand one and the not so obvious, but more crucial, eye-foot component — the cleanest possible shot making is a by-product of a perfectly timed final positional step, occurring in the same time frame as ball on string impact.

Good players, the one's that we immediately notice who make it look easy, do not get set, according to a tired old adage that's not only a huge misperception, but one that somehow still lives on in club land. Tour pros and better club players use a more energized brand of footwork to, if you will, stalk the ball in order to set up for their final stride into the shot.

When well executed a feeling of effortlessness is experienced often resulting in an amazingly powerful and penetrating shot — the kinetic chain at its best, firing on all cylinders.

This kind of on-stride shot making is, surprisingly to many, at its natural, athletic best — even if you do not possess the Federer fluidity and especially if you know who Jack Kramer was — when on the run in pursuit of an opponent's well-placed ball.

Equally perplexing for even more players is the fact that shots directed right at them, so common in doubles play in particular with two players defending the court, are more difficult in that they require continuous small adjustment steps, commonly referred to as "stutter steps," often in place with no place to go, until the final hitting step can be taken. Never stand waiting motionless, planted with your feet in cement, because the ball is "right to you!" Always keep your feet moving.

So, while keeping in mind Steve Heron's foot working mantra, also be cognizant of another given, with a slight twist, regarding human movement: bodies in motion stay in motion, bodies at rest are difficult to get moving.

Positionally Adapting to all the Shots

When playing in the back of the court, an all-important "spacing" component — adjusting to the particular trajectory, speed, spin and bounce point of an approaching ball both laterally *and* the more challenging forward-back positional dynamic as well — is the GPS of the when and where to be in order to best return shots cleanly.

Good news: There are basically only three distinct types of incoming shots that have to be recognized. Get dialed in by first identifying the most common, one that an opponent has struck with nominal speed, clears the net by a margin of approximately 3 to 4 feet, doesn't land particularly deep in the court, and stays relatively low off the bounce.

Allowing this ball to descend from its post-bounce high point down into your "wheelhouse" — knee to mid-thigh high — represents the most anatomically natural hitting zone where good things usually happen.

Approaching balls that exhibit a pronounced "rainbow" trajectory, with or without topspin, most often at a notably slower pace in club land with similar depth, signals a different positional tactic. Now, instead of attempting to allow this high-bouncing floater to drop low – that ill-advised one dimensional quagmire - it's far more efficient, doable, reliable and aggressive to meet this ball right at its apex or highest point after bouncing. Not only will this tactic rob your opponent of some recovery time, but also simultaneously allow you to dictate play versus these "fluff-a-nutters" instead of vice versa.

You'll also have to respond quickly to the occasional fast-approaching "laser beam" that lands extremely deep and has considerable "gas" off the bounce. These shots must be played on the rise, or immediately after the ball has bounced at a height no higher than shin to knee high. Trying to escape by retreating farther back into the court is best left to incredibly fit speedsters like Rafa Nadal.

Holding your ground, getting down low, and absorbing the blow on the short hop with a smothering and slowed swing will keep you in the point and send an intimidating message to your opponent as well: "Is that all you've got!"

At times awkward "in-betweeners" will complicate matters in that a hitting position that suits an approaching ball best is not quite achievable even with the best footwork. In those instances striking the ball in front, no matter what, as it's descending or ascending, trumps all.

Reading and differentiating opponent's shots, then adjusting your spacing accordingly — particularly the forward-back aspect — versus the one way only approach mentioned earlier will allow you to produce your best and most efficient ground strokes and insure that you're playing the ball instead of the ball playing you.

The partners to be could be somewhat familiar, or never have played together previously. No matter.

Inevitably the question comes up: "Do you have a preference as to which side you'd like to play?"

The typical answer: "Oh it doesn't matter, I don't care." Doesn't matter? You don't care? What!

It does matter, a great deal. But before we even get into that, there's the matter of the so-called "forehand side" and "backhand side" reference. Not exactly on the mark, but still used after all these years, much like announcing the score "forty-five" versus the correct "forty-fifteen."

Referring to the right side of the court as the forehand side, and the left side as the backhand side is — first and foremost — a slap in the face to all our left-handed friends who, if you've noticed, usually have a knack for playing this game of tennis pretty well.

Right-handed players positioned in the left side "ad-court" (let the correct referencing begin) are afforded an excellent opportunity to "cheat" on their court defending position out on the wing, behind the alley even, to mostly hit their favored forehand all day long. Any incoming probes that do find the backhand are now routinely a mere one-to-two steps away. And opponent forays up the middle, especially when you're teamed with a stationary net man, become inside out cross court forehands moving into the court that can be handled easily, even when struck a bit late with little downside.

Thus, at least in a right-handed world, this side of the court is, in reality, the forehand side where the partner with the more lethal forehand should reside.

Playing the "deuce-court" is an entirely different, and more challenging proposition. Cheating to the center of the court on this side, also to create as many forehand chances as possible and protect one's backhand, has its shortcomings — namely that just about any opponent with a little experience can hit a sharp angle, with a serve or groundstroke, going away from the court that could prove difficult to reach and control when positioned toward the court's center.

So, with court position now having to be played "straight-up," the deuce-court player has to handle the very poachable "inside-out" backhand, of which they will see many from an able team across the net.

Hence, yes, it's actually the backhand side, and where the partner with the more reliable backhand should play.

Postscript: Hitting shots on the run going into-the-court from the wing are far more controlled than those struck on the run going off-the-court, even with the forehand. The former are also far less poachable since club players can be late and unable hit cross court when stretched wide out of court, especially with their backhands, feeding up delicious meatballs to salivating opponents at the net.

So doubles, in large part, and in many ways more so than in singles, features methodically manipulating court position from shot to shot to your advantage, resulting in opponents being maneuvered out of position.

Who does it to whom first, best, wins.

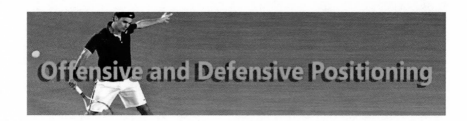

While visiting an out of town club last weekend, I overheard a player announce to his doubles group immediately after completing play: "I don't know why you guys wanted to stop after just three sets, I could've easily played another one."

The pro, whom I knew, also standing within earshot, looked at me, shrugged and shook his head to stealthily disassociate himself from this particular member.

His statement was by no means a proclamation of his boundless energy or superb fitness, it was, however, an unknowing confession of his doubles "style" of net play — the motionless, non-participating net man.

Earlier, I casually observed this group and the player in question. When at the net he consistently positioned himself as close to the net as possible — a mere racket's length away — normally only appropriate for very young children, and as close to the alley as possible without actually stepping on the singles sideline. He stood absolutely still, never moving from that spot, with his head swiveling wildly back and forth — like some possessed character in an Exorcist movie — to observe the action.

He removed himself from the fray, leaving his partner to cover four-fifths of the court. I can only surmise, since he and his partner lost, that he probably blamed him for poor back court play.

Club doubles is played mostly in the one-up, one-back alignment. Playing it well requires a constant shifting back and forth by the opposing net players between an offensive position (one that creates an opportunity to poach) and a defensive position (one that defends against the poach) that's stressed earlier and again here since so many never seem to fully get this, or be motivated to just do it.

At the beginning of each point, the net player on the serving team should be positioned offensively. That's approximately in the middle of the service box in order to pick-off (the "poaching" reference) any errant returns that are reachable.

Conversely, as in defense, the receiving team's net player is positioned in close proximity to the service box "T" in order to defend the middle of the court from an opposing poacher.

Once the defending net player's partner makes a successful return — one that's sufficiently, typically cross court and safely out of the poacher's range — the net partner then transitions immediately into the "up position" to, hopefully, have an opportunity to snag the opposition's cross court counter.

Upon failing to be a factor in the initial offensive position on the serving team, this net player has to then transition back toward the defending position mentioned earlier near the "T" to fend off any interceptions of their partner's shots from the back.

Back and forth it goes. Over and over. All match long. This takes effort, energized footwork, constant movement, and a commitment to the task versus the approach of our always fresh as a daisy friend.

Other challenging teamwork, positioning issues abound in doubles play, but the offense-defense aspect of net play is essential if you're going to play true doubles versus four players stuck in a mere facsimile of actual doubles play with its flowing team dynamic.

Don't Forget to Breathe When Striking

Yes, still more on this all-important, and mostly neglected, component of playing your best.

Breathing at the ball-striking moment is a key synchronizer for success. Yet, most club players are consistent "breath-holders" at the moment of truth.

It's interesting that this particular lack of modeling tour player habits is in complete opposition to the norm, where all else is embraced.

Curious?

Holding your breath while simultaneously striking shots is, simply, not a good thing. Would you hold your breath while exercising at the gym? Of course not. The trainer would be all over you. Would you go out for a brisk walk, jog, or a serious run and hold your breath for a moment or two every few seconds? How would that turn out?

But encountering both slow and fast-flying yellow spheres can be emotionally stressful at the ball-on-racket moment - let the breath holding begin. And it can be especially physically undermining for a hustling go-getter as well. Double whammy.

In the past, many have been repelled from breathing — exhaling through the contact zone — since it has commonly been referred to as "grunting." Bad connotation for many.

Way back in the early '70s of televised tennis (PBS was the first) Jimmy Connors became the Founding Father of the "modern" grunt. On the women's side Monica Seles came along a decade later.

The audible exhalation/grunt arrived.

In today's game, to make perception matters worse, we've got high pitched ear piercing screaming practiced by many of the top women, and a few men as well albeit at a lower octave.

A past US Open Series final from Palo Alto once pitted the two top practitioners on tour, Maria Sharapova and Victoria Azarenka, against each other.

First, I turned the volume down, and then completely off. They made Venus and Serena sound like whispering choir girls.

No wonder you're still not buying into it. But, no way around it, if you're going to play your best, that is be relatively unconscious — meaning no overt left brain analysis while swinging a relaxed stick — with low muscle tension and reduced emotional stress, you're going to have to accept the physicality of breathing out when connecting with the ball.

No need to adjust the volume when Roger Federer is playing – unless it's up - since he never buries the decibel meter needle. You can't even hear him, but believe me, he is breathing. Therein lies the good news - you do not have to awaken half the neighborhood every time you play a shot. And, as a club player, you won't be drawing any unwanted attention to yourself.

Nonetheless, you should be exhaling through impact, and there's the more friendly term to embrace going forward: exhaling. You'll immediately reap the play better benefits, especially not experiencing being seriously out of breath and unnecessarily elevating your heart rate into a physically stressed zone.

A good way to begin is to quietly say "yes" as you are striking your shots. This replicates exhaling reasonably well and easy to do. And, like Roger, it will be mostly completely inaudible to others.

Sustain it on the "long" strokes to their end — forehands, backhands, serves, overheads, serve returns, and lobbing. Make it brief when volleying at the net — the "short" strokes.

Eventually it will transform itself from "yes" into your own signature exhalation "sound" (not a grunt), and you'll become a smooth stroking machine while simultaneously keeping your gas tank full.

Play Freely to Avoid Paralysis Through Analysis

In the spirit of don't drink and drive, don't think and hit. Reviewing an 8-point check list while simultaneously striking a moving ball is next to impossible.

But sometimes you do just that to try and play better. Unfortunately, you will play worse.

Why? Because all that left brain-driven analytical thought will literally glaze your eyes over and result in, at best, only a peripheral sighting of the ball — a disaster in the making.

"Then how am I supposed to watch the ball, judge spacing, visualize my shot, ready the racket by turning my hips/shoulders, keep my footwork energized, relax my grip, time my hitting step, breathe out at impact, and follow through all at the same time?"

That's the million dollar question I'm constantly being asked by challenged multi-taskers.

Answer: You'll only be able to manage it from muscle memory, established through the proper repetition of the above noted core fundamentals in a practice environment.

Unfortunately, those in the habit of playing matches day in and day out without ever practicing — hitting with a friend, getting on the ball machine, or just drop-hitting by yourself and/or serving without point pressure — is very limiting. Add the misguided warm-up habits of club players that reinforce so little of what's needed to play your best and you've got a big problem with game stagnation.

You don't think about how to swallow or how to walk for example. No need, it's reliably right there on your inner hard-drive.

It's the same with your game, but only if the basic Ps and Qs have been dialed-in through even occasional practice.

Tennis is an interval sport — intense action followed by brief timeouts prior to the start of the next point — and requires being in the moment, but also allows for being out of the moment. Just do the same during the point (your player persona), followed by, if necessary, figuring out how to do it better (your self-coach persona) during the time in between.

Again, in the midst of a point there can be only two tasks to focus on: 1) watching the ball, 2) visualizing both your shot's intended direction and margin

144

to the net.

That's it! I joke with players that "it's hard to be that stupid."

The appropriate mechanical and movement necessities are either going to reflexively happen or not happen. They can only be "monitored" kinesthetically — defined as "a sense that perceives bodily movement, position, and weight."

Play freely. *Let* it happen. Do not *make* it happen — the square peg into the round hole syndrome – not just pseudo psychology.

So, bottom line, what does it take to stop this undermining in-point paralysis through analysis?

Short answer: courage, conviction, trust. Easily said.

Giving your Judgmental Self up to the ball and a shot flight plan is no easy proposition, especially if your game is flawed with technical inefficiencies that you recognize but don't know how to correct. Self-doubt creeps in, distracts and the dominos fall one by one.

Managing the required finite/gross motor skills during the action are accomplished through "feel." Being in touch with your physical being without thinking about it is the considerable trick.

In earlier times, as referred to previously, long before the proliferation of sports psychologists, players who on occasion performed at a level well beyond their norm were often identified as being "unconscious," or "playing out of their mind."

Precisely.

Use Their Pace and Laugh in Their Face

One of the great equalizers in tennis is the ability to effectively negate an opponent's power game — their shots that have extra speed, and depth with an accompanying explosive bounce.

Dealing with these penetrating "$100 balls," the ones that can be run down, represents an exceptional opportunity to send a challenging message to an opponent fully expecting a winning outcome: "Is that all you've got?"

Being consistently able to absorb, smother and neutralize any big blasts, nothing more, and routinely re-directing them back across the net will get an opponent's attention in short order (note the jaw drops).

Too often, upon recognizing an incoming bomb, players panic and foolishly fight the ball, attempting to match or even surpass its pace.

No, no, no. Pouring gasoline on a fire will not bring the desired result. The goal is to just ride out the storm and re-level the playing field.

There is nothing more frustrating to a player who has just launched their best stuff than to see it come back — seemingly effortlessly — without making a dent.

Surprisingly, even experienced veterans will sometimes take umbrage and begin attempting to hit not only harder, but closer to the lines as well – what Djokovic forces upon everyone - a sure-fire formula for self-destruction.

Voila. You've got 'em. You're in their head.

The two most satisfying shot outcomes in tennis are: a) hitting a clean winner or service ace — the obvious one, b) observing an opponent's shaken demeanor when you're continually parrying *their* A-game with relative ease and luring them increasingly into unforced errors — the not so obvious other one.

For me personally, it's the latter. What fun, particularly since one's own power quotient typically drops off once you've graduated into age group play and learning to be a "counter puncher" becomes begrudgingly attractive.

The technique involved in this demoralizing tactic is to prepare the racket very quickly — albeit softly versus the temptation to overgrip the racket in full fight-or-flight mode — and then immediately, seamlessly initiating the forward movement of it through the ball at as slow a rate of speed as is possible.

Again: Absorb, smother, use.

A tricky gear change at first try — this fast to slow — but absolutely learnable and downloaded into your motor subconscious quickly enough. The resulting capability to diffuse that $100 ball and transform it into an equalizing $50 response, one that lands deep enough to not be capitalized upon, is one of the biggest difference makers in the game.

Knowing that you can handle pace comfortably is a huge confidence builder, and will give you membership into an entirely different play group.

When you do find yourself up against opponents with known firepower and they hit an unreachable winner, just say "nice shot." No worries. They won the point, you didn't lose it.

But if you're generally not able to handle pace on balls in your court coverage zone then you've lost the point right then and there without even forcing one more shot. And any thoughts of being invited to sub-in with that really good foursome are best put to rest.

As a solid all-around player I know likes to say: "Just use their pace and laugh in their face."

Trust me, you'll like it.

Gearing Up Mentally and Physically

One of the dictionary definitions of ritual is: "a customarily repeated act or series of acts."

The use of rituals in tennis just prior to serving and receiving — the two most important shots in the game that are initiated from an always-challenging static start — is easily observed in the pro game and essential in creating a whole body rhythm and positive unconsciousness for all. They are deeply ingrained, idiosyncratic and highly valued among both the sport's stars and journeymen alike.

They are even utilized in between points — the toweling off and the inspection of the balls offered up by the ball kids — as the players lead up to taking position to serve or return.

And surely you've all noticed Rafa Nadal's "shorts tugging" tick. Interesting.

These individually customized routines are universal and exist throughout all of sport, and even in daily life as well. Have you ever considered that you brush your teeth and dress yourself in the exact same manner every morning?

Baseball batters, of course, rule the roost. Watching their elaborate fidgeting with uniforms, caps, batting gloves and batting helmets before even stepping into the batter's box where they then repeat a few practice swings can, at times, seem interminable.

The list goes on with golfers famously doing their wiggling and waggling as they ready to hit. And then there are the basketball players with their lively ball bouncing and body dance before shooting a free throw.

In tennis, when the moment of serving is at hand, experienced players first look across the net and visualize the intended flight of the serve. This is followed by a number of ball bounces to relax the tossing hand.

Next a little rocking motion back and forth with the ball against the racket strings, and then, hopefully, a feel good state of whole body continuity is achieved along with an uncluttered mind. And then, and only then, the serve is launched.

I'll always remember a Lake Placid club player, Marilyn H., upon first experiencing the immediately positive aspects of developing a serving ritual, saying to me in smiling amazement: "That really gets the kinks out." Exactly.

Returning serve also requires a get-engaged routine well before the serve is struck. Top players often skip laterally in place as the server approaches the line to energize. They then transition into a grounded foot-to-foot weighting while the upper body slowly rotates slightly from left to right, then right to left a number of times since this replicates the very first pivoting movement that the receiver must make once the serve is struck.

Today, Serena Williams' return ritual, with all of its signature gyrations, is arguably the best in the women's or men's game. She is clearly committed to connecting to the moment in harmony with an opponent about to unleash their best.

Going forward always take the time to properly, "gear-up" both physically and mentally prior to starting a point either serving or returning.

Standing absolutely still, with not a muscle stirring, is analogous to shutting your car engine off at a red traffic light. Keep the motor revving. The difference will immediately strike a chord.

Settling to the Return Task

More on rituals.

It's those mano a mano moments in sports that are most welcome by the best competitors. The occasional penalty shots in hockey and soccer, and the game-ending shootouts.

In sports like tennis and baseball, these one-on-one moments occur repeatedly, and represent the core component characteristic of each. Server versus returner. Pitcher versus hitter.

Every point in tennis begins with this same dynamic and is precisely why the serve and return are the No. 1 and No. 2 most important shots in the game. Why on earth club players commonly forgo even a little serve-return practice in a friendly pre-match warmup, and instead lower their playing bar by embracing "FBI," is hard to explain. Then, to be fair, should it not follow that the receiver then announce "FRI" (first return in)?

As the returner, one faces the task of taking on an essentially "free shot" from the server, who gets two chances! Unfair? Not necessarily.

You can absorb a heavy, well-placed serve and just block it back into play. You can attack a weak delivery, a not unusual opportunity in club land. Or, you can play a neutral, safe return for serves somewhere in between.

The good news is that all serves are "short." Since they must land in a service box that's a mere 13 feet wide and extends only 21 feet beyond a 3-foot plus net barrier in a court that's 39 feet long per side, "deep" serves pale in comparison to deep, in-point backcourt balls.

That's very fair, and there's generous spacing - 40 feet from service line to fence - to choose the best position to lock onto the server's speed, spin and bounce height. Cake.

The bigger challenge is negating the lurking downside of the static start inherent in the return. Anywhere from 10 to 30 seconds elapse prior to the start of the server-returner duel on every point. How you fill that time is crucial in remaining engaged and connected.

Overcoming the potentially undermining nature of static states is prevalent in sport. In baseball, you can picture the batter taking numerous practice swings prior to the pitch. In golf, it's the "wiggling" and "waggling" before hitting.

In tennis this component is especially necessity on the return – and of course the serve as well - and are the "rituals" typically referred to, which every heady player at any level embraces and ultimately puts their own signature on.

First, after pacing about - do not ever stand still between points - make an educated guess on position. Prior to even arriving there visualizing the return should already be taking place, picturing both your intended direction and margin to the net in your mind's eye.

Then settle in by swaying your shoulders, with the racket, a bit side to side - after all, turning, pivoting, and preparing the racket is always the first move once the serve is recognized. Also, include a subtle foot-to-foot weight transfer to keep the feet stimulated and ready to go. Feel the ready to rock rhythm.

A perfectly timed split-step will lock your eyes onto the ball at serve impact, maximize your reaction to its direction, and contribute to maintaining ball-tracking from contact, to bounce point, and right into your racket.

Develop your own ritual. Embellish it. You'll soon be viewing the return as a viable opportunity.

PART THREE: Website Essays

The Easy Balls are not Easy

How many times have you heard your peers mumbling something like this after a perceived bad miss: "C'mton, how can you miss a ball right to you?" How many times have you thought the same thing?

Yet these "easy balls" are from it. They negate the advantages inherent in the repeated axiom, "bodies in motion stay in motion." Instead they enable the opposite, "bodies at rest stay at rest." Make no mistake about it, this is no easy conundrum. But it's not unusual at all for players to misperceive the difficulty inherent in handling these kinds of balls, particularly in doubles where you're only covering a small part of the back court and the balls are right in your zone.

Balls that require lateral or forward movement trigger the bodies in motion response. The natural athleticism triggered in hitting-on-the-run recall one's motor skill memory and fully support ball striking timing. It just flows.

Incoming balls right at you, body shots, disable this process and lead to static positioning, i.e. just standing there and waiting. That would be analogous to turning your car's engine off at a red traffic light, resulting in a disconnection from the task at hand versus keeping the motor idling until the light turns green even though you're stationary. On the tennis court that's a recipe for repeated "how could I miss that ball" unforced errors.

If that's not enough, factor in that it's much more difficult to read the bounce angle on a ball that's right in front of you than it is if it's off to one side.

Stutter steps become the only viable solution. Back to Jimmy Connors, the best proponent of this good footwork component ever. Not the fastest player of his era, but the best at staying in motion when balls were approaching right at him. Although not going anywhere, Jimmy would take 3,4,5,6,7 little steps before launching his shot. Eye-foot coordination supporting eye-hand coordination. That's how it works! Why do you think he goes down as one of the very best returners of all-time? Footwork.

So forget about the "get-set" cue I still hear being bandied about far too often. Do not get planted. Do not stand there doing nothing, waiting for the ball which, in the absence of physicality, always leads to over conscious negative thinking and its accompanying glazed-over poor ball tracking. Instead "set-up," utilizing those stutter steps, to create the same no-brainer athleticism that occurs so naturally when you're on the run.

Good stutter-stepping footwork seemingly doesn't matter, until it does.

Adapting to playing on these two very different surfaces, not an uncommon frequent requirement for club players – unlike tour players whose year is divided into periods of play on one particular surface - is simple enough, but underappreciated by most and not even on the radar screen of some. Sure, everyone recognizes that clay courts are far more forgiving on the body, particularly in areas of an older median age like Florida in particular, but there's more to the mix than just that.

If the majority of your tennis is played on soft courts, then, going in, you should be acutely aware that opponent's shots will have a considerably quicker bounce, especially if the amount of sand mixed into the final color coating – this determines the court's speed - is on the thin side, or they are in need of resurfacing.

So what does that mean? It means that your margin of error regarding the timing of your racket preparation on your groundies will not be very forgiving, as it can be, somewhat, on clay. If you're a bit late in preparing you'll experience mishits, racket twisting, and bobble-heading resulting from the poor ball tracking that goes hand-in-hand when the ball is playing you instead of the other way around. So, you'd better have the take-back loaded by the time the approaching ball bounces. Note: I am not saying "run with the racket back." Instead, time the finish of your prep with the ball's bounce based upon the speed at which it is traveling.

When transitioning from hard to clay the #1 challenge is to amp up your footwork. Clay courts, even good ones, can be an adventure in shot timing – particularly when the court is not groomed immediately before play - since a consistently true bounce, unlike hard courts, is not guaranteed. Factor in that the duration of time elapsing between an opponent's strike of the ball and yours is slightly longer, a more energized ball "stalking" to "fill" the extra time is exactly what that amped footwork is needed to achieve good positioning, previously identified, simply, as being at the right place at the right time to make your shot. Martina Navratolova lately has started referring to this, in the spirit of shot selection, as "position selection!"

Because hard courts are faster, the average height off the bounce is lower, resulting in a generally lower strike zone with many balls right in your anatomically ideal knee-high to thigh-high wheelhouse. Clay bounces on average are higher requiring a much broader strike zone, including all the way up to chest, shoulder, and head high, that is unless you're a track star and insist on backing up all the way to the windscreen if necessary – resulting in being as far away as possible from the net and the opponent(s) - to allow the ball to get into that low hitting zone. Good luck with that.

Clay courts also require a serious commitment to patience: a) expect the ball to come back; b) don't even mind. It's okay. Third, fourth ball rally panic, leading to pressing and suddenly trying to "do something" when no real opportunity yet exists – it's just rally ball! - is foolhardy and will result in a stream of unforced errors that will ruin your day.

Shot making on the asphalt is far more rewarded so a more aggressive mind set is possible since you'll be more able to dictate play. Just don't get delusional because you happen to make a freaky low percentage winner every once in a while and begin to think that's the "routine you." Some patience is still required.

The footing on the two surfaces is also quite different. If you're transitioning from your usual hard courts to clay try "skating" at first – literally shuffling somewhat from ball to ball - to get a feel for the surface traction, i.e. not being able to stop and start on a dime. If the challenge is the other way around then you're going to have to pick your feet up off the playing surface as a countermeasure to the much higher friction coefficient of shoe rubber to court. You might hear a little shoe "squeaking." Good, it means you're moving!

Regarding doubles play, poaching is more doable on hard surfaces since opponents are not able to "hold" their shots quite as long - as they can on clay - when either returning serve or playing a groundie from the back, and, by going behind you, can catch you on an early bus to the next county.

Lastly, learning to slide into your shots on the dirt like the big boys and girls takes practice and is a learned skill. Some never get it down – would you believe Andre Agassi, a former French Open champion, remains, even today, among the many. Maria Sharapova referred to her own difficulties on clay as, "A cow on ice."

Try practicing on a wood floor in your stocking feet. See, nothing to it!

Clay to Hard,
Hard to Clay

Adapting to playing on these two very different surfaces, not an uncommon frequent requirement for club players - unlike tour players whose year is divided into periods of play on one particular surface - is simple enough, but underappreciated by most and not even on the radar screen of some. Sure, everyone recognizes that clay courts are far more forgiving on the body, particularly in areas of an older median age like Florida in particular, but there's more to the mix than just that.

If the majority of your tennis is played on soft courts, then, going in, you should be acutely aware that opponent's shots will have considerably more "gas off the bounce" on hard, especially if the amount of sand mixed into the final color coating - this determines the court's speed - is on the thin side, or they are in need of resurfacing.

So what does that mean? It means that your margin of error regarding the timing of your racket preparation on your groundies will not be very forgiving, as it can be, somewhat, on clay. If you're a bit late in preparing you'll experience mis-hits, racket twisting, and bobble-heading resulting from the poor ball tracking that goes hand-in-hand when the ball is playing you instead of the other way around. So, you'd better have the take-back finished by the time the approaching ball bounces. Note: I am not saying "run with the racket back." Instead, time the finish of your prep with the ball's bounce based upon the speed at which it is traveling.

When transitioning from hard to clay the #1 challenge is to amp up your footwork. Clay courts, even good ones, can be an adventure in shot timing - particularly when the court is not groomed immediately before play - since a consistently true bounce, unlike hard courts, is not guaranteed. Factor in that the duration of time elapsing between an opponent's strike of the ball and yours is slightly longer, a more energized ball "stalking" to "fill" the extra time is exactly what that amped footwork is needed to achieve - good positioning or being at the right place at the right time to make your shot. Martina Navratolova lately has started referring to this, in the spirit of shot selection, as "position selection!"

Because hard courts are fester, the average height off the bounce is lower, resulting in a generally lower strike zone with many balls right in your anatomically ideal knee-high to thigh-high wheelhouse. Clay bounces on average are higher requiring a much broader strike zone, including all the way up to chest, shoulder, and head high, that is unless you're a track star and insist on backing up all the way to the windscreen if necessary - getting as far away as possible from the net and the opponent(s)? - to allow the ball to get into that low hitting zone. Good luck with that.

Clay courts also require a serious commitment to patience: a) expect the ball to come back; b) don't even mind. It's okay. Third, fourth ball rally panic, leading to pressing and suddenly trying to "do something" when no real opportunity yet exists - it's just rally ball! - is foolhardy and will result in a stream of unforced errors that will ruin your day. Shot making on the asphalt is far more rewarded so a more aggressive mind set is possible since you'll be more able to dictate play... just don't get delusional because you happen to make a freaky low percentage winner every once in a while and begin to think that's the "routine you." Some patience is still required.

The footing on the two surfaces is also quite different. If you're transitioning from your usual hard courts to clay try "skating" at first - literally shuffling somewhat from ball to ball - to get a feel for the surface traction, i.e. not being able to stop and start on a dime. If the challenge is the other way around then you're going to have to pick your feet up off the playing surface as a countermeasure to the much higher friction coefficient of shoe rubber to court. You might hear a little shoe "squeaking." Good, it means you're moving!

Regarding doubles play, poaching is more doable on hard surfaces since opponents are not able to "hold" their shots quite as long – as they can on clay - when either returning serve or playing a groundie from the back, and, by going behind you, can catch you on an early bus to the next county.

Lastly, learning to slide into your shots on the dirt like the big boys and girls takes practice and is a learned skill. Some never get it down - would you believe Andre Agassi, a former French Open champion, remains, even today, among the many. Nonetheless, the main ingredient is getting down very low and timing your slide's end right at the ball striking moment. Practice on a wooden floor in your stocking feet. See, nothing to it!

Hard Courts, Soft Courts, and Your Body's Adaptation

Too often to not notice, I repeatedly experience a very curious impression that my top of the line footwear creates an even softer, more cushioned ride when playing on hard courts – which I rarely do - compared to when I'm playing on clay. What? Yet, I get the exact same sense when just walking from the parking lot to the clubhouse on the cement sidewalk. Subscribing to the conventional wisdom, how can that possibly be? Somehow I have to be misperceiving this.

Perhaps not. Recent running studies, some products of small control groups, others based on biomechanical modeling, indicate that the human body, the most amazing self-righting machine, automatically adjusts to different surface hardness in order to keep the forces on the feet, ankles, knees, and hips as minimal as possible.

According to Dr. Stuart Warden, director of Translational Musculoskeletal Research at Indiana University, "If you run on a hard surface, your body decreases its stiffness. Your knees and hips flex more. On a soft surface, your legs stiffen."

An example used by Warden compares the body's auto-response when jumping off a table on to the floor, to landing on a trampoline. With the former you'd soften your knees at touchdown to better absorb the shock, which wouldn't be necessary at all and, interestingly, not auto-employed in the latter dynamic with its practically cancelled out landing impact.

Playing well on clay, the "soft" surface, does require considerably more footwork. This takes form in stutter steps which become, even on a well-groomed surface like the ones at the French Open, where an absolutely true bounce is not always the norm that it always is on a hard court, the sheer number of foot plants is far greater – especially in close quarter doubles where more adjustment steps are needed in comparison to on-the-run singles – than on true bounce hard surfaces.

In a recent on court seminar presentation to fellow professionals – at the Tennis Hall of Fame's indoor hard courts – I warmed-up for about ten minutes with a good young junior as the attendees started arriving. To my amazement, in both instances, I dialed-in my groundies in no time at all – with an acute awareness of a less physical footwork stress than on the clay that I spend twelve months a year on – and found myself moving and striking balls with exceptional rhythm and relative ease.

Perhaps this repeating perception of mine is indeed a product of my body, smartly, softening-up its g-force foot strikes as needed. Conversely, is it possible that when I'm on soft surfaces – where the conventional wisdom does tell us, has always told us, that this is the more forgiving playing surface on the joints – my body becomes innately less attentive to absorbing foot strike shock?

Still, one might raise the question of braking from shot-to-shot, and its joint bearing consequences from surface to surface. Stopping on clay is far more forgiving in that you literally cannot stop on a dime, which you will absolutely be capable of on hard surfaces – unless you're one of the modern day specimens who can actually slide on hard courts (are they using shoes with a different rubber compound?). The "dirt" will afford you a bit of slide-room, or more, depending on your foot speed to the ball and the condition of the court. Then again, timely movement into and out of the shot making moment can cancel-out the potential costs of "dime-stopping" on the hard stuff.

Ever notice, on congested roadways with numerous traffic lights, how some drivers race to the next red light only to jam on the brakes when they get there, while others accelerate and decelerate smoothly and efficiently, just as all good hard surface tennis movers do.

And consider how you instinctively utilized very light foot plants whenever you found yourself crossing the sun baked, red hot pavement adjacent to those childhood beaches and lakefronts barefoot. Speaking of barefoot, I would be remiss not to acknowledge the relatively new running barefoot movement, and also the accompanying running minimalist footwear now being marketed that goes with it, ignited mostly by Christopher McDougall's best-selling book, *Born To Run*, about the Mexican outback Indian's phenomenal endurance, injury free running deep in the totally isolated Copper Canyon completely without modern day "motion control" footwear.

In any event, when you do find yourself on hard court surfaces, be conscious of maximizing your body's apparent innate ability to cushion your ride. And, when on clay, avoid carelessly clunking around because you're conditioned to thinking that you're on a "soft" court and wearing $120 shoes and your bullet proof.

Since I am on clay almost all the time, the outsoles of those expensive shoes take forever to wear out. The insoles, however, are a completely different matter. They wear out and lose their cushioning relatively quickly – about 40 hours for me. Yet, for the average player, it happens so incrementally it can sneak up on you, that is until you start hurting and you wonder why since your shoes are "only 3 months old."

Currently, Adidas, last I knew, provides the very best, well cushioned, longest lasting insoles in their tennis line, which are interchangeable among all brands. At times I would wait for online sales of second tier models in their line at Tennis Warehouse, and acquire a few pairs at a time just for the insoles, which I would then rotate daily (6 pair) in my K-Swiss Big Shots.

When they are not in use they are placed in the sunlight to aerate them, and dry them out in my high humidity environment, which helps refresh the all-important "inner" cushioning.

Today, with my podiatrist informing me that my feet are shot, I'm recommending an insole sandwich of SofSole Thin Fits with BackJoy inserts, available online on Amazon, especially if you have, or have had, any chronic hip, knee, ankle, or foot problems.

Improving your skill to move lightly and quickly on top of the court will contribute to achieving more viable hitting positions - on any surface – resulting in you not only performing at your very best but also contribute markedly to injury prevention and fatigue reduction.

 # Just Talking Tennis Heads or More?

I'm betting that audible breathing, especially very audible breathing, just popped into your head. And you're right, it's the obvious physical "talking-head" component, but by no means the only one, and that's where the nuances get interesting.

One that I'd wager on that is seldom, if ever, even considered or monitored, is playing slack-jawed. Take a few minutes tomorrow and observe your peer's jaw status during shot making. You'll be very surprised to see all sorts of clenched, distorted lower jaw positions right at impact. Not good as it creates tension that radiates through your entire body, including the arm(s) swinging the racket. It's all connected as my massage therapist likes to say.

Then there's squinting to enhance one's vision. No big deal. That's been around and documented for a long time. What actually results is a changing of the eye's shape, and an altering of the light allowed – less - to enter. Just walk out of your house into a bright sunny day without sunglasses or a cap and your autopilot squinting switch will go off.

But that's not it. The latest deal is going consciously bug-eyed – observe Djokovic - to trigger better ball-tracking and visual enhancement, particularly at the ball striking moment. It's certainly not unusual to see magazine and newspaper images of professional tennis players doing exactly this.

At the urging of one of my lessons clients, a true student of the game and whose primary coach has him incorporating this, I gave it a try. No doubt there's merit regarding one's focusing on the ball, but the surprising aspect for me was a quieting of the mind. A thought dissolver. No doubt, as this technique becomes more familiar, some TV announcer, or writer, or pro will come up with a catch phrase for its practice. I'm going with "big-eyed" for now. "Bug-eyed," although literally accurate, somehow just doesn't cut it.

Now, before getting back to, once again, breathing technique, consider player "shot vocalizing." No, I'm not just referring to plain old grunting, or screaming as practiced by some. I'm talking about employing different tonal qualities, even two syllable enunciations - compared to the usual one - and the like that are linked to the shot making task. Common example: many two-handed backhand pro players make a completely different sound when going to a one-handed slice out of necessity.

Why? Power shot vs more finesse and feel. A more all-out voluminous exhalation morphs instantly into one of relative quiet.

Still on breathing, who would ever think about flaring their nostrils – yes I'm serious - for more efficient breathing? For starters, remember that a number of companies in the 90's introduced "breathing strips," a band-aid like stick-on that adheres to the upper nose to stretch and expand one's nasal passages once applied. Football players really embraced them for a while, still do in both college and pros, and so did the Jensen brothers doubles team who preceded the Bryan brothers as the premier U.S. Davis Cup pair.

Nostril flaring, when done spontaneously, indicates the body's auto effort to make breathing more efficient. This is true in both humans and animals. Racehorses epitomize this expansion when under physical duress on the track.

Utilizing this technique during the shot making moment – just prior to letting the racket go during the inhalation stage – ends up, as it turns out, creating a greater " back pressure" that will increase O2 uptake by 10-20%, and simultaneously effect better lung elasticity prior to the mouth-breathing exhalation, grunting phase.

Still not a fan of the "grunting" word, but it's out there and here to stay.

So yes, there's more to this than just, simply, a talking head that's audibly exhaling, grunting. Realizing an even better brand of your current best tennis can be readily augmented by: 1) playing slack-jawed for greater physical relaxation, 2) going big-eyed at the ball striking moment, 3) flaring your nostrils and utilizing nose-breathing in the final inhalation moment prior to making your shot, and then mouth breathing, exhaling in the ball striking moment.

Keep in mind that learning new techniques takes practice before they become naturally occurring, or reflexive.

Supporting Your Game

You've put in the time on the practice court – you've paid your dues. You've invested your hard earned money into lessons and coaching. Yet, achieving improved mechanics and technical skill, even high level ball striking skills, will not pay the dividends that you're banking on if you fail to consistently support those abilities.

Q. – What is the most important skill in tennis?

A. – Watching the ball!

Q. – What is the most difficult skill in tennis?

A. – Watching the ball!

Yes, it is indeed a skill, one that not only has to be developed, improved upon, and monitored day in and day out, but one that must be reinvented in every single warm-up on a daily basis.

Besides paying close attention to the optimal moment to strike your shot – that's what you're watching the ball for – always maintain a relatively still head while you're in the act of tracking the ball. If you are a frequent "bobble header" you will not only adversely affect your timing but also have difficulty finding the racket's sweet spot.

How many times do we hear world class player's state in press conferences after an especially good on-court performance: "I saw the ball really well today."

Don't be confused about this since you claim that you "saw" the ball. But that was through your periphery – that's not good enough. Sure, you can "see" through your periphery, but you must focus intensely on the flying yellow sphere as best you can since the human eye is somewhat limited, but, thankfully, they do receive help from the brain.

And don't ever stop remembering Rod Laver's classic take on the challenging game of tennis that can be so frustrating to so many: "It's a simple game. It's just not easy."

VISUALIZE...REALIZE:
The Mind Body Connection

When working with players I make a habit of asking them, particularly after they've experienced a particularly ugly unforced error, exactly what their intentions were for their shot. It is not unusual at all for them to admit, typically after a moment of deliberation, that they really did *not* have a clear idea of what they wanted to do with the ball beyond "over there somewhere." That's just not going to get it done reliably. Even with sound mechanics you're not going to be able to play the tennis that you're truly capable of playing with that kind of "quarterbacking."

Once explained, some players have an innate knack for picturing their shots in advance of striking the ball – "chess on the run" according to late author and tennis enthusiast David Foster Wallace. Unfortunately, these individuals are few and far between. Most players have a grossly underdeveloped use of their right brain hemisphere – the picturing area, i.e. thinking in pictures. Instead they mostly analytically "think" from their left brain resulting in interrupted/distracted ball watching. Interestingly, left-handers are more predisposed to visualizing their shots since their hard wiring is right brain driven.

As a young "flash and dash" right-handed serve and volley specialist, I also enjoyed success hitting clean passing shots in singles and low returns in doubles versus other serve and volleyers and net rushers, the tactical norm of the day when players were without the howitzer-like rackets and the rapid recoil strings of today giving them the time to get into the net. Yet, curiously, although armed with the same forehand and backhand skill, my backcourt game was a completely unreliable crap-shoot, lacking in both confidence and consistency. A complete mystery.

Eventually, although many years later - we all coached ourselves back then and knew nothing about visualization; no one even used that terminology – it finally became obvious to me that I needed a "target" and excelled when I had one. An opponent coming in, or already at the net, triggered, from years of playing experience, an unconscious ability to clearly picture – in my right brain mind's eye – exactly where I wanted my shots to go. Both the player, and the net itself or the "window" immediately above it, provided unknowing reference points both directionally with regard to the court and marginally with regard to the top of the net. It was only then that I became a credible back courter if I needed or chose to be one - just in time for the 35's. Oh well.

Amazingly, some thirty years later, developing visualization skills in club land remains mostly untaught and unaddressed. Such a pity. When a Roger Federer states, as noted earlier on, that he believes his greatest skill is his ability to first recognize an opponent's approaching ball with all of its speed, spin, and trajectory, and then "see" his own response faster than anyone else, giving him comparatively more time for the actual striking of that ball, it's time to take notice.

Golfers develop this skill more readily and easily than tennis players since all of their shots are hit from a static start – unlike tennis players who enjoy that luxury only on serve and return of serve. First the look at the fairway or the green. Then the personalized wiggle-waggle routine. Then another look or two followed by another moment of wiggling and waggling, and finally the swing. They are visualizing early on in the development of their golf game!

Not so in tennis. Surprisingly, even accomplished, veteran ball strikers are often unconsciously hoping for success instead of "seeing" success through positive visualization prior to every ball struck, including in the midst of a live point - back to Wallace's "chess on the run."

This lack of clear cognizance of a shot's precise purpose undermines a perfectly good player's mechanics and otherwise sound games in a big way, resulting in launching mishit "bricks," giving points away needlessly, and playing ugly at times.

Perform this exercise in your mind's eye to get started:

1. Picture the color yellow

2. Picture a yellow tennis ball

3. Picture a yellow tennis ball passing over the middle of the net by a 3 foot margin with a rainbow trajectory landing halfway between the service line and the baseline.

These "pictures" occur lightning fast compared to slow and distracted analytical thinking. Once integrated into your game the results will totally surprise you - connecting your mind and body through visualization with the motor areas of the brain and the spinal cord handling the "details."

Visualize…Realize.

Finally, who better than new golf superstar, Jordan Spieth, to put it so succinctly: "The more specific you are about your shot's intention, the less you miss by."

PLAYER DISCONNECTION

Leonardo da Vinci didn't play tennis, but the king eclectic of his time related to how it should be played when he said, "…like a sailor who enters a ship without a helm or compass, and who can never be certain whither he is going."

How do you dial-in your shot trajectories and bounce points if you're without a "flight plan"? How do you correct errors if you're unaware of precisely what your shot's "flight" characteristics were supposed to be? This is precisely when you start choking – holding your breath for dear life and hoping you don't miss.

Conversely, how can you be in a good shot-making position when you're not observing an opponent's margin-to-the-net and its accompanying trajectory and, as a result in part, where their shot is going to bounce?

The court, particularly in singles, is very forgiving. An aircraft carrier deck laterally, and vertically unlimited since no one is crossing and picking-off your somewhat high-over-the net shots intended to create depth. That doubles reference makes it quite another story.

Rogue poachers abound, and the hitting lanes are primarily cross court and 50% less forgiving than in singles, alleys included. Simply being consistently cognizant – that means every single shot struck – of intended ball flight "paths" in relation to the net, and how they convert to spotting the ball on the court, will elevate your game .5 on the NRTP scale in a matter of hours. Now you're making any needed adjustments on the fly and nipping in the bud those bad patches, which can cost you a close match.

Know the margins that you're playing within. Again, visualize them by *thinking in pictures*. Use the net and the lines as reference points, always creating safety and room for error without stifling aggressiveness.

More than anything, unless it's a total mismatch in playing skill, it's you, not them, who determine the level of your performance, which you have total control over.

PREPARING TO START THE POINT:
Serving and Receiving

Fully cognizant of its importance, I couldn't help but take note of the meticulous pre-pitch routine of New York Yankee veteran Andy Pettitte - always clutch in the big moments – during a past World Series, and weigh-in some more as it relates to tennis. At the same time it was equally interesting to observe the pre-hit routines of the star players who were facing him. The idiosyncratic patterned rituals, always performed move-by-move in precisely the same order, collectively leading up to the very fleeting moment when the ball is released at high speed, and the batter attempts to put it in play (or out of play – home run) from a mere 60'6" away, or choose not to. It's that classic mano-a-mano moment of truth again.

Upon receiving the ball from the catcher for the next pitch, Pettitte immediately proceeds to immerse himself in his intricate ritual – unique to him – leading up to his next delivery, all aimed at creating a confident and familiar comfort zone from which to throw.

First, catching the ball from the catcher. Then the same every time round about, no hurry walk back to the mound and then onto the rubber. The multiple tugs at different parts of his uniform and cap. The shoulder shrugging. The ball in glove placement below his sight line and in front of his body while reading the sign from the catcher. The deep breath. The focused moment of visualizing the intended pitch's speed, trajectory, and location. And finally, the coiling up of his body and the fully committed, no self-doubt release of the pitch. This all taking place simultaneously with the hitter performing his own rituals to ready himself.

Sound familiar? The exact same scenario takes place in tennis between the server and the receiver or returner, and in about the same time frame. At the tour level the depth of these rituals are readily apparent – think Rafael Nadal's shorts "tug," or the Novak Djokovic's extended ball bouncing to name just two.

These guys do not dare leave home without them, but do not confuse this with superstition. Not the same! Yet, these kinds of rituals, which are also absolutely necessary for you to perform your best before serving or returning, are often vague and inconsistent in club players at best, and in between point time, worse yet, is mostly picking up balls and not much more in terms of preparation to play the next point.

Rituals are defined by Webster as "a customarily repeated act or action or series of acts." They are very much acquired habits, that in sports, and life, create a sense of well-being and purpose as one prepares to embark on a given activity or task. Do you not brush your teeth in the same fashion every single time? Do you not put your clothes on in the same order every single morning to start the day? These learned habits are ritualistic in nature, and are most beneficial in life and especially in sport where performing finite motor skills under pressure is the order of the day.

On the court, once any given point ends, the preparation leading up to a positive start of the next one begins with self-belief for both the server and the returner. From the server's perspective it starts with taking one's time gathering the balls.

Do not rush mindlessly helter skelter from point to point. Haste still makes waste in any venue. Always exhibit a positive body language – those observing should not be able to discern whether you have won the point or not! At the same time the process of deciding upon the speed, spin, and trajectory over the net - by thinking in pictures, or by visualizing your intended "flight plan" – begins and is finalized for your first serve as you approach the line. If you've seen any televised tennis recently the computerized line calling system, Hawkeye, perfectly illustrates the path of any ball in question through a thick yellow line, with the court as background (not coincidentally the ball color), from shot in question that traces its trajectory from impact to the in-or-out bounce point, and then continues on a bit farther after the bounce illustrating the shot's angle of ascent as well.

Then there's the settling-in to your serving position, the deep breath to relax, and further visualization reinforcement – picturing a successful serve before you launch it. Now the rhythmic ball bouncing to relax further – please, don't do Djokovic – followed by the ball-on-racket rhythmic rocking of some kind to get the left and right arm in sync along with the entire body, and the final look across the net visualization before launching one's service motion with total commitment or zero self-doubt.

The receiver's routine is very much the same. The gathering of balls for the server as necessary. The walk-up to the desired returning position at a comfortable, easy pace. The energizing in place – the revving of the engine if you will – by skipping laterally foot-to-foot. Then the settling into the return position featuring a rhythmic side-to-side upper body movement – including a slight shifting of weight from foot-to-foot that mimics the hip-shoulder rotation needed to prepare the racket once the serve is actually struck. Simultaneously, visualizing both the intended return – flight plan again - from the forehand wing, and from the backhand side as well.

Embrace the fact that the serve and the return are the only shots that you have plenty of time to pre-visualize, all others are on the fly - "Chess on the run," according to the late novelist and tennis enthusiast David Foster Wallace.

These actions and thoughts take place, ideally, in precisely the same sequence on each and every point, i.e. the term "rituals." They will pay big dividends if you develop your very own routines and stick with them religiously – lean on them, believe in them!

Take a moment sometime soon and observe the best ball strikers on Earth – see Tennis Channel or, better yet, attend a tour event in your area - going through their own elaborate and idiosyncratic rituals prior to starting their points.

Also take special note of the always positive in-between-point body language and the on-a-mission game faces! Call it a cheat sheet of sorts to bolster your ball striking game and enhance your overall chance for success mentally-emotionally as well.

Ready. Set. Go!

Relax – It's Just a Rally Ball

Far too often club players find themselves uncomfortable and apprehensive when locked in a backcourt cross court exchange in doubles for no good reason. Relax! It's just a "rally ball." Don't sweat it. There's nothing wrong with being willing to stalemate an opponent from the back of the court. Stalemating isn't losing, as so many wrongly seem to perceive in the heat of battle, it's actually a winning strategy! A message is sent that you do not give away points through panicked, unforced, unnecessary errors by insecurely trying to force a square peg into the first round hole in sight as quickly as possible.

Demonstrating to opponents that you are unflappable, and not prone to impatience and impulsiveness at the 3rd or 4th ball, puts tremendous pressure on them, an invitation if you will, for them to come up with the goods prematurely. Temp them to make the first move. Let them play. Let them get antsy. Believe me, it's as satisfying as hitting a winner to hang tough while continuously pushing their self-destruct button.

What fun!

An ideal variation on this theme is to recognize when the approaching ball is a particularly inviting opportunity for you, a ball that's going to be right in your strong side wheelhouse. By increasing your racket speed through the ball ever so slightly – say 10-15% max – you'll be able to strike a more penetrating ball, delivered with stealth, hopefully deep or at an opportune angle. Since they will absolutely fail to recognize the subtle change in your swing rate, they will be completely surprised by the extra penetration off the bounce.

In addition, your partner at the net in doubles, cognizant of what is transpiring – that the opponent is about to have their hands full - is now free to roam unencumbered and poach aggressively. Another message sent. Double whammy!

Go ahead and observe almost any match, at almost any level, anywhere in clubland. These matches are not won with brilliant shot making, they are lost through impatience and the over the top, unrealistic shot selection that always accompanies it.

This is so easy to achieve once committed, you could even hum along the Simon & Garfunkel lyric simultaneously, "Slow down, you're movin' too fast, ...cruisn' along and feelin' groovy."

Letting Them Play for Peak Performance in Clubland

Have you ever noticed that even after you have warmed-up like a champ, making very few errors along with a high percentage of practice serves in, you can then proceed to play a match riddled with unforced errors from start to finish? If that's a "yes" read on.

In a good warm-up you expect the ball to come back over the net. In fact you want it to. That's your mind set. After all, you're trying to hit as many shots as possible in the allotted time to hopefully dial in your true game.

Yet, all too often, players unconsciously change that mind set once the match begins. They stop playing *with* the individual across the net, and begin playing *against* them. Why? Because they now become outcome driven instead of performance driven.

Begin to recognize that the essential difference between warming-up and match play is that now you're keeping score. That's it. It's still just a game, not a life or death struggle. The elevated pressure you feel, particularly at the beginning of a match, but at pivotal times in the match as well, is a product of the "with vs against" transformation. The square pegs you're now producing no longer fit into the round holes you successfully dialed in during the warm-up, and you're in for an exercise in frustration.

My personal mind set is this: a) I expect the ball to come back, b) I don't even mind! And that goes for doubles as well as singles. The minute I become delusional in my expectations – setting unrealistic shot making goals and/or deserting the present for the future or the past – I become an error machine. After all, this is the game I have arrived with, so I'm going to be true to it. Of course I'm going to play within my capabilities regarding pace of shot and margin to both the net and the lines in order to play consistently. And sure, I'll strike every ball as cleanly as possible – as if it's the last one I will ever have the opportunity of hitting. I will not try to make winners! I will remain relentless in making appropriate placements instead, defend the court ferociously, and let the chips ultimately fall where they may.

You must be willing to engage the opposition if you're going to have a fighting chance of prevailing in the end. They will make numerous gifts to you with their own unforced errors if you give them half a chance. All you have to do is turn on the Tennis Channel and observe professional players "trading" in a long neutral exchange until one player begins to gain an advantage, and then typically works that advantage, without rushing, to a favorable conclusion. And these are the best tennis players on the planet!

So, at the end of the day, if you're secure enough to let them play, and go with the natural on-court flow, then you will have a great opportunity to play your best and that's what you should be asking of your Self.

Not so amazingly, you'll increase your wins and reduce your losses as well.

Smart Shots

An often occurring talking point with both lesson clients and club members is my previously mentioned racket(s). They are clearly very old, their beat-up appearance featuring badly scuffed bumpers along with chipped and fading paint a dead giveaway. Instead of explaining why I choose to wield an antiquated stick with its "intellifiber" tech, I simply point out the small, now barely legible marketing slogan at the top of the frame: "smarter racquet ~ better game."

A laugh is always shared without any further explanation. Truth be told it's the closest feel, albeit stiffer, to the wood sticks that I grew up with and honed my game on. Always the coach, it then becomes a perfect segue for me to happily offer some unsolicited advice that's core to just about every club player's game, advice that's coupled with why these old rackets appear to still work pretty well: Play aggressively but patiently, play with controllable pace, play with safe margins to the lines and the net, impart optimal spin, i.e. smart shots.

Yes, low risk tennis reaps the greatest dividends - not trying harder, trying better. When necessary, remind yourself on changeovers to stick to your game plan if you're getting too amped up, and going too big with small, high risk margins leading to far too many giveaway, unforced errors...a trap easily fallen into.

At a seminar I once presented - translated from English! - on teaching mental toughness skills at an Austrian Coaches Conference in Innsbruck, I recall the immediate pen-to-paper reaction I observed among the approximately 100 professionals courtside upon declaring right out of the gate that I believed visualization was the #1 inner toughness component, the one that ignites and enables all else, especially the core advice mentioned earlier.

I'm still drinking that Kool-Aid® years later and encourage all my students to embrace it, stick with it, and trust it. No if and buts about it. And what's the worst possible resulting scenario? No guarantees you'll get the W, but you'll absolutely play better.

In a variation on the aforementioned racket slogan, how about this instead; "smarter player ~ better game."

Consider one of the Merriam-Webster dictionary's definitions of smart: "containing a microprocessor for limited computing capability." Exactly. We're talking about playing tennis, not sending a probe to Mars. It truly is not rocket science.

Processing the situation presented by the incoming shot - fast recognition, then visualizing the correct response equaling shot selection: $r + v = ss$. It doesn't take an inordinate amount of personal computing power to accomplish that simple task. Think that cave man thing and commit to doing it.

In contrast there are far too many who, particularly when under pressure, strike balls hoping the tennis gods will look over them. Hoping they don't screw up! Really? That's not your inner microprocessor malfunctioning, that's your microprocessor not functioning at all.

Avoid at all costs: Ready, fire, aim.

Get smart. Stay smart. Play better, a lot better.

Playing Scared

Just about every time I walk through the courts during a league match I see players playing scared, afraid to make a mistake. This is not what "playing within yourself" means.

This happens to even the stars in professional football every Sunday, mostly to kickers, quarterbacks, and coaches as well on game day.

These are individuals making millions of dollars for their expertise and talent but who, like you, are also under pressure, in their arena to win or, unlike you, lose their job. The Dallas Cowboys head coach, Jason Garrett, took it on the chin in 2014 from the well-respected football pundits for poor game management.

"Jason is coaching scared with a defeatist attitude," said one. Another noted, "The pressure has gotten to Jason, and he's really over-coaching." Tennis player translation: too cautious, over thinking, pressing.

When Garrett eventually responded to this criticism he declared, in so many words, that the best players are indeed the mentally toughest players, and the best teams are the mentally toughest teams. How about that comment from the physically tough, violent, and rough and tumble football culture-

First of all relax, everyone feels pressure, whether it's internally or externally produced. It's not going away, ever! What did the all-time great jazz musician, Miles Davis, say about performance anxiety? "If you're not nervous, you ain't listenin'."

That's a good nervous.

So, on the court, you'd better get used to it and learn counter measures to deal with it comfortably, head-on in order to neutralize it as much as possible within the performance equation.

How? By becoming a shot-in and shot-out, point-in and point-out, and day-in and day-out:

- audible breather
- crystal clear visualizer
- keen ball tracker
- energized foot worker
- relaxed gripper
- early racket prepper

- free stroker

- possessor of both a positive game face at ball-on-racket moment, and a positive body language as well.

That's it. It's that simple, but, as we all know, and I regularly and readily admit, not that easy, particularly if you do not make these core components an integral part of your game every single day - beginning in the warm-up - whether it's a team practice, a friendly doubles, a ball machine session, solo serving practice, or a league or you're not nervous, you tournament match.

Another match play paralyzer is over-respecting opponents, what I refer to as the "non-swagger." These opposing players are across the net from you because they are, give or take a little, the same NTRP level as you. So why the defeatist perception going-in that they're probably better than you?

Back to reminding you to "play within yourself," exactly what does that mean? Swinging the racket through the ball only as fast as you can control on a consistent basis. No more, no less! It also refers to allowing yourself safe margins for error with regard to both the lines and the net while always remaining aggressive. And, never to be underestimated, if your primary focus is, "I have to win this," or, "I can't lose that," you will forever be relegated to not playing your best tennis, and match play improvement will be elusive at best.

Fearlessly engaging opponents - versus the all too common avoidance mode - and letting the chips, again, fall where they may, is the very most you can do.

Icing the Server
When Receiving In The Big Moments

Professional football is mostly perceived as a very physical, violent game. All you have to do is YouTube "NFL violent hits" and you'll see what I mean, not to mention the recent recognition of the "concussion problem." However football, despite the carnage, also has myriad psychological elements to it as well. One that has recently come to the forefront is the practice of team's overt effort in attempting to rattle the state of mind of the opposing team's field goal kicker. The tactic is referred to as "icing," and involves the defensive team calling a time-out at the very last moment prior to the kicker, who is already queued up physically, mentally, emotionally, and ready to attempt the kick with the outcome of the game often on the line.

Studies have proven that it is very effective in that kickers on average, when "iced," drop-off in their normal success rate by 15% - 20%! Nothing like disrupting the kicker's preparation ritual by shutting him down and making him wait another few minutes, restart his ritual, and give him time to think some more about the ramifications of failure with 52 teammates, who, unlike the kickers, get their uniforms dirty, depending on the outcome.

In tennis, particularly in the important moments, the server experiences the same kind of pressure as the field goal kicker – the parallel is striking - particularly on points that are pivotal in deciding a game or particularly in a match's ultimate outcome.

Tennis rules junkies love to spout off about how the receiver must play to the pace of the server. True, but only if that's a "reasonable" pace of the server which is most often left out of the equation, i.e. you are not expected to resign yourself to being either purposely or inadvertently "quick served" prior to being fully settled in with your own return "walk-up" and ritual.

During these big moments make it a point to take that little bit of extra time – that's reasonable extra time without violating the rules of sportsmanship – and make the server wait that extra ten seconds or so while you legitimately, for example, take a moment to fiddle with your strings, adjust your cap or visor while toweling your forehead off with your wristband, or take the long way around to your actual receiving court position.

Note: Answering cell phone – which I've actually witnessed in league play - as depicted in the accompanying image is not an option.

At the same time, since the scenario is that it's a close match that is potentially up for grabs, you'll have a better opportunity to settle your Self to the task at hand while you are controlling the pacing, or time in between points, and giving the server a little ice time simultaneously.

Football teams actually rehearse icing their own kickers in practice so that they can experience dealing with it and render it ineffective. Back on the tennis court, if you reverse roles and put yourself in the server's sneakers, and you're being iced, you can learn countermeasures from two of football's best pressure proof kickers.

Joe Nedney of the 49ers and Atlanta's Matt Bryant, two of the best, embrace very different but effective strategies that work for them. Bryant typically drapes a towel over his helmet, once back on the sidelines during the time-out, and doesn't even think about the game! Instead his focus goes to his family which he explains: "I try to find a happy place." Nedney's approach is more combative: "You want to ice me? Great. You're still going to lose the game and you're going to have one less time out. That's the only mentality you can have."

Personally, I can recall a close match, in my final year of tournaments years ago - I was aspiring to be #1 on the Florida USTA 35's circuit and doing well - with a respected opponent of some reputation. This pompous jerk, as it turned out that day, repeatedly insisted on walking 1-2 courts away – we were the only match playing on a bank of 4 courts at the time – to retrieve the third ball when I was serving whenever the opportunity presented itself. This guy invented icing! When I confronted him in no uncertain terms he flipped his lid – I had apparently violated his presumed sanctity – and he, in a tantrum, demanded an on-court referee. I was fortunate, I then did not have to come up with a solution that day in dealing with such blatant gamesmanship. The referee went ahead and enforced that he play to a reasonable pace leading to his undoing.

Nonetheless, pressure in sport is universally experienced. Even curlers have to deal with it – okay, that's not really a sport is it. Never mind. Yet, the term "mental toughness" was, in part, born out of it. Unlike the above described incident, you'll have to be cognizant of coming up with a solution to deal with icing positively when you're the one being made to wait. Conversely, you'll also be in control of those instances when you have a legit opportunity to fairly apply a bit of the icing tactic onto them.

Always keep in mind that it's your court, your tennis balls, and the opponent is there for your playing pleasure. Be selfish but also be fair minded and a good sportsman. But, take charge and stay in charge. Buy them a coke later.

 # Top 10 Stress Reducers

10. Practice the skills – new or improved – worked on in a lesson before your next match, including friendlies.

9. Practice, minimally, at least one time between every two matches, including friendlies.

8. Stay in the present – one ball, one point, one game, one set at a time. Don't fret over past mistakes or a daunting score line.

7. Take your time between points, particularly when misfiring and the tendency is to rush to begin the next point to right yourself.

6. Do not stand still in between points. Keep pacing back and forth and then "energize-up" just prior to the start of the point whether receiving, serving, or positioned at the net in doubles.

5. Do not "get set" or "plant" when making your shots. Take the final foot-working step - "setting up" - while in the act of hitting... same time frame. Step 'n strike.

4. Maintain a relatively low grip tension in the ready position and through shot impact. Do not strangle the racket.

3. Breathe – inhale just before you launch your racket into the ball, exhale through the point of impact and follow through with a relaxed jaw. Discover your own signature sound.

2. Watch the ball into your racket, then remain connected to it in its outgoing path with a still head – no bobble-heading or swivel-heading. Only the ball – not the opponent, not the court, both of which are best viewed in your periphery only. You'll then perceive the action as taking place more slowly.

1. Visualize your shot intentions every single time – both directionally and marginally to the net. Picture its intended trajectory over the net. The power of visualization on a tennis court is immense. See success in your mind's eye.

Collectively, these 10 steps will be instrumental in reducing any over consciousness during play. You may recall a previous reference, commonly made in earlier times, regarding individuals playing at a level well beyond their norm: "He's unconscious."

Exactly.

SELF-TALK: Good, Bad or Indifferent

Everyone does it in one form or another, at every level of the game, particularly in a heated, closely contested match that's up for grabs. You've seen it. You've heard it. You've mostly likely done it.

Certainly there have been a few stoic ones at the top of the game that you never heard a peep out of, nor, for that matter, seldom displayed any accompanying facial or body language, positive or negative. Bjorn Borg immediately comes to mind. Chris Evert and Arthur Ashe were other notable examples from an earlier time.

Today's closest representative would have to be Roger Federer, who seldom reveals anything to his opponents and, almost without exception, just goes about his business.

Negative self-talk is seldom, if ever, productive. Only John McEnroe, in his heyday, could go on a complete out-of-control rant, at himself, and then somehow get right back to playing brilliantly on the very next point. Turning a high negative into a high positive is tricky stuff. Nonetheless, in his book, *You Cannot Be Serious*, he indicates he would have been far better off without all the McBrat outbursts.

Do not fall victim to that on your court. It's tempting. In the spirit of something I recently said, in a different but related context, to one of my players who was insisting on playing right on top of the baseline like Andre Agassi used to; "You're no Agassi." Gotta be real. So lose any histrionics born out of unrealistic play and gain control of your emotions since you're no McEnroe either.

Interestingly, what's the biggest difference in Andy Murray's game since Ivan Lendl, the sour, dour Czech legend began coaching him about a year ago? Not the ball striking to any noticeable degree. Yes, his physical fitness is right there at the top, but that's not the defining component either. It's Murray ditching all the gut wrenching drama for all to see with all the emotionally exhausting, roller coasting baggage. It's the above the neck fitness that's made the difference.

The judge and jury in you always gets in the way of the player within. Tim Galwey, in his groundbreaking book *The Inner Game*, was, as noted earlier, the first to really articulate our conflicting on-court personas with his "Self-One" and "Self-Two" depictions. One being the free flowing player just doing it, completely unencumbered mentally and emotionally, trusting and accepting the game they arrived with despite any flaws. The other being the unforgiving, judgmental, unrealistic goal setting, vitriol-spewing, bad twin who's never satisfied with himself and thus, can never really succeed.

These individuals tend to carry-on audible, running conversations with themselves, sometimes expletive loaded, after seemingly every point lost, whether on an error or even in response to an opponent's winner. One could call it a bad temper. Too simple. Another could say it's a deflection of embarrassment over the shots they're missing, implying to all in view, including the opponent, that they never miss those shots.

I'm embarrassed when I witness these players conversing with themselves in the 3rd person: "Oh c'mon Kenny, you never miss this many shots," as if it's the first time it has ever happened.

Jimmy Connors, well known for his uncanny ability to incite positive support from a crowd, never talked negatively to himself, only the officials. He did engage in chatter with his fans in response to their cheers and urging such as, "I'm trying as hard as I can." Or, "This is what they want; this is what they come for," while yelling into a courtside microphone. Best of all: "He's going to have to pass me 62 times," referencing his attacking the net style of play in one of his memorable U.S. Open triumphs against an opponent 15 plus years his junior.

"Shut-up and compete," isn't that what the noted corporate consultant Tom Peters used to dispense for boatloads of money when preaching his gospel to middle-managers at the IBMs of the world?

Positive self-talk is another matter entirely. You see, and quietly hear – even lip read – some of the best pro tour players having motivating, solution-oriented conversations with themselves to stay on task no matter what the adversity they're facing. Some are completely silent, even lip reading produces nothing, but their body and facial language reveal that they're never going away.

As much as I do not like listening to Maria Sharapova, I really like watching her. Not so much in the point, but between points when she, without fail, positions herself about halfway between the baseline and the court's end, back to the net, staring into and fiddling with her strings, huddling positively with herself for a few seconds prior to turning and walking purposely, all business, expressionless steely-eyed, back to the baseline to serve or return the next point. Never a deviation in her re-booting.

Modeling your on-court demeanor and style of competing after one of the non-fist pumping, determined, undeterred quiet ones – think Giles Simon and Simona Halep - is your best path to greater success, self-satisfaction and game improvement. And a little class. Why would you do otherwise?

Jaw Dropping

No, I'm not referring to what occurs after witnessing a truly amazing event, one that was so incredible that it was both figuratively and literally a jaw dropper. I am referring to the ideal manner in which you position your jaw when on the court in general, and more specifically to the moment at which you're striking the ball - slack jawed (see image).

Consider for a moment those individuals who find it necessary to wear a mouth guard to negate their serious teeth grinding response to stressful dream states. Even if you, like most, do not find a mouth guard necessary, I'm sure that on occasion you wake up with the realization that you experienced what might have been an anxious night In dream land.

Next time you're walking through your dub or park to your court take a moment and observe player's faces at the shot making moment. What you see will, first and foremost, amaze you, and then probably elicit a chuckling smile. They'll be players fiercely baring their teeth, ones with eyes bulging, ones with eyes squinting, and many with jaws held tight with the lower portion often misaligned to one side. Some of these facial expressions are reminiscent of threatened characters in chainsaw movies.

Even players who breathe - exhaling through their stroke to promote relaxation - can be victims of excessive muscle tension specifically triggered by the signature sound that they make, especially in club land.

That audible sound should, in its "melody" if you will, facilitate relaxation instead, not the heightened fight-or-flight state our ancient ancestors experienced at the site of a large predator bearing down on them. It should not draw you into an in-between-zone that's either too tentative or too jacked-up.

The signature sounds of today's tour professionals are, interestingly, all over the board from shrieking to more combative grunts to more serene and even keeled tones to the mostly inaudible.

I still clearly recall just about everyone naively poking fun at Pete Sampras' ever present slack jawed state both during and in between points back in his prime. They didn't get it folks. Perhaps they were too conditioned previously by the Connors-McEnroe sounds and sights of fury. I have no idea whether or not Pete learned that, along with the relaxed tonal quality of his exhalations, or it just came naturally along with his easy going manner. I suspect the latter. I do know that he was, and still is on the Senior Tour, an unbelievably good role model regarding that component's role in enhancing one's overall mental toughness in a game fraught with never ending stressful situations.

Try it. You'll see and feel the difference.

Playing In the Wind

Upon first viewing Rafael Nadal's movement, both to the ball and in defending the court against Andy Murray in the recent Indian Wells final, I immediately thought that his problematic knee must be acting up. Rafa was a non-stop shuffling, stutter-stepping machine on a mission. Surely, I decided, he must be hurting to such an extent that he can't run normally. Then the announcing crew let it be known that the players were experiencing swirling wind gusts up to 45 mph in the sunken stadium.

Murray, perhaps the smoothest mover in the game today, is a glider who barely appears to touch the court, an incarnation of perhaps the smoothest ever, the "Big Cat," Miroslav Mecir, mentioned previously. Yet, in the conditions being produced in the California desert, this normally exceptional ability is not rewarded in the wind without serious adjustments.

Even with coach Uncle Toni not present, Nadal's team had him impeccably prepared to deal effectively with the challenge: 1) never stop moving your feet to adjust to each balls varying and erratic flight, 2) stay aggressive with shot pace to minimize the winds effect, 3) watch the ball *exceptionally well* all the way into the racket, 4) keep the balls safely away from the lines for extra safe margins. Nadal won "easily" 6-1, 6-2 over the currently recognized world #2.

My hometown, coastal Punta Gorda, Florida takes no backseat to the desert when it comes to having to play in the wind. Accept the fact that you will be hard pressed to play your A-game. Know going in that you're in for a physically punishing day if you're truly committed to following Nadal's lead. If it is doubles that you're playing keep it simple and be willing to engage in conservative cross court exchanges to repeatedly give less physically and mentally resilient opponents another chance to give you a free point with an unforced error.

Love to watch them unravel!

Andre Agassi once stated: "I don't mind playing in the wind because everyone else hates it." Taking the ball early didn't hurt.

RESPECTING THE GAME:
Top 10 Do's & Don'ts

Tennis is a global game that is infused with tradition. Etiquette and protocol - born out of respecting the game and those you are playing it with and against - are both expected and required to maximize a positive experience for all, including spectators impacting it.

Too often, out of ignorance, things happen that are outside of the realm of optimal player interaction, i.e. conducting oneself with class, and can border on poor sportsmanship.

Here are a few friendly reminders to abide by:

- Know the proper pre-match warm-up protocol.

- The server is responsible for announcing the score before every point begins.

- Absolutely do not try to gain any unfair advantage in line calling by making statements like: "I think it was out" or "I'm not sure, can we play it over?" If there is any reasonable doubt then the ball is good. Period. End of story!

- Make all line calls immediately, clearly, and audibly.

- Avoid interrupting play by returning clearly out serves. Either let them go or softly direct them into the net near the net post. One exception: the serve is so close to the line you're already committed to returning it, but then realize at impact that it was slightly out. Make the call as quickly as possible and apologize for putting the ball in play.

- If your opponents play an out ball keep playing. It's their call, not yours.

- If you play an out ball, but it's too late to make the call in good conscience, the point is yours if the opponents stop playing because they thought it was out. It's your call, not theirs.

- When returning an errant ball to an adjacent court wait until that court's point is completed and announce, "Ct. 3, coming, or incoming." Do not just send it in indiscriminately.

- There is no additional practice allowed once a match is underway. That includes gathering balls after a changeover and firing in a few practice serves while everyone else is getting a drink or toweling off. Also included is players forgoing their changeover time so they can have a quick hit.

- When a spectator of another match applaud all good play. It's always impressive to witness Venus and Serena's mother doing just that. If your teammates, or friends, win a well-played point that ends on a bad error by the opposition always qualify your support with "good point." Cheering big time after the opponent's every error is best left for the world stage. It's considered boorish to engage in that level of partisanship in club land where you're probably going to interact with those same individuals going forward. Why create hard feelings?

Hopefully, at the end of the day, you've been proactive, not combative, in attempting to educate any fellow players not with the program. In a worst case scenario with those who do not get it, and are not interested in getting it, do not let their errant ways get to you and disrupt your play. Always maintain your mental toughness- cool, calm, and collected - and use the situation to your advantage.

My favorite among Einstein's "Three Rules of Work" mentioned before is the following succinct mind set: "In difficulty lies opportunity."

Making Your Lessons Stick

There are a number of tired, old adages that are tossed around clubs everywhere. "You'll get worse after a lesson," is one that tennis pros shake their collective head at and is a bunch of nonsense as well. But it often becomes a reality due to the way in which player's follow-up after their lessons, particularly if their bad habits were especially idiosyncratic and they had become somewhat adept at managing these inefficiencies.

The best athletes are always the worst offenders, which makes perfect sense in that they are the best at managing inefficient play due to their exceptional natural ability.

So, what is it that players do immediately after receiving coaching? They go right out and play, expecting an immediate wholesale change in their technique, instead of diligently practicing - on the ball machine, with a hitting partner, or even drop-hitting – what they've learned.

Naturally, they quickly, under the pressure of match play, revert back to their state of secure mediocrity, albeit secure – the reason for scheduling the lesson in the first place - which is where they will reside for the rest of their club "career" if they fail to change their ways.

It's very frustrating when one of these same individuals goes out of their way to inform their pro that their game "is now worse," despite the obvious success that they experienced – and happily recognized - with their new/altered techniques during the lesson.

I know I cringe in frustration when it happens to me, and it does, even though I know I clearly and quickly identified – after 50 years of teaching experience with thousands of players – the problem(s). This is my fault, since I neglected to make sure that they understood the need for practice first immediately after.

It's paramount for all coaches to finish every lesson with a fervent directive that they're going to need to practice hundreds of reps to erase the old muscle memory and establish the new on their, if you will, 'hard drive' before jumping back into the fray. You cannot think about mechanics. You have to just feel it. That takes practice, and lots of it if you're serious about becoming a better player. That's why you need the reps.

It's always interesting to note that tour players are totally dedicated to practicing constantly to both maintain their skills and to continue to improve. Yet, club players, who claim that they want to get better, treat practice like the mercurial ex-NBA super star Allen Iverson. He once said, in response to a question at a press conference after a loss on a day when he missed the pre-game shoot-around, "Practice? Practice?? You talking about practice???"

But let's face it, you're probably not possessing the world class athletic gifts of an Allen Iverson on a tennis court.

Commit to doing the right thing after your next lesson. You'll reap the rewards and really get your money's worth too.

Never Too Late for *Older Dogs*

I'm back on my soap box encouraging older players – and demonstrating to them on court every day - that, yes, older dogs can learn new tricks. This after overhearing a couple of closed minded naysayers proclaiming that you cannot, that you are resigned to a flawed game if you're of a certain age. Are these folks victims of their own lame acceptance of mediocrity, or just too lazy to really try?

I thought I had put this misperception to bed a few years ago in my first book, *More Than Just the Strokes*. Apparently these guys didn't read it, or they refuse to open their minds up to the possibilities if they did.

Allow me to remind those in doubt that none other than former world #1s Jimmy Connors, Pete Sampras, and Andre Agassi disagree with such a negative stance. Connors said, while dominating the Seniors Tour a few years back, "I think I can strike the ball better now than I could 15 years ago. And I think I anticipate better than I did in the past." Agassi, according to his coach, Darren Cahill, was still more than holding his own at the end of his career because "he never trained [practiced] to maintain, he trained to improve." And Pistol Pete, not long after he retired, offered, "Honestly, I think the best tennis I played was when I was older. I was ten times the player as I got older than when I was really dominating." Okay? Got it? You can keep getting better despite the physical realities that come with chronological advancement.

Still not on board, and, as a result, warming-up for two minutes at most so that you "won't get too tired to play," or announcing, "let's not waste any more time warming-up," and then proclaiming "f.b.i." to start the match?

Okay, here's some more evidence.

You may recall the 80+ year's young player I noted earlier, a top 10 ITF 80 & over player, who works out with me 1-2 times per week in the Northeast summers to stay sharp and to, yes, continue to improve, which she most definitely has by being recognized by the USTA to represent our country in international team play.

There's another 80+ player that I'll be working with tomorrow, a recreational player, who this summer developed, I kid-you-not, a one-handed topspin backhand that she said she wanted to learn after watching Roger Federer's on television.

And then there's also a slightly older gentleman who has acquired, and relishes, an uncanny backhand overhead over the past couple of summers right in front of me.

Who knew!

189

In the news not long ago we learned that 61 year old marathon swimmer, Diana Nyad, failed in her attempt to swim from Cuba to Key West – that's if you can even refer to her effort as a failure. This was her second attempt, the first, 32 years ago when she was 29, also ended without fulfillment. After having to give it up after 29 hours in the water – still mentally strong but physically gassed - she addressed the press candidly: "I'm almost 62 years old. I'm standing here at the prime of life. I think this is the prime, when one reaches this age. You still have a body that's strong, but now you have a better mind." I had the pleasure of meeting her on an airplane back when she was doing television commentary for CBS at the US Open. Her effort and comments came as no surprise at all to me after that one conversation with her. She exuded always aspiring higher.

Yeah, sure you're slower, less flexible, less powerful, and somewhat vision impaired compared to your youth, or even 10 years ago. So what? Does that mean you have to resign your Self to standing pat with your game? I think not! You can still continue to improve your ball striking skills, anticipations skills, strategy and tactics, mental toughness, and more

So, c'mon, it's time to lose the tired "old dogs" cliché once and for all, get to work, and have even more fun meeting the challenge.

Note: Nyad finally succeeded in her quest not long ago.

Why Coaching

Because athletes – amateur and professional alike – in all sports, particularly the individual ones, often misperceive their performance, both the failures and the successes. Nothing new there. Worse yet, they can be in denial and, amazingly, simultaneously without viable solutions.

In his recent book, *Perplexities of Consciousness*, Eric Schwitzgebal contends that our powers of introspection are not always an accurate recounting of events, and that in reality our conscious experience of being on the inside is often confused and contradictory. Just ask both doubles teams to reconstruct the points regarding the correct game score – 40-30 or 30-40 for example. And that's just regarding the score line, never mind the mechanical nuances, or lack thereof, of that inside-out forehand you have trouble with.

But in club tennis, where everyone prefers the winning experience to the losing one, most go it alone without even periodic coaching or tune-ups. The resulting underachievement of their potential for better performances – the ability to more consistently make one's existing good shots and reduce the occurrences of one's bad shots - along with the burden of not really understanding the reasons for an off-day, or a prolonged slump where they're "plateauing," is extremely limiting.

Running Coach Terence Mahon believes that the biggest challenge of self-coaching is honestly evaluating how you're really doing. He said, "Athletes are used to looking at one day. But if you look at one day of training [playing], you are not seeing the whole map. Coaches are working off of the experience not only of that athlete but of many before them." And over many years.

It's a rarity on the professional tennis tour when an accomplished player is without a coach. But Jo-Wilfried Tsonga is doing just that lately. He parted ways with his coach in the middle of the 2011 campaign, and then enjoyed a resurgence in the season's second half which has afforded him an excellent chance to qualify for the final 8 showdown in London that year. An acrobatic, athletic player, it's believed that he made the change because he felt too reigned-in and "cookie-cuttered."

That can happen in club land as well, facilitated by well-intentioned one-way-is-the-only-way coaches.

In the end it's paramount that club pros challenge – if retained - player's erroneous self-evaluations on why they are struggling, for example, with their high backhand mechanics or second serve mind set. Simultaneously, players with eons less experience and game knowledge must be open minded, avoid defensiveness and being argumentative, and realize that the coach is with them, not against them. If it's not a good player-coach fit, then either party should take initiative and suggest a new direction with no hard feelings.

By the way, if the pro-coach is inept at proficiently demonstrating any aspect of ball striking mechanics, or unable to impart the mental-emotional nuances of the game, that's another red flag indicating it's time to move on.

But the coach also has a huge responsibility to not cross the line: Interfering with a player's natural, inner athletic approach to the game, their brain hard wiring, and the percentage breakdown of how they best receive instruction – visually (seeing it), auditorily (hearing it), kinesthetically (feeling it).

At the end of the day it still takes two to tango.

Practice, Practice, Practice

The number of frequent tennis players enjoying our athletic game across the nation, and worldwide as well - multiple millions, is impressive to say the least. Yet, despite their good intentions and regular commitment to the game, whether recreational or competitive, their typical lack of practice time is so frustrating since, in this instance, they are short changing themselves and their level of play.

Roger Federer, in the throes of a sub-par performance - for him – way back in the first 4 months of the 2009 campaign, explained that, besides any lingering effects of mononucleosis, his biggest set-back was a "lack of practice time." Are you with me so far? Arguably the most gifted tennis player of all time is regretting, and understanding, that not being able to practice as much as he was normally accustomed to took its toll.

Over the years many of the playing and coaching tennis legends, willing to share their considerable insights over a span of a couple of generations - some things do not change - have weighed-in on this subject.

Here's my Top 10 Sampling for you to consider for your game:

1. "Progress and improvement do not come in big bunches, they come in little pieces." - Arthur Ashe

2. "Practice may not make things perfect, but it sure makes things better." - Brad Gilbert

3. "Try to find a mix of stronger and weaker practice partners. Against weaker players, you can work on your weaknesses. Against the stronger players, you'll have to use your strengths." - Fred Stolle

4. "An hour of hard practice is better than going through the motions." - Pete Sampras

5. "Spend more time preparing and less time regretting." - Virginia Wade

6. "When I struggled with myself and had to build myself up, I did it on the practice court." - Margaret Smith Court

7. "Champions [at any level] keep playing until they get it right." - Billie Jean King

8. "There's no excuse for a poor serve - serving well is simply a matter of practice." - Pancho Gonzales

9. "If the pain of losing to people is greater than the pain of making changes, then by all means, make the changes." - Vic Braden

10. "Everyone needs a coach...who can see what you're doing when you cannot." - Pete Sampras

Again, back on the soap box, playing set after set, day after day, is not the way to achieve your personal best.

One of the definitions of practice is "to perform or work at repeatedly so as to become proficient."

And, yes, practice with the right person can be fun too!

Take Your Eye Off the Ball

I know what you're thinking. You cannot be serious! Take your eye *off* the ball? I'm talking about learning more about how to play the game by regularly observing how the sport's best players do it, and not the point. Unless you're a very accomplished and experienced player, you learn very little by watching tour level singles points unfold - you might not yet have the ball striking and movement skills to tap into that level of strategy and tactics - amounting to concentrating mostly on nothing more than the ball going back and forth. Nothing gained in terms of your own on-court performance, although just casually enjoying a well-played tennis match is cool too.

But, when taking in big time tennis, whether it's live - if you're fortunate enough to be attending an ATP/WTA event in your area - or simply on the tube, try taking the time and making an effort to isolate one player and singularly observe their technique, both above and below the waist. From that you can really improve your own game, even in the comfort of your living room, perhaps even with a cool refreshing drink in hand. Can't beat that.

Professional players certainly do put their own signature on their style of play, and good coaching encourages them to do that since tennis is most definitely not a cookie cutter game and has lots of room for athletic interpretation. Yet, you cannot miss the striking similarities from player to player, men or women: the relationship of the take back with the approaching ball, the perfectly timed split stepping, the open and closed hitting positions, the serve and return rituals, the service toss, how they run balls down and then recover effortlessly and right on time, the head-still ball tracking, the "one club only" grip changing, and the breathing (no please, not the screaming, not that!) to name a few of the essential core components of the game.

These, and others, are the difference makers between the good you and the bad you. Let's not even get into the ugly. There's no getting around them if you want to play your best and keep improving, even if you've witnessed firsthand the move from white balls to yellow ones.

Just take a look at world class player Marion Bartoli if you need convincing - the poster child of idiosyncratic style if there ever was one. Yet, these interpretive basics are the really important stuff, versus, for example, concentrating on by-product issues like "where's the 'right' place for my forehand follow through to *always* end up?," the nonsensical, one dimensional kind of crap espoused by some club pro talking heads with cookie cutters in hand.

And, at the same time it's too bad more tour doubles isn't aired, beyond the occasional Davis Cup and Fed Cup ties, since doubles is the most popular game worldwide. It would be all good for all if we could see more and more top flight doubles, and hopefully enjoy an antidote to seeing four clubbers on the court in that anti-model hybrid singles-doubles mode, or whatever it is, seen far too often.

Sure, it can prove to be a very fast game to follow, especially the men – think Bryan brothers, but it's still four players interacting in a space only 25% larger than the one for singles – just like you - so there's a lot going on. Positioning as a team always in motion is everything, which last I time I looked, was still a bit sketchy in the club scene.

Observing how it's done best, when possible - the way a team works seamlessly together in both defending the court and moving forward together on offense whenever the opportunity presents - will pay doubles dividends in your league too. Just make sure that your regular partner is sitting next to you when you watch and learn, or they'll be on your no-call list in no time flat.

Actively modeling your game after a particular tour player's game, or a particular doubles team, one that strikes a chord for how you'd love to be able to play, and always aspire to play, will bleed into your motor subconscious with empowering results. How's that for an opportunity?

Learning for nothing, lessons for free!

Summer School Courtside Crib Sheet

Trouble shooting your game in the heat of competition is not as easy as it sounds. The great Arthur Ashe, a Hall of Famer, was known to have kept notes in his racket bag which he would refer to on changeovers. Not a bad idea for serious club players who actually want to get better. No doubt it included key reminders regarding both what it took to play his own game well, and I suspect some thoughts on how to best deal with the opponent at hand.

Here's a Top Ten Crib Sheet to get you through when your game is not firing on all cylinders:

10. Did you arrive early enough to prepare both physically and mentally?

9. Are you pacing yourself between points or rushing around with your hair on fire?

8. Are you split stepping at every opponent's strike of the ball or standing lump like?

7. Is your racket loaded and prepared early enough or still in the holster?

6. Are you using loosening rituals on both serve and serve return or mimicking a robot?

5. Are you strangling your grip in fear or optimally relaxed?

4. Are you breathing at impact or holding your breath for dear life?

3. Are you visualizing your shots or just hoping for a good result?

2. Are you really watching the ball or only seeing it fleetingly through your periphery?

1. Did you remember to keep this list in your racket bag or did you leave it on the kitchen counter next to the grocery or hardware store list?

ARE YOU A THUDDER, A TWANGER, OR A PINGER: Racket Dampeners

It's very unusual to visit tennis courts in any setting and see players without one in their racket these days. The more popular term, "shock absorbers," coupled with the never ending tennis elbow stories that put players on the healing shelf, have popularized these little rubber accessories that are attached to the mains just below the cross strings at the racket's throat.

But do they actually reduce the string's vibrations to your arm, or, are they, more than anything else - as this article might be suggesting – just auditory input changers? The manufacturers, of course, claim every shock absorbing benefit known to mankind. More on that later.

In my own dampener lexicon "pingers" are those players who do not make use of them at all - particularly tour pros like Roger Federer among some others - resulting in a high pitched impact sound. "Twangers" use one of the many types of quarter size ones available that fit snugly between the two central main strings as previously noted – first popularized mainly by Pete Sampras with his O-ring" and utilized by numerous pros and club players alike - producing a medium pitched sound but only when the ball is struck in the sweet spot. "Thudders" prefer the worm like type - favored by a preponderance of club players but almost no tour pros - that thread through nearly all the main strings, yet still below the bottom cross string, delivering a low pitched sound in and out of the sweet spot.

Personally, although for a decade I've preferred the long bands, I recently switched to a small one for a quick check-in on my sweet spot consistency. Conclusion: It did make me a more acutely auditory aware of any off center strikes that would ping a bit, but I did switch back after a couple of weeks after deciding that, regardless of the sound, I became convinced that there really was some greater level of shock dampening benefit. Once a thudder, always a thudder?

Racket manufacturers have tried building them into the racket's grommet strips extending up from the throat piece - a hybrid of the smaller ones and the "worms" - in the form of inch long "string sleeves" for the center four mains as one example. Those applications were short lived.

Andre Agassi, during his breakout teenage years when he had the long fake locks, the jean shorts, and the bright graphic shirts, introduced tying a rubber band around the mains at the throat. I recall Head, his racket sponsor, actually packaging a facsimile for retail sale at one point. A special rubber compound originated from a Brazilian rubber plantation no doubt.

My own take on the topic is that they do have a dual effect, both in dampening some of the vibration, but, mostly, in altering the auditory input creating a perception of more solid, sweet spot ball striking.

On a more scientific note, in 1999 the prestigious Journal of Sports Medicine published a study on the topic: "The Effect of Tennis Racket String Vibration Dampers on Racket Handle Vibrations and Discomfort Following Impacts." Here's their bottom line: "Vibration traces from an accelerometer mounted on the racket handle revealed that string vibration dampers quickly absorbed high-frequency string vibration without attenuating the lower frequency frame vibration, in conclusion, we found no evidence to support the contention that string vibration dampers reduce hand and arm impact discomfort." Here's a bit more: "...damper mass is not significant compared with frame mass, so elastomeric dampers installed in the string mesh cannot absorb a significant amount of frame vibration energy." Key word being "significant."

So perhaps that's why Mr. Federer and other notables at the top find them completely unnecessary.

Nonetheless, I'm sticking with: If you think it works, then it does.

THE IMPOSSIBLE: Accelerating and Decelerating Simultaneously

That's wrong. Sure it's possible. Players do it all the time. People do It in life too. Can you drive your car with one foot on the gas and one foot on the brake at the same time. Sure. Ever get in a NYC taxi? Ever drive behind the proverbial little old lady in a 40 mph zone and she's going 20 with the brake lights on. Lots of brake jobs in the making, and over worked engines as well. It's often the same observing well intentioned, trying hard club players who do the very same thing with their strokes - accelerating to the ball while decelerating, holding back the racket simultaneously, and then stopping the follow through as soon as possible. Tennis elbow anyone? Not to mention lots of chronically tired arms and perceived weak wrists.

So where should your follow-through stop? It doesn't! It decelerates through the full range of your follow-through and silkily drops back into the ready position with the greatest of ease.

While on topic, understand that rackets and strings by themselves do not give you tennis elbow. You do. Of course, both the racket and string choice and the string tension have to match your game and physical prowess. That's a given, or you're asking for trouble. A bad fit will cause you to alter your previously injury free strokes from your norm. This is what does the damage. Talk to your pro who knows your game better than you do. Consult with your stringer and/or pro shop. Get on the "right" page for you. And don't be switching rackets every six months because there's a sale, or company X has a new model out and you've fallen for the marketing hype -always that latest blend of perfect control and power featuring the latest greatest technology.

Find a racket you like, strung with a string you like, at a tension you like that performs well for you, and doesn't cause any change in your hard earned technique, and then stick with it. You'll always be able to find string. And you'll find discontinued models as well if you really want to (contact billwrigley@comcast.net). And you can experiment in tension changes typically in 2-3 pound increments. My stringer just found a brand new example of my very dated racket that over the years has become hardwired to my strokes and my game.

And if you're not a particularly clean, smooth ball striker - and you should be aware of that - then find an experienced pro who can get you to both technically understand and kinesthetically feel the difference in striking a powerful shot cleanly with effortless control.

Bending The Serve In

Because learning this skill is exactly where many club players, even aspiring higher ones, stall-out, and their serve literally flat-lines permanently – very limiting - here's more.

If you're still one of those players who serves exclusively flat on 1st serve after playing for a few years or more, and you tentatively tap in your 2nd serve meekly without any spin – advantage receiver, it's well past the time you should learn to bend-it-in.

Long ago, or if you're relatively new to the game, you settled on a serving grip that either is or closely resembles your forehand grip. It's a grip that on serve squares the face of the racket to the ball at impact. This results in imparting little spin to assist gravity in bringing the ball down – when the air pressure above the ball becomes enhanced with the ball rotating 15 to 20 to 25 times per second - into a relatively small service box that's in close proximity to the net barrier. Not much margin for error available there for a ball struck flat with pace but lacking rotation.

That means the viable pass-through-space immediately above the net is very small and unforgiving on a first serve, and then, as a result of a typically low 1st serve percentage among these players, promotes the "chicken-little" puff-ball second serve which should be reserved for beginners and novices only!

Here's how you can graduate to spin in one practice session completely by yourself. Whatever your existing flat serve grip currently is rotate the racket in your hand 1/16th to 1/8th of an inch to the right. Voila. This will create a slightly – all that's needed - angular racket face at impact causing the ball to rotate through the air and give gravity a boost.

You will immediately see a change in the ball's in-flight trajectory from the previous laser beam like flight to one that slightly curves right to left and arcs downward as well. Just visualize those great graphics utilized by the Hawkeye line calling replay technology that's now commonplace in televised tennis. That's what you're visualizing.

In the beginning stages of its development, the ball will go left of the intended target and into the net. This will necessitate literally aiming "wrong" – over compensating by visualizing the target being to right of the actual intended target and by aiming considerably higher over the net than previously – until the neuromuscular magic has a chance to adapt. Your brain is smarter than you are. Let it happen.

Once settled-in you can begin to alter your toss, and possibly your grip still further, to gain either more "rainbow" trajectory – the bending spin serve, or greater right-to-left movement with reduced arc – a slice or slider, or a combo platter of the two. A useful rule of thumb regarding toss location to achieve placement in the box is: left creates right, right creates left. Placing your toss both closer to you and to the left will force you to "hit-up" on the ball at approximately the 1:00 side of the ball (seemingly over), while to the right, yet still in front like a "flattie" toss will allow you to hit more "around" the 2:00 side of the ball.

This will require some solitary practice time – fun to me! But players often fall short on this necessity and then complicate matters by prematurely introducing their new bender or slice exclusively on second serve. Yup, you guessed it, the double faults come in bunches and the technique is quickly abandoned as undoable and impractical. And the giving-up on it begins.

When first unveiling it – in a friendly! – use the technique on 1st serve only. The pressures off and you can swing freely and begin to create a new muscle memory. The percentages will eventually come up a bit and, on 2nd serve, you can still get the ball in play just as you have previously.

In time, again with practice, your success on 1st serve will improve dramatically, at which time you can then begin to use your new bender-slice appropriately in 2nd serve situations and go back to your "big" 1st serve and live happily ever after.

Maintaining the same racket head speed utilized on a 1st serve is crucial when learning to spin-bend-slice the ball in on the 2nd. This will create greater ball rotation to clear the net safely and bring the ball into the service box, not to mention avoiding conflicted muscle memory.

Remember what tennis legend, and founder of the pro tour as we know, Jack Kramer said, which will ring true as long as the game is played: "You're only as good as your second serve."

So how about committing to learning one starting today.

202

BALL BOUNCING and the SERVE

Still relevant after all these years. Just about everyone does it, from tour level on down to club and park mortals, but c'mon, how many bounces of the ball does it take to ready oneself prior to serving?

The great Pete Sampras was one bounce and slam, bam, thank you ma'am. The annoying antithesis to the game's greatest server of all-time, is unquestionably Novak Djokovic. Although he's thankfully abbreviated this part of his ritual in the past year – mostly because the inside word was that his peers we're fed up with it, not to mention how tedious it was to the game's money managers – it was not unusual at all for the Serbian to bounce the ball well into the teens before every first serve. That would be analogous to a baseball batter insisting on as many practice swings prior to the pitcher releasing the ball. Or, a basketball free throw shooter doing the same ball bouncing routine prior to letting the shot the go.

Ridiculous.

Jimmy Connors, towards the end of his career and especially during his last hurrah at the '91 US Open, would go to the bounce, bounce, bounce routine now and then, although not because he needed that much time to get focused, but because the then 39 year old needed an extra blow versus the 20 something young bucks he was still taking down.

Okay, fair enough.

Another legend, Boris Becker, would cradle-dribble the ball with his racket repeatedly while approaching the line to serve – as many pros do today – but once there he would start his distinct ritual sans any ball bouncing at all.

Back to the question, of course there's no right or wrong here, but, on average, how many bounces should it take to achieve pre-serve relaxation along with serve selection and its accompanying visualization before launching? That's entirely up to you, but don't treat it haphazardly. Rituals are extremely important on both serve and the return.

Be earnest in developing a sense of timing, pacing, and preparation that's feels right for you, whether it's no bounces, a couple, or a few. And be consistent – although it's not unusual for even the very best to vary their bounce count from 1st to 2nd serve (Djokovic typically halves the number on his 2nd serve) - particularly when you're struggling. Rushing, or abbreviating your normal ritual, will never solve any serving problems. But, conversely, becoming overly deliberate can lead to over consciousness, never a good thing either.

Find *your* deal.

The Elusive Service Toss

More thoughts on this key to serving well.

Tossing the ball up into the right place – for both you personally and the type of serve that you're hitting – is analogous to being in the right place at just the right time for all the other shots. Unfortunately, it's more difficult than it sounds since it's accomplished with your non-dominant hand/arm, and a bit tricky as well. If not placed properly, and consistently, there is little hope of possessing a reliable serve.

Let's first address the arm's position both prior to launching the ball, and during the release itself. Palm down? Of course not. Palm up? Surprisingly perhaps, another of course not. An anatomically neutral position – identical to the natural position that your arm assumes while hanging by your side – is what you should be striving for. This position is first realized typically with the ball resting against the racket strings in your finger-tips – preferably below the sweet spot - as one begins their service "ritual."

Next, it is important to know that the ball, once released, should be devoid of any spin or rotation. This is best accomplished by releasing the ball at your arm's point of full extension while moving upward. Simply open your hand up, do not roll it off of your fingers!

Muscle tension, or a complete lack thereof, is the key in establishing a consistently repeatable finite tossing range of motion. This relaxation is established simultaneously in the tossing arm and the hitting arm by initiating a slight rocking motion in the Ritual Stage – which you see utilized by so many tour players - prior to initiating the toss, creating a necessary synergy between the two.

The main beneficiary of this action is actually the tossing arm, a modified tossing rehearsal if you will, although the hitting arm is influenced as well into not rushing into its "loaded" position with counter-productive muscle tension. Ideally, the weight of a completely relaxed, "dead arm" moving upward establishes all the natural momentum necessary to propel a mere 2 oz. ball out of one's hand and into a sufficiently high, hit-able zone. Always remember: relaxed muscles are athletically intelligent, tight ones are dumb as a door knob and do not lend themselves to replication.

Young children are able to learn this fairly quickly using the "hot potato-egg toss" analogy. When urged to toss the ball up very carefully and lightly without breaking the egg, versus the sudden quick release hot potato version, a consistent result is accomplished in minutes. They get it! When smash-the-egg (ball) at a point that is as high as they can reach with the racket is added to the equation, a reasonably smooth transition from Stage 1 (preparing to strike the ball) to Stage 2 (striking the ball) is achieved. A full-fledged serve is born almost immediately exhibiting a viable throwing motion instead of the completely inefficient scratch-your-back half-serve that's taught (malpractice!) to beginners and novices, and that has caused long term problems for so many players, young and old alike.

So go slow, easy, extend, release, and then let it go!

The Third Groundstroke

"Rotating his body in midair, a testament to that core strength, he smoked a pair of inside-out forehands for winners, swinging one way while his entire body drifted the other and somehow making it all look natural." Another spot-on Jon Wertheim insightful description of Roger Federer - from his book, *Strokes of Genius*, about the 2008 Wimbledon Federer-Nadal classic final - running around his backhand, well into the ad side of the court, to unleash those severely angled laser beams that gets it just right. Done effectively opposing righties hate it since it stretches them out wide to their backhand. Only left-handers, with Nadal at the very top of a global list, are able to counter it effectively most of the time.

There was a time in tennis when running around your backhand was considered both a sign of weakness and bad form. Not so, thankfully, for some time now, with the best players on the planet, who clearly do not have problematic backhands, utilizing the tactic at every possible opportunity. You should too, unless you're one of those rare individuals in club land who are not more accomplished off the forehand wing and view the backhand as their strength. That stated, in those instances when you're jammed by a ball approaching your belt buckle, it is still athletically more natural to move away from it by playing a forehand versus a backhand, and yes, even including two-handers who, unlike one-handed players, also fully rotate in making their shot.

The first move, upon recognizing the opportunity, is pivoting by rotating one's hips and shoulders away from the approaching shot. Creating space by initially moving the hitting shoulder/hip back towards the back fence, back pedaling to get the ball where you want it, and finally launching an open stance forehand that drives off the hitting side leg - right leg for right-handers –while elevating off the court, and then landing on the left leg while simultaneously moving away from the ball just as Wertheim described it (see image).

Ideally, you're going to hit freely with accentuated racket head speed up and over this ball generating very aggressive topspin for both safety in net clearance and some additional penetration off the bounce as well. You'll also buy a bit of extra recovery time to cover any well-struck down-the-line singles counter, or an especially lucky late stab that could catch you by surprise at the net in doubles.

Still in doubles, the run-around can be employed most liberally in the ad court well into the alley - including "cheating" on initial position - and even beyond since any response up the now somewhat exposed middle, especially when paired with a timid net player, can be run down easily back into the court with a very doable forehand. A lefty can achieve a similar result playing in the deuce court, albeit having to contend with the righty's forehand response.

So, in life it's prudent to avoid giving anyone the run around. On the tennis court go ahead and feel free.

John Isner's "GOOD MISS"

At the end of the 2010 pro tour, it was easy to regard American John Isner as one of the tour's newest, best, brightest, and insightful stars. Here are some of the reasons why:

- Not because of his Wimbledon marathon victory

- Not because he chose to grow up in a normal, home town setting under the tutelage of his local club pro/coach instead of attending a live-in tennis academy/factory.

- Not because he attended and actually graduated from college.

- Not because he has steadily risen in the rankings into the world's top 20.

- Not because he gave world #3 Novak Djokovic all he could handle in the USA vs Serbia (eventual champion) Davis Cup tie earlier in the year, losing in 5 close sets on slow red clay in Belgrade in front of a hostile crowd after fending off a number of match points in the 5th set.

- And not even because he remains both exceedingly likeable and humble, unlike certain other American notables at that time who wore out their welcome among so many fans with repeated boorish and unsportsmanlike behavior.

As a teacher/coach I especially like him because of his core philosophy of how to play the game, which makes him a consistent "gamer" - he never goes away - and is an integral part of his success: "If you miss, make sure it's a good miss."

In club doubles this can be exemplified by missing the meat and potatoes cross court return from the backcourt – when forced out wide - with either your (right hander) forehand from the deuce court or the backhand in the ad court, just wide. Striking the ball just a bit too early will land the ball just out, an Isner "good miss."

But, if too often you've allowed yourself to be late in making the cross court return, then the ball-is-playing-you – reactive tennis - and you've most likely coughed up a sitter to a waiting net man. This, in the John Isner lexicon, represents a bad miss. If not corrected immediately, i.e. early on in the match, by "chancing" a good miss wide - even if the point is lost – it can often initiate the beginnings of a loss in confidence, tentativeness, and an unrecoverable downward spiral.

Conversely, if you do inadvertently strike the ball a bit too early, resulting in that miss just outside of the doubles line, you are very much proactive by playing-the-ball aggressively instead of the other way around. This slight timing error will, in short order, fix itself without any accumulation of damaging negative thoughts - particularly the fear of being poached, plus you've sent a strong message to your opponents that you will not retreat into a reactive, self-doubting shell.

Some other ways to perceive forms of embracing "good misses":

- Use overcompensation when struggling to find the right timing, i.e. strike the ball seemingly too early, or too far in front, and take the chance that it might be out in order to find the optimal moment of contact in relation to your body position - the result is, surprisingly, more often than not a successful shot, and a recalibration is quickly achieved.

- Always remain aggressive - but not overzealous - in terms of shot pace, albeit with bigger margins to the lines for safety as necessary until you're able to dial-in penetrating placements closer to the lines.

- Never try harder when struggling, try softer, more relaxed, smoother... stay with it instead of tensing up, fighting it, and becoming against it.

- Keep going for your shots versus becoming tentative and timid because you know that you will find it since you know it's there, but just taking a little longer than your norm to realize - it happens.

Keep remembering, if you're playing league tennis the opponents are in your class. They are not significantly better players than you so don't fall victim to perceiving them in that way! If they were significantly better they would be rated at a much higher level and not playing in your division.

Since it is a relatively even playing field tilt it in your favor by never, ever allowing the ball to dictate to you. Play through any tentativeness and any timidity that's experienced. Keep it simple and solid. Be real of course by playing within yourself, but never lose this "contest" with your Self! It's often the most important one.

Isner's American female contemporary at the time, Melanie Oudin, whose promising career was derailed by dysfunctional family selfishness after a brilliant U.S. Open performance, had a motivating message embossed on her footwear: BELIEVE.

Good advice to hold onto.

Cutting Off The Angle.. Vertically

It's always gratifying when players are able to inform their pros that, yes, they are aware of "cutting off the angle" laterally on the diagonal when playing the net to reduce the size of the passing lanes, especially in doubles with those 4 ½ foot wide alleys. Yet these very same players are often not cognizant of utilizing the same positional tactic when at the net and defending against an opponent's obvious attempt at a defensive lob over them from a stretched low, short ball position in and around the service line or closer.

Close!

Instead, too many defensively retreat back towards their service line, taking pressure off the hitter, and allowing the lob attempt to increasingly gain height and become fully airborne. This results in either becoming a difficult to play ball, or a completely unplayable one that successfully sails over them as they back paddle in futile pursuit, then requiring a last ditch partner rescue effort that typically has a bad ending.

Just another reason why the lob is so effective in club doubles but seldom at the professional level.

In these instances of opponents attempting what should be deemed a poor shot selection, one that's allowed to become a viable one in the above noted scenario, closing aggressively forward, closing straight at the opponent in close proximity to the net, will also "cut off the angle." But this time it's vertically, in effect shutting down the ascending lobbing lane early on and creating an easy volley at a defenseless opponent well before their lob has an opportunity to get up and over them and becomes too high to handle effectively, if at all.

This aggressive positional response represents a big step for club players to become a far more effective net player, much more than just being a good volleyer - not at all the same thing.

The Most Neglected Shot in the Game

Q. What's the most ignored shot, in terms of practice time devoted to it, in tennis? **A.** The return of serve.

Second in importance behind the serve regarding getting the ball in play, and arguably number two in the difficulty department as well, this is very curious. And, even the pre-match warm-up provides very limited return practice if you follow protocol - at the tour level it is not often that anyone will even attempt it, preferring instead to concentrate on their serves, although the women are more likely than their male counterparts.

Although still a forehand or backhand, it is differentiated from in-the-point ground strokes hit on the run because it is launched from a static start. Therefor more demanding.

Because it is a static start shot, developing a consciously repeatable ritual - *exactly* the same each and every time - one that will eventually morph into becoming as automatic and unconscious as walking, is enormously important. So many players, either unenlightened, complacent or both, arrive at their chosen return position with nothing in mind, and then stand there motionless imitating a mannequin at Macy's.

After a point is completed make it a habit to inhale and exhale deeply and quiet your mind for a few seconds. Then visualize your flight plan for your next return - one for both the forehand and backhand wing - and release any telltale tension in your jaw, neck, shoulders, and arms and hands while you make your way slowly and methodically to the next receiving position. Since there's nothing worse than allowing yourself to be quick served, either intentionally or unintentionally, always approach your chosen spot from well behind the baseline while facing the server. Walk well past the baseline if you're coming from the court proper. If necessary, once you've turned around wave off any server rushing you with your hand up until you've had time to completely settle in.

Once there, re-energize as necessary by laterally skipping side-to-side, foot-to-foot, followed by the ritual stage typically consisting of hips and shoulders rotating slightly side to side with the racket in sync. This will enhance both relaxation and rhythm and create a predisposition for the initial take-back-turn-pivot that's completed by the time the ball is passing over the net after your split step was landed at the server's impact.

Now footwork becomes crucial and is fully engaged in either chasing down

211

a serve that stretches you out wide or into the center of the court, or through stutter-stepping, those small, rapid fire adjustment steps that keep you connected to serves right into your strike zone, or ones that are jamming you.

Nonetheless, solid, reliable returning isn't going to happen without exceptional ball tracking, beginning at impact, to the service box bounce point - a common place to "lose it" - and finally into the in front hitting zone where you intend to strike it based upon your pre-visualized shot selection.

During this always the same sequence of events, from approaching your position, to settling in, to serve recognition, and up to the moment of ball-on-racket impact, your head must remain very still if you're going to see the ball well. Bobble-heading, or lifting your head up and back as you're striking the ball, minimally guarantees return misdirection and often causes completely shanked mishits.

Returning serve is ultimately about timing through both eye-hand and eye-foot coordination working in tandem - the elusive right place, right time component. Teaming up with the approaching ball, working with it versus fighting it, supports the physical components of smoothness versus lunging or jerking at the ball, and also promotes a positive and comfortable mindset that will produce your best results.

Need a model? There is no one better at preparing to return serve than Serena Williams. Her ritual from a point's end leads up to, and is aimed at, a perfectly timed total focus on the ball and its intended outcome, with clearly nothing else entering the picture. Her beautifully managed tabula rasa moment.

I'll leave you with a reminder of a return dynamic that you experience periodically. The ball is served. It appears as if it's on track to be in. You ready yourself. You start your racket at the ball, but, at the very last moment you realize that it's just out and you, physically unable to stop the racket but with any pressure suddenly eliminated, completely relax and go through with the return.

The result? Almost always a mind boggling, perfectly timed, silky smooth, and effortlessly powerful shot with a GPS like guided result.

Try replicating that feeling all the time.

SERVING SUCCESS:
Warming-Up vs Match Play

Have you ever noticed that it is not so unusual to warm-up your serve solidly prior to the start of a match and then proceed to begin the match serving badly? If you've never experienced that, then stop right here and begin making your travel plans to the next tour "qualies." If it does strike a chord, please continue.

When warming-up, there is of course zero-expectations of a return, resulting in far better ball watching – focusing on striking the ball at what you perceive to be the optimal moment for your tossing style. Yet, once it's show time and the match begins, there is a tendency to pull your head down prematurely prior to making contact, to ready yourself for the now-expected return. There goes your first serve percentage right in the dumpster, and maybe confidence problems with your second serve as well.

One-time world #1, Kim Clijsters, recipient of a wild card at a past U.S. Open while in the midst of a very on-track comeback after a two year "retirement," clearly understands this dilemma when she said on the event's opening day, "My mistake is that I don't always finish off my movement the way I should. I'm kind of already preparing myself for the next shot, while I didn't even finish my serve yet."

Once again, the late Vic Braden had a laughable take on this in addition to some of his other previous mentioned ones: "There's only one ball, you've got it, what's the hurry?" Well said as usual, not to mention that club players, whose serves seldom approach even 90 mph, comparatively have oodles of extra time to prepare for their opponent's return.

Now factor in that every single time in your life, from early childhood, that you threw any object – balls, snowballs, rocks, spitballs – you looked where you were throwing. Since serving is a throwing motion, there exists - depending upon your previous life/sports experience - a great deal of potentially undermining conditioning to overcome.

So, when taking your first few practice serves, absolutely make sure, first and foremost, every time out, that you're keeping your head up and not carelessly pulling your head down too early. And, because you're hopefully always trying to place your delivery into a specific service box quadrant with appropriate margin to the net – even with your practice serves - keep in mind the advice I kiddingly offer to those a bit complacent about this all-important moment, "If the court moves during your toss, I'll let you know."

Enjoy your new, upgraded serving percentage.

Debunking the Modern Game

Make that the so-called "modern game." There's a serious faux pas resulting from such an inappropriate label, one which tennis has now been saddled with for a few years by both those whose job it is to create marketing hype for the financial welfare of the game, and especially those who, no doubt sincerely, promote some imaginary new, narrow instructional genre.

The result? The now fully embraced connotation, or fallout, is that all that preceded this new is outdated and irrelevant. To discredit all that has come before what's current is a sharp stick in the collective eye of the uber-talents who, over many years, built the foundation upon which today's game is played at its highest level.

The great Rod Laver, whom you've by now learned I mention often in this work, was not the only facsimile of what's being played today. Go ahead and view him on YouTube. Looks like Federer with a wood racket. Sure, the advances in equipment have led to some adaptations in ground stroke ball striking in particular, but the game is still the game.

Pete Sampras is another example, and let us not leave out Martina Navratolova.

If anything the chatter should be focused on the fact that the game has evolved into being a one dimensional one – big banging from the back of the court – but that wouldn't sell, and would be a glowing testimonial to its modernism.

The golf pro at my club explained to me that, after watching last year's Wimbledon final, he became bored because every point seemed to be played exactly the same.

Fair point. I often experience that myself when watching, although it's wonderful to see Federer coming in more and more as he ages.

Yes, of course, the athletes of today have become bigger, stronger, faster, quicker in all sports, best exemplified in sports such as track and field and swimming where stop watches plot the steady advances in human physiology. Think Usane Bolt, Michael Phelps, and Dara Torres who, like Navratolova, continued to excel into her forties.

Does that mean that Jesse Owens, Roger Bannister, Mark Spitz, and Wilma Rudolph are written off – disrespected even – as negatively antiquated? I think not!

Did those in the Jack Kramer, Pancho Gonzales era, and the pundits covering them, reduce the earlier Bill Tilden dominance as old fashioned and somehow unworthy?

Or, did Tiger Woods, or the golf writers and television announcers, ever arrogantly diminish the accomplishments or idiosyncratic playing style of Arnold Palmer with those tiny little club faces?

No, nothing but respect. So why now in tennis?

Exactly what is this "modern game" that we're supposed to be embracing? Consider the primary example of how the game is being taught – completely unachievable for most club players - by the new breed of USPTA influenced coaches of today. A Western grip on the forehand, or even an extreme Western grip, is now favored in order to not prioritize striking the ball in front of one's body, purposely allowing it to travel well into the backside of the hitting zone. Why? In order to make contact off of one's back hip to facilitate the necessity of brushing violently up the backside of the ball, with maxed out racket speed, in a fully-opened stance from well behind the baseline!

Does the rash of tour hip injuries come to mind, the kind that ended the careers of two fairly recent world #1 modern day warriors, Guga Kuerten and Magnus Larsen, along with a host of other finely tuned tennis athletes using their bodies inefficiently? And what's up with the myriad injuries that Rafael Nadal has suffered while strutting *the* "modern" approach?

Is that how Roger Federer, relatively injury free at 34, and today's premier model player, plays his forehand in this new day and age? No! He strikes it well ahead of his body with mostly an Eastern forehand grip, even when slightly open-stanced, in order to hit *through* the ball, albeit with some topspin to bend it into the court at the higher shot speed of today's game, just as Rod Laver did back in his day but with that far less lethal Dunlop Maxply Fort and slower balls, but with that tree trunk of a forearm.

While practicing recently with a former world class player whose game came of age in the '80s, compared to my, by comparison, ancient development in the '60s, an interested sports savvy spectator remarked to me after our session: "It was interesting to see the difference between your games." Upon asking him whose game more closely resembled Federer's game – key word being *resembled* – his response was that my game was a closer match.

- The more flattened out forehand, with some topspin, versus the more loopy topspin of my practice partner.

- My more versatile one-handed backhand, both with topspin and a skidding slice, compared to his one-dimensional, two-handed topspin stroke.

Today we have these lightweight frames – the biggest difference between the rackets of today and those first generation graphites introduced in the late '70s – ones that these bigger, stronger players, male and female, can accelerate through the ball with blazing speed.

Interestingly, those that choose to flatten out their groundies, best exemplified by Juan Martin del Potro's convincing win over Federer at the '09 US Open doing just that, were and still are praised – curious and contradictory – for *their* ball

215

striking approach by these same TV announcing crews espousing "modern" times. And when you consider Maria Sharapova among others, and Lindsey Davenport before her, the "modern" tennis being advocated by today's teachers as the Holy Grail is not always the case even at the professional level.

So then why did Jimmy Connors and John McEnroe continue to play somewhat flat off the ground, even in their later years, when their equipment had been ultimately turboized? Because they could! Because they were taught how to hit through the ball when the opportunity presented itself while still incorporating the nuances of spin, including underspin when appropriate, versus those who seldom ever deviate from leaving fuzzless bald spots on the backs of balls while feverishly hitting up on them to the nth degree, in full bludgeoning mode – like Americans Jack Sock now and Andy Roddick before him - at times even following through backwards!

So in the end what should we be thinking on this subject? That there is no new game altering, revolutionary, strictly "modern" component. It does not exist. It really is what it is despite the lexicon of the day – a constantly evolving work in progress that's built upon a regimen of long standing, cumulative, basic fundamental core axioms that both children and club players should be tuned into first in their collective evolution and development.

As in life, everything in balance, and everything in moderation is still best.

Poo Poohing Double Strategy Sessions

Yes, these sessions can be misperceived and overrated as the magic elixir for solid doubles play. Hardly the case, although a very handy rationale for struggling players and teams in denial – all they need is better teamwork.

Players certainly do need to understand the constantly changing positional role of the net man from offense to defense – that I continue to harp on right to the end - first and foremost, along with how and when to poach, how to fake poach, how to bait opponents to hit their shot where you want them to hit it, how to properly "switch," when to close (go offensive), when to retreat (go defensive), when to capitalize on a partner's good shot, how to negate incessant lobbing, where to serve to engage your partner, etc. And, yes, many do not understand much of this until they are taught since they have so few teams in their neighborhood to model their doubles games after, not to mention doubles is seldom shown, never mind explained coherently, even on the Tennis Channel (although former world #1 Rene Stubbs did a great series on the Tennis Channel's "Tennis Academy" about a year ago – might be available on their site or on a DVD?).

That stated, all of the above and more can be communicated to motivated players in a couple of sessions. Cake. Whether or not they are able to retain it, or put the appropriate stock in its importance going forward is another issue. Sometimes they will not deviate from bad habits out of a false sense of security in what got them to where they are, and become further entrenched every day with a glass that remains forever half-full in mediocrity. Is there anything more frustrating than observing four players on one court mostly playing singles?

So, assuming that there exists at least a rudimentary sense of positional doubles, what then does it take to play really well? Good shot selection coupled with consistent shot execution! That's *it*. The impatient, insecure penchant, among so many, for attempting low percentage shots after only a couple of shots is startling. Thread-the-needle consistent shot making is a difficult proposition. Then, even when appropriate high percentage shot tactics are patiently embraced, club player execution is, shall we say, often less than stellar.

That's the big, often unrecognized, problem.

Why is that among individuals who've been playing 5 and 6 times per week for years? Because they choose to never practice double's shot making. Never! Mind boggling.

They cannot hit deep, un-poachable, penetrating cross court groundstrokes with any dependability. The same goes for the necessary sharply angled return (specifically to make it un-poachable if the net man has covered the line) when positioned short in the court and stretched wide out on the wing. They often inadvertently feed shoulder high meatballs to opponents at the net, by still trying to go deep, and get their partners killed. And, maddeningly, they mostly serve into the opponent's strength, especially in the deuce court, stifling their net man. Etcetera. No matter, they continue to blabber about how better "doubles teamwork" being all that they need to get to that next level, which they typically don't aspire to anyway despite their claims – "I won't be able to play with my friends." - and play mind numbing messy match, after match, after match.

For me, worst of all, is when I ask players what their intentions were after having to fight off, or reach for, a very difficult ball unsuccessfully. They typically say incredulously: "Oh, I was just trying to get it over," and this is a 4.0 player saying this. What? The clever ones attempt to cover their tracks by attempting an after the fact "correct" answer even though they were visualizing absolutely zip, instead, I'm assuming, hoping for divine intervention.

There are offensive possibilities, there are defensive necessities, and there are "rally balls" when it is neither – it's that, uncomfortable for some, a stalemate. Don't blink first. You're not losing when engaged in a dueling cross court exchange from the back of the court – the meat and potatoes of club doubles. You're winning! That has to be your perception, otherwise you're going to impulsively do something, candidly, stupid.

Chill, it'll be alright!

If you can make enough simple, penetrating shots, or angled ones when appropriate, your net man will take care of business, and you'll be able to come in and join him on occasion. Suddenly, those allegedly great players that you claim to have faced aren't so terrific anymore. Of course, if you typically cannot, your doubles game isn't the problem, it's your inability to make shots that your partner, and you, can capitalize on, versus the all too often alternative of delivering shots that you and your partner end up getting victimized by, especially by those who lob, lob, lob.

When a Roger Federer reasons, as mentioned earlier on, that his lack of form is because, for whatever reason, was due to lack of practice time, he's referring mostly to maintaining – in your instance improving – executing his shots.

Club players, are you really listening?

Club Doubles' Increasingly Missing Link

Why is it that so many players respect and admire those who have the desire and ability to successfully poach, yet are repelled by others who have the desire and shot making ability to reverse the dynamic and take advantage of opposing net players whenever possible by going right at them?

So let me see if I've got this right. On an even playing field it's perfectly acceptable for the net man to take advantage of the backcourt player and his net partner, but not okay for a backcourt player to take advantage of an opposing net man. Q. Why is that? A. I don't have a clue.

Let's review the allegedly taboo scenario. Back courter moves into no-man's land to jump on a short sitter – could be return of serve, particularly second serve - and chooses to attack the player at the net, now exposed because of their partner's weak shot, by directing a shot right at their belt buckle. Why not? This tactic is singularly aimed at handcuffing them, taking time away from them, and also sending a message that poaching will be discouraged.

I like to lightheartedly refer to this shot as the "navel destroyer."

But, there's no malice involved. It is totally legitimate. It's simply taking advantage of an opponent's court position just as a poacher also does to a vulnerable net opposite, albeit right at their shoelaces. Those who are offended by it, and take it as some personal affront, need to get over it or stick to singles.

Yet it can happen in singles as well. I can recall an Ivan Lendl winning press conference back when he ruled the world for 2-3 years from the back of the court with his big, heavy, penetrating ball off either wing. A reporter informed Lendl that his opponent that day had taken offense at his habit of drilling him when he chose to come to the net, behind ineffective, light weight approach shots as it turned out. The world #1's comment, delivered in his monotone Czech inflected English, was priceless: "Then tell him not to come in."

Think about it. In this instance the guy comes in to take advantage, and instead is taken advantage of, and then whines about getting taken to the woodshed.

Where was his mental toughness?

In the spirit of "if you can't take the heat get out of the kitchen," don't play the net if you're only okay with dishing it out (poaching), but not cool about being the dishee.

So it's an interesting irony that it's okay to poach and take advantage but not okay to be taken advantage of, particularly in the lower NTRP designations, and, dare I say, most often among pre-Title IX women players with little or no previous sport's background.

Now, however, here's an important qualifier: If a net player is completely defenseless - and has already demonstrated that previously - and you've got the sitter of all sitters in your sights, you can still easily win the point and cut an opponent some slack at the same time by simply passing them.

Don't be boorish, unsportsmanlike, and a bully. Once a mismatch is realized, just go for the pass. Nothing sacrificed.

Conversely, it's also prudent, when all is clearly lost, for the endangered net player to concede the point by turning away from the salivating opponent loading up. Holding your ground is analogous to staring down a gorilla in a small room. Not a good idea, and asking to suffer the consequences.

If an inviting ball does accidentally get away from you and you do accidentally hit someone then immediately put your hand up – the universal sign – to indicate that you're sorry. If that's not enough try adding a little levity to the moment by offering: "Trust me, if I was trying to hit you there would be nothing to worry about." Then smile and buy them a coke after the match.

If you do find yourself teamed up with a partner who repeatedly is setting you up for the kill, follow Lendl's advice - don't play the net, stay back, make them do something different, and wait for a short ball to come in.

The Standing Around Syndrome

You've all heard the now classic lament, "There's no crying in baseball," proclaimed in total frustration by Tom Hanks, team manager in "A League of Their Own," a movie about women's start-up big league baseball during WWII. In the very same spirit, there's no standing around in tennis!

Well over 50% of the time you spend on the tennis court in match play takes place in between the points, especially in doubles where the points tend to end sooner than in singles. How one utilizes this these continuous mini-time outs is key in staying mentally and emotionally focused and physically engaged leading up to the next point.

If you could Google Earth a good close-up sampling of tennis clubs around the land you would notice it immediately: that otherwise motivated players, seeking competitive success, unfortunately stand absolutely still - in place, not a muscle stirring, completely static - once a point ends.

Here's an analogy I frequently offer up for consideration. Do you put your car in P and then turn the engine off when waiting for a red traffic light to turn green? Naturally, if you did, you wouldn't be ready to go once the signal turned green, and you would be slow starting. Similarly, you're not ready to play after standing around completely motionless for ten to fifteen to twenty seconds waiting for the next point to begin.

The best club players, and of course tour professionals, spend their in-between point time pacing back and forth, going nowhere but moving, staying physical, the tiger in the cage, often focused on and fiddling with their strings, making every effort to stay relaxed and fully engaged in the present, ready to spring both quickly and smoothly into action when the action goes green.

Going forward, start making the brief moment that you're striking the ball the *only* time that you're going to be relatively still - and perfectly balanced - for the fleeting moment, a mere split second, that it takes to swing the racket.

It's man always in motion.

Defeating the Poacher

I'm sure that you've experienced playing against exceptional net players in club land who are not only adept volleyers, but, more daunting, skilled poachers in doubles as well. They tend to be an annoying bunch who do not allow the luxury of an unchallenged, meat and potatoes cross court return of serve to start a point. When operating in concert with a good server – meaning a server with pinpoint placement versus one sporting big power – they can become a nightmare to deal with.

They poach, they fake poach, and they position themselves in the middle of the service box on serve tempting you to try and thread an overly ambitious needle down the line.

However, there are two primary counter measures. Constantly avoiding them, and having to hit sharp shooter returns out of their reach into the center of the court, without periodic counter attacks, only empowers them to run wild on you with no consequences. Since no one at any level can take the offensive, or be comfortable, when the ball is hit with some authority right at them, you must be willing, and enthusiastic about, taking them on, early on once they have shown their hand, even if you lose a couple of points in the process. A well placed ball into their midsection – addressed from a different perspective earlier - even if they're already in motion, will completely handcuff them, typically leading to an outright error or a feeble response. A message is sent with regard to them thinking that they'll be able to roam freely versus you!

Naturally, lobbing is the other viable option, particularly when you've got your hands full with a tough serve on your weaker side. Going over the eager poacher – I am not implying a perfect offensive topspin lob but instead a standard lob that's especially high (approximately 40' at its apex) and intended to land in the middle of no man's land – allows you and your partner to then close and take full control of the net, completely changing the dynamic of the point and perhaps the match.

Okay, so that's all good, but please let us not forget that if you've got a good ball to hit, *hit it,* that's what they make 'em for! A "match" featuring a lob contest when viable shots were there for the taking, becomes a counter-productive exercise in lowering the bar over the long haul, the antithesis of aspiring higher.

Go for it – green light tennis!

Very much analogous to "get a life," is "get a game!"

222